Using Video

Using Video

Psychological and Social Applications

Edited by
Peter W. Dowrick
Department of Psychology, University of Alaska

Simon J. Biggs
Community Psychology Group, Department of Social Services, London Borough of Newham

JOHN WILEY AND SONS
Chichester · New York · Brisbane · Toronto · Singapore

Library of Congress Cataloging in Publication Data:
Main entry under title:

Using video.

  Bibliography: p.
  Includes index.
  1. Psychological research—Audio-visual aids. 2. Psychology, Applied—
Audio-visual aids. I. Dowrick, Peter W. II. Biggs, Simon J.
BF76.5.U83 1983   150'.28   82-20058
ISBN 0 471 90093 1

British Library Cataloguing in Publication Data:

Using video.
  1. Psychology—Methodology. 2. Psychological research. 3. Video tape
records and recording. I. Dowrick, Peter W. II. Biggs, Simon J.
150'.72   BF38.5
ISBN 0 471 90093 1

Phototypeset by Input Typesetting Ltd., London SW19 8DR
and printed by Pitman Press, Bath, Avon.

For Verna May and George

and

Doreen and Ron

Contributors

TIM BETTS — Queen Elizabeth Hospital, Birmingham

SIMON J. BIGGS — Department of Social Services, Newham, London

SALLY CASSWELL — University of Auckland, New Zealand

ANDY CLARKE — Max Planck Institut fur Psychiatrie, Munich, W. Germany

PETER W. DOWRICK — University of Alaska, Anchorage, U.S.A.

HEINER ELLGRING — Max Planck Institut fur Psychiatrie, Munich, W. Germany

OWEN D. W. HARGIE — Ulster Polytechnic, Northern Ireland

LEONARD HENNY — Sociologisch Institut, Utrecht, Holland

RAY E. HOSFORD — University of California, Santa Barbara, U.S.A.

BRIAN KIELY — Hollymoor Hospital, Birmingham

GABRIELLE M. MAXWELL — University of Otago, New Zealand

MICHAEL E. MILLS — University of California, Santa Barbara, U.S.A.

CELIA McREA — Queens University, Belfast

JUDITH K. PRINGLE — University of Otago, New Zealand

CHARLES M. RENNE — National Jewish Hospital, Denver, U.S.A.

CHRISTINE Y. M. SAUNDERS — Ulster Polytechnic, Northern Ireland

JOHN SHOTTER — University of Nottingham

ANGELA B. SUMMERFIELD — Birkbeck College, London

PETER TROWER — Hollymoor Hospital, Birmingham

HARALD G. WALLBOTT — Universitat Giessen, W. Germany

GLEN WASEK — Harvard University, Cambridge, U.S.A.

Contents

Preface

This book brings together international contributions to the use of videotape in studying and influencing human behaviour. The aim has been to develop a comprehensive review of the scientific and therapeutic endeavours variously connected by the video medium. In the last 20 years rapid advances in technology have stimulated a vastly mushrooming growth in applications of videotape recording and replay. From its inception, inspired by the fascination of self-confrontation, the field has sprouted diverse methods and purposes, backed by very sparse theory. We believe that it is now timely to attempt a serious integration of this field, notwithstanding the difficulties in doing so. We hope that this volume, the outcome of our endeavour, will serve as a handbook for video users who seek models of specific techniques or styles of approach in using their equipment. Also, we hope to offer a concept of video as a special medium, partly from the general picture emerging from video in practice and partly from specific theoretical contributions.

Inevitably, our attempts to integrate have left some holes. To some extent this is a result of being able only to sample the field; but more importantly there are some genuine gaps to which attention deserves to be drawn: long assumed rationales overdue for testing, worn therapeutic strategies with no empirical evidence, potential areas for research not yet addressed. In our attempt to present a picture 'complete' with gaps, we designed the scope of the book largely before we identified the contributors. Most chapters, therefore, are determined by our perception of the issues most needing to be discussed, not simply determined by the specialties of conveniently located colleagues (a criticism of many edited collections). Individual authors did their part by developing original manuscripts to fit the total concept. As editors, we divided our responsibilities somewhat unevenly throughout all sections, and it is hoped that difficulties of communicating across the miles have not resulted in too great differences in style.

The contributions are separated into three sections, each with an introduction of its own. The first section provides a survey of applications, existing and potential. There are discussions of recording logistics, analysis and review for both beginning and sophisticated users. In the second section the practice of video as a direct change agent is explored, particularly via replay to subjects, trainees, clients or members of the community. Diverse applications, from medical conditions to community action, are surveyed and evaluated. Most chapters in these two sections include a 'case study' to illustrate general principles in a practical manner. The third section explores some of the implications which emerge from the earlier chapters. In particular there are discussions of theories, implicit and explicit, behind the use of video, and attempts to evaluate the state of the art and future directions.

Many people, in far flung corners of the world, contributed to this book. Each author has his or her support network gratefully, if anonymously, acknowledged here. As editors, we thank especially Bob Madigan and Robert Edelman for reviewing our chapters and Cheri Johnson and Sheila King who went out of their way to assist with manuscript preparation.

Peter W. Dowrick
Anchorage, Alaska, United States

Simon J. Biggs
London, United Kingdom

April 1982

Using Video
Edited by P. W. Dowrick and S. J. Biggs
© 1983 John Wiley & Sons Ltd

PART I

INTRODUCTION (RESEARCH)

Peter W. Dowrick

Human behaviour under the eye of the camera

The first section of this book devotes seven chapters to the description of video recording in the pursuit of understanding human behaviour. Video recordings are useful for the initial scientific analysis of people's actions and interactions, and also for documenting and transmitting that knowledge. The following chapters present information on typical subject matter and how it may be recorded, stored and analysed.

In Chapter 1 Angela Summerfield introduces the sense of rapid history which can be traced in video technology. In parallel with the changes in complexity of equipment over the past two decades, there has been increasing sophistication in the kinds of social interactions to be brought under the 'eye of the camera'. Dr Summerfield deals briefly with practical issues (such as the importance of recording content over aesthetics), treated in more depth in Chapters 4 and 7, and illustrates how these have been applied to the study of conversation (e.g. how conversation may be regulated by non-verbal exchanges).

The distinction between individual action and social interaction can be a fine one. In crowds where people have similar (or at least mutually dependent) purposes, behaviour is best seen as interactive—and this is touched upon in Chapter 1. However, crossing a crowded street, at Oxford Circus in the heart of London for example, can be a very impersonal matter—studies of which are mentioned in Chapter 2. As we get further from social situations, the most relevant behaviours and their settings vary more dramatically. With these variations come very different practical considerations for the use of video recording. In her concisely informative chapter Sally Casswell offers a sample of diverse applications. The common threads and idiosyncracies of video related anthropological studies, psychiatric diagnosis and court proceedings are explored. In some cases video is used not for data documentation but as the stimulus situation to *elicit* the behaviour of interest. However, most usefully Dr Casswell concentrates on the application of video to the understanding of physical skills, her own work with drivers intoxicated with marijuana being most innovative and described in sufficient detail to inspire other researchers. Both of these chapters end with speculations on the future of human behaviour.

Whereas the issue of how the camera is affected by the recording situation has been dealt with so far, Chapter 3 concentrates on the reverse—how the presence of recording equipment will affect the behaviour of those being observed. Chuck Renne provides considerable practical detail on ethical concerns and describes how different populations may react to the camera. He draws on his knowledge of the field at large and derives specific examples from his experience with children in an asthma hospital.

Data collected on video recordings then need to be analysed—the topic of Chapter 4. Gay Maxwell and Judy Pringle discuss the advantages of video recordings for improving reliability and validity checks and provide useful pointers for the integration of recording analysis and research design. The fine working model of Gay Maxwell's social skills training and analysis laboratory lends a background to the considerations that the authors propose when making decisions about methods of analysis from types of measurements and ratings to single frame versus continuous replay—whichever may be most suited to an investigator's specific interests.

More specialized data interpretation can be achieved by interfacing video recording decks with a computer. In Chapter 5 Andy Clarke and Heiner Ellgring elaborate the practical advantages of doing this interface and offer advice on how to go about it. In particular, they discuss how tapes can be encoded for situations in which you may have voluminous recordings and wish to merge short sequences for easy comparison. They illustrate this in the case of tracking non-verbal mood indicators as they change over the course of depression therapy.

In Chapter 6 Tim Betts expands upon the value of video libraries. Practicalities arise in terms of how physically to develop and maintain a library. Also addressed by Dr Betts are the issues surrounding retrieval and distribution, which raise some idiosyncracies not encountered in other media.

In the final chapter of this section Harald Wallbott provides a condensed handbook on the technology and handling of video equipment. Readers still learning to use their cameras and recorders will find useful guidance on such topics as ensuring reasonable picture and sound under variable conditions. For those users with more experience there is information on special effects, partial masking and split screens. The section ends with a view to the future (digital recording, random access, miniaturization) and possible implications for physiological research.

Using Video
Edited by P. W. Dowrick and S. J. Biggs
© 1983 John Wiley & Sons Ltd

Chapter 1

Recording Social Interaction

Angela B. Summerfield

Department of Psychology, Birkbeck College, University of London

What is social interaction?

What kind of behaviour can be described as social interaction? How far does the definition stretch? These questions need to be answered before video can be considered as a recording medium.

Psychological studies of human social behaviour have too often been restricted to investigations of two to five person units conversing under rather limited conditions in a laboratory environment. However, the term 'social interaction' extends to many other social situations, whether occurring naturally or contrived by the investigator. Anthropologists study social behaviour in industrialized as well as primitive societies. Their techniques of participant observation have been adopted by other social scientists who have been interested in such phenomena as football hooliganism, riots, rituals and leisure activities. All of these situations meet the two criteria that social interaction involves communication between individuals with the aim of achieving a common goal. In the study of social interaction, boundaries between disciplines are often hazy and behavioural scientists of different disciplinary origins may study the same phenomena from different viewpoints. They may even do so as members of an interdisciplinary team using a common method such as video.

Past uses of video in recording social interaction

Video has directly succeeded film and the use of trained observers in the study of social interaction. Its ready availability from the mid sixties onwards led to its use in many studies of non-verbal communication, as well as in applied work on social skills. Harper, Wiens and Matarazzo (1978) give a detailed account of recent research on non-verbal communication and much of the work they describe involved the use of video recordings. Examples of applications in this area include studies of facial expression, of the use of emotional categories, of cultural determinants of non-verbal behaviour, of individual differences in movement and gesture, eye contact and other aspects of looking and the study of personal space. Video has allowed significant methodological improvements to be made in the study of non-verbal communication, because it allows greater ease in the collection of data and more opportunity for repeated examination of the visual record. Since earlier studies of non-verbal communication had quite often used still photographs, the transition from an emphasis on static behaviour to a dynamic, sequential emphasis has been critical. A comparable account of the use of video in clinically orientated studies of social behaviour can be found in Berger (1978). Much of this book concentrates on a specialized sub-variety, namely two-person psychotherapeutic interactions, but some consideration is given to the uses of videotape in studying family therapy as well as encounter groups, and also to clinical teaching. In these cases video recordings were made so that they could be used as feedback for the groups. The increasing value placed on these tapes during the course of a group's history is stressed.

The possibilities of video are only just becoming apparent to workers on social interaction, but what can be seen from these studies is that full use of the medium may only occur after an extended stage of using video to mimic what the observer sees in real life. In other words, the opportunities associated with more than one camera angle, close-ups, slow-motion and other specialized techniques are introduced comparatively late in the history of a particular research field. There seems to be a time-lag before investigators actively manipulate the possibilities of the medium and accept the potential richness of the material which becomes available. These trends are considered in more detail below.

Basic considerations in planning a recording

The first requirement in recording social interaction is to decide on the aim of the investigation and as a consequence which aspects of the interaction need preservation and attention. Since any interactive situation presents a rich complexity of information, some degree of selectivity is essential. It is only after the criteria for selection have been established that it is possible to concentrate on making the record as accurate and as detailed an approximation to the reality as possible.

As Maxwell says elsewhere in this volume (Chapter 4), before the advent of video in the sixties most investigators used trained observers to record social interaction, while a minority were able to afford the expenses of film. The use of observers sets certain limits and opens up certain possibilities for investigations. In particular, they can be trained to make inferences or judgements about what they observe, so they may describe not only the behavioural components of what they see and hear but also the constrictions they put upon them. They may omit the component stage entirely. So, for example, an observer might rate the degree of anger or hostility without making any intermediate record of the behaviours which led him to that opinion. Since judgements of this kind necessarily reflect the social norms of the observer's culture as to what constitutes anger, hostility or some other trait, the results of such studies are inevitably culture-specific. Until the availability of video it was impossible in most cases for a colleague in a different culture to establish the basis on which the judgements were made. Good practice in the use of video for recording social interaction therefore includes storing video records and making them available to colleagues for inspection. The spread of this practice is likely to result both in greater caution in the interpretation of data and also in less parochial conclusions being drawn from them.

It remains to be seen how the study of social interaction will shift now that most research workers have access to adequate video recording methods. At present the theoretical development of many aspects of the study of social interaction is clearly related to the technical limitations of the empirical work on which it is based. Studies carried out in the field with portable video equipment are likely to have a somewhat different impact on the future development of social interaction research.

More significantly, however, the whole tradition of theory and research in social interaction has been based largely on work carried out live with trained observers of the type cited above. The curious blend of descriptions of behaviour on the one hand and inferences on the other which characterize this work has made it difficult for research workers to develop new methods of analysis which take into account not only the enduring nature of video recordings in contrast to live observation, but also their special characteristics and limitations. Too often investigators have fallen back on the implicit assumption that the video camera sees what the human eye sees, which even a little consideration will reveal as not being the case. It cannot be said too emphatically that the video record is itself a sample of the original natural interaction and those behaviours selected for observation on the record are in their turn a second sub-sample of that.

A pleasing example of a method of analysis which in contrast was developed very much in the context of video is the Facial Action Coding System (FACS), devised by Ekman and Friesen (1978) as a method of analysing the fine muscular changes in the face which make up facial expression. This technique therefore avoids any problems of cultural specificity in interpretation. FACS analysis can be exceedingly time-consuming, involving as it can frequent reruns and slow-motion or frame-by-frame analysis of the tape, but such a method would be unthinkable if observers alone were available and film is less readily suited to it than video. The characteristics of video recordings allow FACS analysis a degree of precision and detail which is absent from more traditional methods of analysis in facial expression in the context of social interaction and which have only been partially overcome by earlier forms of component analysis. Clearly a study which is designed from the beginning to allow FACS analysis is a very different one from one which has to be fitted into a more traditional framework.

Data collection by video

A perpetual trap for researchers using video is the sophistication of the production styles used in commercial television. The varying shots, the inserts and the special effects are there to attract viewers and prevent them switching to rival channels. Such methods can often be counterproductive in interaction research where the purpose is to produce a detailed and comprehensive record rather than to encourage the viewer to fill in the gaps from his imagination. This mistake is particularly likely to happen when recording is delegated to technical or other staff who do not fully understand the principles underlying the research or how the tapes will be analysed. Their implicit aim then becomes to produce an 'interesting' series of pictures rather than a comprehensive and accurate one. Suitable research tapes are, however, often boring to the casual viewer.

The first question the investigator needs to ask himself is which variables are being studied.

Hartup (1979) provides a valuable framework for structuring social interaction in order to decide what type of recording to make. He subdivides it as follows, basing his classification on the concept of the 'social act', which occurs between individuals or their surrogates:

1. *Frequencies.* This category includes the presence or absence of an act and how often it occurs. Example: making eye-contact with another person.
2. *Latencies.* The length of time it takes an individual to respond to a situation. Example: latency of response in answering a question.
3. *Intensities.* The degree of magnitude of the response. Example: loudness of voice when expressing an emotion.
4. *Durations.* The length of time a behaviour continues. This has two aspects, the length of time for the total unit and the proportion of the total time taken up by the units of this type. Example: amount of time spent clasping hands.
5. *Densities.* Amount of time devoted to a particular class of behaviour. Example: amount of time spent touching others.
6. *Sequences.* The order in which social acts occur. Example: turn-taking in conversation.

If the investigator evaluates the interaction he hopes to study in relation to these categories, a more precise idea of how the recording should be made and where special attention to detail is needed will be provided.

However, it is apparent that in order to record any of these dimensions of behaviour, the investigator needs a clear, consistent and unambiguous record of the interaction which has taken place. Because of the two-dimensional nature of video this may present problems, even in recording the interaction of dyads. A number of ingenious methods have been developed, for instance, for capturing two-person interactions in such a way that eye-contact may be observed. Latencies which can be observed in the auditory modality, such as delays in speaking, present less of a problem, but intensities in visually observed behaviour, such as gestures, are not always easy to measure accurately because of the limited number of directions from which video pictures may be taken at any one time. Similarly, durations of behaviours can only be rated accurately if the behaviours themselves are present on a clear form on the tape.

These problems are necessarily compounded when the investigator wishes to study groups of three or more people rather than dyads. It is rarely possible to make individual recordings of each participant as well as of the group as a whole. Even if it were feasible, there remains the problem of how to relate these separate records to each other. For this reason, studies of social interaction in groups using video tend either to be rather superficial or anecdotal in the type of analysis employed or, alternatively, to utilize only a partial analysis of the interaction, based on an overall picture of the whole group in which some behaviours of members are obscured for at least part of the time by the physical positions of the others. These problems are far from being solved, although a partial solution can be achieved by making one recording with a camera directly above the centre of the group and others with cameras focusing on two or three members at a time. These pictures can then be displayed simultaneously on a split screen.

The second consideration concerns which persons from which angles need to be included in the picture to produce a satisfactory sample of the interaction for this purpose. One also needs to bear in mind whether the record will be used for any additional purpose such as feedback to a social skills training group or as teaching material in an academic course. In general it is difficult to make tapes which satisfy more than one aim, and multipurpose recording should be avoided whenever possible.

It is not the purpose of this book to provide the degree of technical detail which is needed to produce high quality pictures with a particular make of equipment. More general advice can, however, be given.

Recordings in controlled settings

Certain general considerations apply to recordings made in controlled settings for both research purposes and for other reasons, such as clinical teaching and feedback.

It is often possible to use a special room which has been set aside for this purpose. If a choice is available, the room should be quiet, it should have matt surfaces which do not reflect light and it should be as free as possible from intrusive and confusing visual detail. This does not mean that it should be clinically bare, since too antiseptic an environment is likely to stress subjects and lead them to interact in a less natural way. However, heavily patterned wallpaper, carpets and other furnishings may distract those who subsequently score the tape. A more ambitious recording room which is to be used regularly for recording can be improved by sound-dampening of the walls and ceilings with one of the variety of tiles and hangings which are now available for this purpose. A large one-way mirror is also useful since videotaping through a mirror with a low-light camera is less distracting for subjects than if cameras are present in the same room. Any mirror should extend as near to the floor as possible so that shots of feet are not impeded and young children crawling up to the mirror are not hidden from view. Comfortable chairs and perhaps a table will make the room seem more familiar to subjects. A transparent table made of perspex or a similar material can be used so that subjects' legs and feet are not hidden. Good results have been obtained with such transparent furniture at the Social Psychology Laboratory, Justus-Liebig University, Giessen, West Germany.

It is advisable to show subjects the recording equipment before their session and allow them to examine it if they wish. The presence of a camera in the room is not necessarily in itself socially disruptive, although a remote control camera unit may be indirectly disturbing if it is noisy. Most social interaction skills are deeply ingrained in the individual's behavioural repertoire and are unlikely to disintegrate unless he is exceptionally highly stressed by the recording environment. Time and opportunity for inspection and settling in should minimize this problem. Subjects should be told that they are free to leave at any time if they wish. It is most unusual for this to happen, but the offer seems to be reassuring. In fact, many subjects report that they forget about the presence of the camera after the first few minutes. Some subjects may ask to view the recordings afterwards and investigators should decide in advance what they wish to do, since it can be difficult to resist a determined group.

Research recordings

Recordings which are to be used for research purposes present special problems, even if a properly designed recording studio is available. The investigator continually has to trade off his wish to have as few different records as possible against the problems of achieving clear and complete pictures with only one or perhaps two fixed cameras. However, good quality research has been carried out by investigators with very limited facilities. The most important factor is to ensure that the method of analysis which will be used is not overambitious in relation to the type of recordings which realistically can be made. In other words, the investigator needs to decide which aspects of the interaction are really salient for him, obtain as clear and detailed pictures as possible of them and resign himself to the fact that other aspects of the interaction are likely to be incompletely or ambiguously represented.

This book is not designed to cover the making of sound recordings, but much research on social interaction involves an analysis of verbal material and voice qualities as well as what can be recorded visually. Most videotape recorders have rather poor quality sound for research purposes and the reader is advised to consult specialist books which explain how to make separate sound recordings. These can then be linked with the video picture via a time-code on the videotape.

Recordings for applied purposes

Recordings of social interaction may be made in controlled settings in order to provide material for a variety of applications. These include tapes for teaching purposes and recordings for feeding back information to participants in the interaction about their own interactive skills. Illustrative material of these types requires quite different aims in its collection from those of research records. Such material is frequently used selectively, whether to demonstrate an interviewing style or to draw trainees' attention to some point a group leader is making about their behaviour. The tape therefore needs to be psychologically apt rather than relentlessly comprehensive. Such recordings benefit from the use of close-ups, juxtaposition of images, fading of one image into another and a whole range of other techniques which are available. It is still important, however, that the camera work should be done by those professionally responsible for the material. It is very difficult for assistants who are untrained in the social or medical sciences to construe the situation in the same way and therefore to make the appropriate recording. Institutions which insist that a training in electronics is necessary before handling a camera should be resisted strongly. Recordings made by the group leaders or trainers may produce rather less technically sophisticated results than would otherwise be the case, but there are benefits in terms of social and psychological pertinence rather than visual perfection.

When recordings are to be used for video feedback in a group situation there is a case for allowing group members to make the recordings themselves, instead of, or preferably in addition to, using those made by the trainer or therapist. This activity increases group cohesion and, despite a loss of technical refinements, such recordings tell much about how participants perceive the interaction and what they see as the most important aspects of their collective behaviour. Thus a patient recording a marital interaction in his therapy group may concentrate almost entirely on the face of the wife, while eliminating the husband from the picture. Such recordings reflect what the camera operator sees in the mind's eye, if not with the real eye. A comparison of recordings made by different group members can also be helpful in showing up different viewpoints, as well as emphasizing that video is a way of achieving democratization—of giving power and knowledge to group members as well as to the leader.

Keeping a video record of a group's progress allows members to see that learning has occurred over time. Such records can also be encouraging to professionals working with chronically ill patients or with mentally handicapped children. Video recordings taken at intervals help them to notice small improvements which might otherwise have been overlooked. Here again the same principle applies: the record should be selective and highlight social behaviours of particular interest. Making such records in a controlled setting allows the superior recording environment to offset to some extent the problems caused by inexperienced camera operators.

Recordings in natural settings

Recordings which are made in natural settings pose different problems. They are frequently characterized by interruptions, blurrings and many changes of camera position, as well as the intrusion into the picture of irrelevant objects or people who are not involved in the study. Some principles can be applied in order to minimize these difficulties.

Firstly, the investigator should be very clear indeed about why he is carrying out the study in a 'natural' setting at all. As Summerfield and Lake (1977) observed, a natural setting is not necessarily more real than a contrived setting; it simply displays a different facet of social experience. Psychologists have been criticized for carrying out too many experiments with college students, but in the same way that college students share some of their most salient characteristics with the rest of the human race, so too do controlled environments have characteristics they share with less contrived ones. In addition, they may avoid some of the irrelevancies of the latter. Ultimately the only satisfactory criterion for recording social interaction in natural settings is that the essence of the social activity in question cannot be captured in any other way.

Certain types of social interaction remain best studied in this manner. Spontaneous displays of crowd violence exemplify this, as do interactions between people who are from a sub-culture reluctant to expose itself in the laboratory. The investigator then needs to decide whether to adopt that tradition of participant observation in which he associates with the group in question and explains the aim of his activities to them or whether he wishes to use more covert methods of acquiring suitable recordings. The ethical questions involved will not be dealt with here, but must be considered. Anyone who plans to take a video camera into a public place should first reflect on the fact that he will attract comments and questions or worse from passers-by. He is also likely in some contexts to be mistaken for a representative of the police, the military or some other group whose surveillance is not valued by the man in the street. Some may respond accordingly. It becomes apparent that video cameras should only be taken into crowds after much forethought and with extreme caution.

More often, however, investigators wish to record some established group in its usual setting, such as a family at home, a class in a school or patients in a hospital ward. The previous development of contact and trust between the investigator and the group in question is essential for studies of this kind. Many visits without video equipment may be needed, not only before trust is established but also before the investigator develops insight into the usual pattern of functioning of the group. His perceptions of what is important and how to record it may then shift radically. Significantly inferior technical standards may have to be accepted in making such recordings. However, groups may be very willing to make minimal changes in their surroundings which do not impair normal functioning and which help in the achievement of more satisfactory recordings.

The most portable equipment is not necessarily the least intrusive in stable natural settings of this type. A little effort in introducing remote control cameras and carefully placed microphones, for instance, is often profitable. The same criteria which apply to research recordings and recordings for applied purposes in controlled settings are equally applicable in natural ones and they will therefore not be considered separately here. The question of whether the presence of recording equipment alters the course of the interaction is one that is no more easily answered here than in other writings on this topic.

Further developments in recording social interaction

With some notable exceptions, such as the efforts of Stephenson and Rutter (1970) and their colleagues to improve methods of recording eye-contact, investigators have not been particularly innovative with regard to video recording techniques. At present the video market is dominated by the increasing use of home video systems. Manufacturers are producing equipment which is relatively cheap, but which does not always have the robustness and the degree of precision in operation that is needed for professional purposes. Full-scale commercial video recording equipment of the type used by television companies is equally unsuitable in price and range of facilities for most readers of this book. Users of video in the social sciences and medicine make up such a tiny proportion of all users that their impact on the policies of video manufacturers is negligible. Organizations such as VIRTUG (Video for Interaction Research and Training Users Group) and Video Informationen in Europe and the *TV in Psychiatry Newsletter* in North America have some degree of liaison with manufacturers, but it is unrealistic to expect that our needs in recording social interaction will be taken into account in relation to new technical developments. Nevertheless, more could be done to make full use of present available equipment for the recording of social interaction. More ingenuity does not inevitably mean more hardware. What can be achieved by selection of shots is not always appreciated by users. The concept of systematically sampling an interaction with video has not been well explored. Some of the problems are likely to remain intractable while video remains a two-dimensional medium and interactions take place in three-dimensional space. There is room, however, for an increase in both technical skill and a more critical approach to the recording of social interaction.

References

Berger, M. M. (Ed.) (1978). *Videotape Techniques in Psychiatric Training and Treatment*, Brunner/Mazel, New York.

Ekman, P., and Friesen, W. V. (1978). *Facial Action Coding System*, Consulting Psychologists Press Inc., Palo Alto.

Harper, R. G., Wiens, A. N., and Matarazzo, J. D. (1978). *Nonverbal Communication: The State of the Art*, Wiley, New York.

Hartup, W. W. (1979). Levels of analysis in the study of social interaction: an historical perspective, in *Social Interaction Analysis: Methodological Issues* (Eds. M. E. Lams, S. J. Suomi and G. R. Stephenson), University of Wisconsin Press, Madison, Wisconsin.

Stephenson, G. M., and Rutter, D. R. (1970). Eye-contact, distance and affiliation: a re-evaluation, *British Journal of Psychology*, **61**, 385–393.

Summerfield, A. B., and Lake, J. A. (1977). Non-verbal and verbal behaviours associated with parting, *British Journal of Psychology*, **68**, 133–136.

Information about the use of an overhead camera and transparent furniture may be obtained from Harald Wallbott, Fachbereich Psychologie, Justus-Liebig Universität, Otto Behagel Strasse 10, D-6300, Giessen, West Germany.

Information about the Video for Interaction Research and Training Users Group (VIRTUG) may be obtained from Dr Angela B. Summerfield, Department of Psychology, Birkbeck College, Malet Street, London WC1E 7HX, England. Dr Wallbott also has information about Video Informationen, a group for German-speaking users. The address for the *TV in Psychiatry Newsletter* is Dr L. Tyhurst, Department of Psychiatry, University of British Columbia, Vancouver, B.C., Canada, V6T 2A1.

Using Video
Edited by P. W. Dowrick and S. J. Biggs
© 1983 John Wiley & Sons Ltd

Chapter 2

Applications of Recording Human Performance

Sally Casswell

University of Auckland

Videotape recording has important applications in the investigation of many aspects of human performance. Often a realistic assessment of a particular piece of human behaviour requires that it is located in the context of the preceding and subsequent events and that the full range of potential cues is recorded. Videotape recording can achieve this simply and inexpensively. The same technology can be used to present, in a controlled setting, a stimulus which adequately represents the complexity of the original situation in order to elicit and measure subsequent reaction. Both of these facets of the use of video recording will be described in this chapter.

Performance under the camera

The majority of the growing number of published applications of video technology to the study of human performance have been concerned with the examination of interpersonal interactions, both verbal and non-verbal (dealt with in detail by Summerfield in Chapter 1 of this volume). The value of video recording to investigations of other aspects of human behaviour is increasingly recognized, however, and a variety of examples have now been published.

One of the special advantages of video technology in studying interpersonal interactions is that having a semi-permanent record of the data available allows flexibility in developing ways of conceptualizing and coding the data after their collection (Duncan and Fiske, 1979). Because of this the number of pilot and pre-pilot studies can be significantly reduced. Despite the need to view the tapes repeatedly in real time the saving in comparison with the practical difficulties of field work can be considerable, and this is of great importance in natural settings which occur infrequently or are difficult and expensive to attend.

Visual anthropology

The discipline of visual anthropology has developed in recognition of the advantages of recording human behaviour in visual form (Collier, 1969). Until recently most of the relatively small amount of visual data collection that was done was carried out using film and still photography; the development of video technology has brought definite technical advantages to the data collection phase of such research. For example, video recordings are cheaper to produce than film, the technology is relatively simple and the results can be checked on the spot (certain video cameras allowing immediate replay without even necessitating the carrying of a monitor into the field). The video camera will cope well with a variety of light levels and the amount of equipment which needs to be taken into the field is easily handled by one person. Video does have disadvantages relative to film—specifically a lack of fine detail in the visual record and the eventual deterioration of the recording. To cope with the former problem the use of brief film segments in conjunction with video recordings may be employed. The deterioration of the record can be circumvented by taking several copies and storing the mistress copy under suitable conditions, or alternatively the technology which now exists to transfer video recordings to film can be employed.

Visual anthropology provides several examples of the use of video to record human behaviour in natural environments. Schaeffer (1975) used video records as one element of data collection in a rural setting in Jamaica during a twelve-month field work period; the recordings covered a variety of major activities of the participants which took place both before, during and after the use of marijuana. As the community had no electricity supply, recordings were made using battery-powered equipment and batteries were recharged in nearby towns. The same author describes the use of video technology to record behaviour in a natural urban setting in a study of architecturally confining spaces. In this study remote controlled video equipment was placed in the homes of participants for 5 to 10 weeks, and reportedly became 'part of the furniture' during the observation period. These videotapes were analysed to determine 'the spacing arrangements within fixed spaces, the structure of communication associated with the use of space, and other behaviour patterns having to do with family life in an urban community' (Schaeffer, 1975). Other studies of family interaction using a kinesics approach (Birdwhistell, 1970) employed video technology to provide long continuous records from which were determined the peak moments of family interaction; these were then filmed using 16 mm film to provide the definition needed for fine grained analysis (Schetlen, cited in Lomax, 1975).

The presentation of visual records of their own behaviour to informants to aid the process of communication with the researcher is a method previously employed by visual anthropology (Krebs, 1975). Filmed sequences or still photographs of people or events are used as the basis of interviews which elicit further information on the conceptual framework of the participants. This method was employed, for example, to research the life experiences of women in Peru (Bunster, 1977). The use of video technology means that the visual record is available immediately; it also allows for slowed and frozen segments as necessary and for a synchronized verbal commentary to be added by the participant using a second auditory channel.

Work and play

This application of video technology has been used in the development of training programmes in a variety of applied areas, including the maintenance of newly developed gas turbine engines (Short, 1972). The video recordings of the actual maintenance operations plus a synchronized audio recording were the basis for later critiques and reviews by experts and produced the research data needed to develop the training programme in a fraction of the time normally needed.

Further examples of this active participation approach come from the field of educational psychology in which considerable use of video technology has taken place. A methodology in which groups of adult learners were videotaped and interactional analyses of the tapes were carried out was designed to minimize the gap between educational research and practice (Farmer, 1971). Similar moves have been made to incorporate the teacher into active participation in educational research (Florio and Walsh, 1976).

Many applications of video recording in the educational area have been self-confrontation for teacher training purposes (Fuller and Manning, 1973) and to a lesser extent the evaluation of teacher behaviour and training (Bedics and Webb, 1971; Duvall and Krepel, 1971; Kysilka and Anderson, 1972). Videotape recordings have also been used to evaluate the effect of specific interventions on children's behaviour. These evaluations include observations of relatively discrete behaviours following fairly small scale interventions (Miller, 1972) through to evaluations based on lengthy recordings of children's behaviour made in their home environment (Connell, 1981). The latter evaluation demonstrated that infants who had experienced a family-oriented intervention programme, as compared with a waiting list control group, spent a greater proportion of their time in interaction with their parents and engaged in more fine motor exploratory behaviour.

Rating schemes based on video recordings which have been especially popular in the classroom setting have been validated by the demonstration of significant correlations between the observers' ratings of students' attention to their tasks in the classroom and academic performance as measured by traditional paper and pencil tests (Ash and Sattler, 1973).

Videotape recorders would seem to have many applications as substitutes for observers of behaviour in public places. The use of time-lapse photography and film recording to investigate issues of environmental design is well developed (Davis and Ayers, 1975). However, studies of environment–behaviour interaction and behaviour such as the consumption of alcohol in public drinking settings have frequently relied on the use of several observers; more permanent and more thorough recordings could be made on videotape. One example of videotape recordings of public behaviour was that of Collett and Marsh (1974) who report an analysis of collision avoidance on a pedestrian crossing at Oxford Circus in London. Portable video recorders and a zoom lens were used and a record was made from the seventh floor of a building overlooking the crossing. The report of this study provides a good example of the way in which the relatively permanent record of events can allow the development and testing of new hypotheses without new observations being made. The analysis demonstrated that the modal passing behaviour of men differed significantly from that of women. Women were more likely to orient themselves away from the person they were passing and were also more likely to draw one or more of their arms across their body while passing. The authors speculate that both of these behaviours are related to women's concern to protect their breasts. The alternative hypotheses that the arm-crossing behaviour was primarily related either to women's greater probability of carrying something or to the modal method of passing were tested out using the existing recordings; both were rejected.

Further areas in which the use of videotape recordings can be expected to increase include research into cultural and recreational performance. Both sporting and performance art movements have been researched using film, and despite the lack of definition in the video record its other technical advantages make it certain that its use will increase in these applications. Video is already used in kinesiological research and the advent of video discs (a development of the technology providing a monitoring of the visual representation comparable to the cinematographic camera) will widen the scope of its application (Hosler, 1973). The advantage of video's portability and simplicity will also make its increasing use in recording performance art certain.

Performance in front of the screen

The facility of video equipment to record and represent a complex sequential set of data cheaply and simply has also led to its use in research settings to present standard stimuli to subjects in order to allow measurement of their responses.

Judgement of feelings

Walkey and Gilmour (1979) have used video recordings in the study of interpersonal distance. Subjects viewed recordings of one person approaching another, such that the direction of approach and the distance between them were randomly varied. The subject was asked to imagine that they were the person being approached on the screen and was asked to rate how comfortable they would feel in each of the scenes. This videotape method was considered by the authors likely to be more valid than pencil and paper measures since the recording could incorporate more of the numerous aspects of the situation which might be relevant. They also considered it to be more reliable than the use of controlled real life situations where even a small change in the behaviour of the assistant could have a considerable effect. In fact, a high positive correlation was found between the video recording method and the controlled real life presentation.

A similar positive correlation between direct and recorded observations was found between the judgements made using a psychiatric rating scale of depression based on face to face observation and after viewing a recording of the same interview (Ziegler and coauthors, 1978). Differences did occur on certain sub-scores and the authors suggest that these differences could be lessened by the use of different camera angles which would allow a larger view of the client (the importance of such technical aspects of recording is discussed by Wallbott, in Chapter 7 of this volume).

Legal and diagnostic judgements

The increasing popularity of the use of videotape recordings in courtroom settings has led to considerable research to evaluate the effect of jurors' judgement and performance of viewing videotaped proceedings as compared with real life (Farmer and coauthors, 1976; Miller, 1976). The studies indicated that watching videotaped material did not cause jurors to behave or decide any differently than they would have at a live trial. The presentation of depositions and full trials on videotape has also enabled research to be easily carried out on the effect of variables such as lawyer credibility and juror communication (Anapol, 1974).

Videotaped presentation of clients for the purpose of psychiatric evaluation has allowed the investigation of cross-national differences in diagnoses (Gurland, 1976). As one of several methods employed, videotapes of clients were shown to a variety of audiences of psychiatrists in many parts of the United Kingdom and United States of America. This allowed close examination of their diagnoses and rating behaviour. The results of this study indicated that different criteria for diagnosis were applied in the two countries.

A further use of recordings of complex behaviour sequences, in this case classroom observations, has enabled the evaluation of different observational coding systems (Borich, Malitz and Kugle, 1978). Again the ability of video recordings to present identical, yet realistic, records of complex behaviour with virtually unlimited replay considerably facilitated the research. These functions could also be performed by film presentations but the practical and financial advantages of video suggest it will be increasingly applied in a variety of different areas.

Implied performance: Indirect recording of behaviour via the environment

The use of video to investigate human performance has also involved the recording of the subject's environment in order to measure indirectly his or her performance. Examples of this come from the field of driving research. This is an area, like social behaviour, in which the performance being studied is an interaction between the driver's behaviour and a continuously changing environment. This makes observation and analysis in the natural environment a complex task.

In situations involving the administration of drugs (Casswell, 1977) and in the monitoring of 'normal' driving performance on the road (Casswell, 1978) a video recorder was used to monitor the driver's environment. In both the field laboratory setting, used to evaluate the effect of drugs on performance, and in the on-the-road situation the recording provided a continuous visual record of the driving environment. The synchronous sound channel was adapted to record the movement of the steering wheel, accelerator, brake and the speed of the vehicle by means of a frequency modulation interface. The availability of the synchronized record allowed the discrimination of vehicle control use on particular parts of both the track and the road. This method provides considerable practical advantages over other methods, the use of event markers for example, particularly in the on-the-road situation.

For recording purposes the camera position was fixed permanently (at driver's eye level, slightly towards the passenger seat). The visual recording was later played back through a monitor with a grid system marked on the screen. Prior work had established the correspondence between different vehicle positions and angles and the recorded image in relation to the grid. It was therefore possible to determine the actual position of the car on selected portions of the roadway during the experimental sessions.

The field laboratory setting was a car race track and subjects were presented with a series of tasks designed to mimic the sequential nature of responding to a natural driving situation. The visual recording was used to measure the overtaking performance of the subjects: the point which they selected as the 'last possible' to pull out to overtake in order to complete the manoeuvre before a marked target area. The speed at which the vehicle was driven during the overtaking manoeuvre was also analysed. A further requirement of the subject was the recognition and response to target names on road signs. The subject's response activated a light which was within the video camera's range and the distance from the sign at which the response took place was estimated from the size of the sign on the video recording. The final measure obtained from the visual recording, as described above, was the lateral placement of the vehicle on several portions of the track. This allowed analysis of the deviations, of amount of 'wobble', in the tracking performance of the subject.

In the field situation the subjects were aware that the recording was taking place but it was thought probable that this was less inhibiting to their performance than an observer in the vehicle would have been. In the on-the-road situation the subjects were not aware that their driving was being monitored. A timing device started the recorder as the subjects were driving the experimental car to the field laboratory setting. Apart from two subjects, one of whom stopped to buy cigarettes and one of whom picked up a hitchhiker (whose head subsequently blocked the camera view), usable data were recorded for a thirty-minute drive. A portion of this was selected for analysis in order to provide comparable data from the same part of the roadway. Analyses from the visual recording (again using the grid system and with the aid of measurements made on the roadway) included the position of the car on the roadway, the response to traffic lights and other signals and the position relative to other vehicles on the road including following and overtaking manoeuvres. Significant differences in driving performance were found between the marijuana users and non-users (in a non-intoxicated state) using this methodology.

The same method of a permanently fixed video camera is now being used to map mental load in car driving (Wildervanck, Mulder and Michon, 1978). The traffic characteristics at various locations and the direction, priorities and speed of the traffic are recorded by means of a video camera mounted behind the windscreen. The driver's physiological response, heart rate and psychomotor response to a subsidiary task are recorded on the auditory channel of the video recorder, again giving a simultaneous recording of aspects of performance in relation to the immediate environment. The use of the video recorder minimizes the experimental effect of observation in a situation in which the level of vigilance and attention is crucial and may be responsive to the presence of observers. It also allows far more reliable coding of the quickly changing environment than is possible from the observations of passengers.

Future directions

During this decade the number of published studies involving the use of videotape recordings has increased considerably in anthropology and even more so in psychology. Currently in the latter discipline video recordings are being used primarily for training and feedback purposes, but research applications are sure to expand in the near future.

The current paradigm shift in social psychology is likely to increase the use of videotape recordings in this area. The move away from the rigorous but sometimes sterile application of the experimental method of observation of individual behaviour in a carefully structured laboratory situation calls for new data collection techniques. A focus on the situational and process variables relevant to human performance implies the need to monitor and analyse sequential social behaviours in context. Allowing as it does for detailed records that can be systematically searched for patterns (Backman, 1979), the use of video recording is particularly suited to this kind of research. The development of new hypotheses and testing them using the same data set is perhaps a less dangerous procedure if the recording contains a relatively complete version of the behaviour and intercoder reliability can be assessed.

The other elements in the 'new paradigm' of social psychology—that men and women are active agents in creating their environment and that the meanings they attribute to their experiences are crucial for an understanding of their behaviour—are also well served by the video technology. The scenario of participant and researcher viewing videotaped recordings of the participant's behaviour and constructing through their interactions a conceptualization of the recorded behaviour is a far cry from the psychological experiment in which manipulations are applied to the black box and selected responses are measured.

An increasing awareness of the need to carry out descriptive studies in natural settings will increase the use of both video recorders and the static camera. These instruments can provide continuous or episodic recordings of performance in a variety of situations (home, workplace and public places), recordings which are subject to repeated detailed analyses. The ethics of the use of video recorders, particularly in public places and with concealed cameras, are likely to be of increasing concern; the practices developed in anthropological research, of signed consent forms and active participation in directing the choice of material, will not apply in all of the projected uses of video recordings. Observations of public behaviour have frequently been carried out by means of pen and paper but the use of video recording may be viewed with more suspicion. Despite these problems the use of video to record human performance both directly and indirectly (through the effects on the environment of the behaviour under study) is certainly likely to increase. It will be one method in a variety used to assess human performance in social situations.

References

Anapol, M. M. (1974). Behind locked doors; an investigation of certain trial and jury variables by means of videotaped trial, *Research in Education*, **9** (5).

Ash, M. J., and Sattler, H. E. (1973). A videotape technique for assessing behavioural correlates of academic performance, *Research in Education*, **8** (8), 62–63.

Backman, C. W. (1979). Epilogue: a new paradigm?, in *Emerging Strategies in Social Psychological Research* (Ed. G. P. Ginsburg), Wiley, New York.

Bedics, R. A., and Webb, J. N. (1971). Measuring the self-evaluation of teaching behaviour through the use of videotape, in *ERIC Educational Documents Abstracts*, CCM Information Corporation, New York.

Birdwhistell, R. L. (1970). *Kinesics and Context*, University of Pennsylvania Press, Philadelphia.

Borich, G. D., Malitz, D., and Kugle, C. L. (1978). Convergent and discriminant validity of a five classroom observation system: testing a model, *Journal of Educational Psychology*, **70** (2), 119–128.

Bunster, X. B. (1977). Talking pictures: field methods and visual mode signs. *Journal of Women in Culture and Society*, **3** (1), 278–293.

Casswell, S. (1977). Cannabis and alcohol effects on closed course driving behaviour, *Proceedings of the Seventh International Conference on Alcohol, Drugs and Traffic Safety, Melbourne*, pp. 238–246.

Casswell, S. (1978). Driving behaviour of cannabis users and non-users in closed-course and normal traffic situations, *Proceedings of the Joint Conference of the American Association for Automotive Medicine and Seventh International Association for Accident and Traffic Medicine*, pp. 330–341.

Collett, P., and Marsh, P. (1974). Patterns of public behaviour: collision avoidance on a pedestrian crossing, *Semotica*, **12**, 281–299.

Collier, J. (1969). *Visual Anthropology*, Holt, Rinehart & Winston, New York.

Connell, D. B. (1981). Videotape perspectives: impact of family oriented intervention, *Resources in Education*, **16** (3), 121.

Davis, G., and Ayers, V. (1975). Photographic recording of Environmental behaviour, in *Behavioural Research Methods in Environmental Design* (Ed. W. Michelson), Halstead Press, New York.

Duncan, S., and Fiske, D. W. (1979). Dynamic patterning in conversation, *American Scientist*, **67**, 90–98.

Duvall, C. R., and Krepel, W. J. (1971). The use of videotape recordings in the analysis of student teaching performance, *Teacher Educator*, **7** (1), 12–16.

Farmer, J. A. (1971). Indigenous, interactional research, *Resources in Education*, **6** (9), 135.

Farmer, L. C., Williams, G. R., Lee, R. E., Cundick, B. P., Howell, R. J., and Rooker, C. K. (1976). Jurors perceptions of trial testimony as a function of the method of presentation, in *Psychology and the Law: Research Frontiers* (Eds. G. Bermant, C. Nemeth and N. Vidmar), D. C. Heath, Lexington, Massachusetts.

Florio, S., and Walsh, M. (1976). The teacher as colleague in classroom research, in *ERIC Educational Documents Abstracts*, MacMillan Information, New York.

Fuller, F. F., and Manning, B. A. (1973). Self-confrontation reviewed: a conceptualization for video playback in teacher education, *Review of Education Research*, **43** (4), 469–528.

Gurland, B. (1976). Aims, organisation and initial studies of the cross-national project, *International Journal of Aging and Human Development*, **7** (4), 283–293.

Hosler, W. (1973). Videotape: a research tool?, *Journal of Physical Education and Recreation*, **48**, 53.

Krebs, S. (1975). The film elicitation techniques, in *Principles of Visual Anthropology* (Ed. P. Hockings), Mouton, Hawthorne, New York.

Kysilka, M., and Anderson, B. (1972). A study to evaluate supervisory feedback for student teachers, in *ERIC Educational Documents Abstracts*, MacMillan Information, New York.

Lomax, A. (1975). Audio visual tools for the analysis of culture style, in *Principles of Visual Anthropology* (Ed. P. Hockings), Mouton, Hawthorne, New York.

Miller, G. (1972). Measuring children's curiosity, *Resources in Education*, **7** (8), 78.

Miller, G. R. (1976). The effects of videotaped trial materials on juror response, in *Psychology and the Law: Research Frontiers* (Eds. G. Bermant, C. Nemeth and N. Vidmar), D. C. Heath, Lexington, Massachusetts.

Schaeffer, J. H. (1975). Videotape: new techniques of observation and analysis in anthropology, in *Principles of Visual Anthropology* (Ed. P. Hockings), Mouton, Hawthorne, New York.

Short, L. G. (1972). Gather data with videotape—or how to put the cart before the horse, *Educational and Industrial Television*, **4** (8), 13–15.

Walkey, F. H., and Gilmour, D. R. (1979). Comparative evaluation of a videotaped measure of interpersonal distance, *Journal of Consulting and Clinical Psychology*, **47** (3), 575–580.

Wildervanck, C., Mulder, G., and Michon, J. A. (1978). Mapping mental load in car driving, *Ergonomics*, **21** (3), 225–229.

Ziegler, V. E., Meyer, D. A., Rosen, S. H., and Biggs, J. T. (1978). Reliability of videotaped Hamilton ratings, *Recent Advances in Biological Psychiatry*, **17**, 119–122.

Using Video
Edited by P. W. Dowrick and S. J. Biggs
© 1983 John Wiley & Sons Ltd

Chapter 3

Considerations of the Participant in Video Recording

Charles M. Renne

National Jewish Hospital, National Asthema Center, Denver

Peter W. Dowrick

University of Alaska, Anchorage

and

Glenn Wasek

Harvard University, Cambridge

The writing of this chapter was supported in part by a National Institute of Heart, Lung and Blood Grant No. HL-22021, and facilitated in part by grants MH-32101 and MH-32469 from the National Institute of Mental Health. We thank Joan Kroll for her contributions to the preparation of this manuscript.

There is an interactive effect between a video recording and its subject: each has an effect on the other. This chapter deals first with the rights of a videotaped participant. Participants must be informed of exactly what will happen in the course of observation, how the tapes will subsequently be used and how they may withdraw from participation if necessary. It is in everyone's best interests to use a form of signed consent, witnessed if possible—certainly where children are subjects. Furthermore, special care must be taken to preserve the context of videotaped information.

Secondly, there is the manner in which participants' behaviour will change under video observation. Specific reactions to being recorded include changes in both personal appearance and focal behaviour. Some generalizations among sub-populations have been made; e.g. highly disturbed or disadvantaged clients tend to react proportionally more to the camera with respect to verbal inhibition. However, both generalized and individual reactions can be ameliorated by planned considerations. Most importantly, participants can become adapted to the recording situations by specific strategies of education and exposure. Furthermore, steps may be taken by the experimenter or therapist to minimize reactive effects either at the recording stage or as part of the data analysis.

Considerations of the participant in video recording

There are two major aspects of the participant's involvement to consider when making videotape recordings. Firstly, there is the protection of the participant from any immediate or subsequent undesirable effects. The second aspect is, in a way, the reverse: 'protecting' the video recording against the atypical reactions by the participant in the recording situation.

Ethical standards and safeguards

Video recording has some special and some general ethical implications. Occasionally there are serious consequences when ethical guidelines are not followed. The principal issue concerns procedures for protecting personal rights when recruiting individuals for projects involving video recording.

Currently, there appears to be a trend towards a heightened awareness of the rights of recipients of human services and research practices—witness the proliferation of articles and books on the topic (e.g. Cohen, 1980; Hannah, Christian and Clark, 1981). Indeed, human rights issues in this connection are still evolving with much variation from one country to the next in defining what these rights are, procedures for safeguarding them and even in the degree of recognition that human rights present a legitimate issue.

Recently in the United States the impetus towards establishing guidelines of ethical procedure has arisen primarily as a consequence of legal challenges concerning the rights of institutionalized persons. The National Commission for the Protection of Human Subjects of Biomedical and Behavioral Research was created partly in response to apparent abuse and the resulting challenges. The Commission formalized sound principles and practices that later served as guidelines for the protection of human rights in other areas. Three central principles were identified: respect for persons, beneficience and justice (National Commission for the Protection of Human Subjects, 1978). Table 1 displays an informed consent document intended to incorporate the first two principles as they apply to video recording practices. The form was developed at the National Asthma Center in Denver, Colorado, where it was used in combination with more general consent forms in research, training and treatment projects. These latter forms included information on the necessity for, or advantages of, using video recording in the projects, and what (if any) alternative recording procedures were available. After the project consent statements were understood by prospective participants, the video recording consent statements were reviewed with them. In view of the 'respect for persons' principle the document was designed to provide complete information, specific to video recording, and to foster understanding of that information by all parties prior to their participation decisions. The principle of 'beneficience' is approached by including information on the risks associated with being video recorded and on strategies for reducing risks or subsequent problems if they arise. It was because of the potential seriousness of these risks and the availability of alternative recording procedures in most projects that the video consent statement was developed.

Violations of privacy and confidentiality are the primary risks associated

VIDEO RECORDING CONSENT STATEMENT

I understand that (1) my identity will be protected in all written references to the video tapes and by audio sound masking of the tapes, when possible, but that some risk of identification remains, for example via facial/visual identification by anyone viewing the video tapes; (2) that all recorded video tapes will be stored in a secure manner with access to them limited to approved project personnel, but that in spite of these precautions, the possibility of unauthorized access to the tapes exists; (3) that all video tapes will be erased immediately upon the date of completion as specified below, unless I provide written consent to extend this time; (4) that reactions or feelings may occur in me as a result of the anticipation of being video recorded, or while being video recorded, which may be uncomfortable or undesired, such as suspiciousness, fear, anxiety, etc., and that while they are usually short-lived, the reactions may at least temporarily influence how I respond toward others. I understand that project personnel will be available to discuss any concerns that I or they may have over my reactions or responses. (5) That I may withdraw this written consent refuse to continue being video recorded, and have all previously recorded tape segments erased at any time with impunity, and without otherwise jeopardizing my participation in the program or the availability of appropriate alternative procedures.

I fully understand the risks to me and the limitations in the procedures described above and I freely and voluntarily consent to the video recording of myself and my dependents for the purpose of *(specify program or project)*_____

_____

Also, I waive the right to view the recorded video tapes, but the video tapes may be viewed and scored, and the information processed and used by those persons specified in the project informed consent document which I have signed, until *(date)* _____ when all recorded video tape must be erased.

_____   _____   I am satisfied that all participants
Signature of Participant(s)   *Date Signed*   have given an informed consent.

_____   _____
                                                             _____
                                                             Signature of Witness

_____   _____

*   *   *   *   *   *   *   *   *   *   *   *   *   *   *   *   *   *   *

RECORDED VIDEO TAPE EXTENSION CONSENT STATEMENT

_____ I do not consent to extend the time or use of recorded video tapes beyond that specified in the original agreement of _____*(date)*.

_____ I do consent to extend the time for use of recorded video tapes by already approved project personnel to _____*(date)*, with the right to withdraw this consent at any time.

_____ I do consent to extend the time for use of recorded video tapes by already approved project personnel to _____*(new date)* for purposes other than that specified in the original agreement of _____*(date)*, with the purpose(s) left to the discretion of _____, and with the right to withdraw this consent at any time.

_____ I do consent to the distribution of my recorded video tapes for unlimited research or training purposes with:

_____ a. No additional proviso(s).
_____ b. The additional proviso that there be no general public viewing unless each video tape is first reviewed and cleared by me personally.

_____   _____   I am satisfied that all participants
Signature of Participant(s)   *Date Signed*   have given an informed consent.

_____   _____
                                                             _____
                                                             Signature of Witness

_____   _____

Table 1 Video recording and recorded videotape extension consent forms

with the video recording method. The method produces permanent visual and auditory records in which it is difficult to ensure anonymity, and the longer that recorded tapes are kept, the greater the risk of exposing their contents to unauthorized persons. The seriousness of these risks demands not only an informed consent statement but also some discussion of safeguarding confidentiality. A minimally informed decision would include a clear statement of the reasons for using video recording and, specifically, who will view the tapes and how they will be stored, processed and erased.

Another risk is that some people react to being video recorded with fear, suspicion or embarrassment. While such reactions are usually temporary and mild, severe reactions occasionally appear with undesirable behavioural by-products, such as aggression or treatment disruption. Participants have a right to know that such reactions can occur, and what they can do about it, including if necessary discontinuing the recording.

Occasionally a project cannot be concluded by an agreed-upon date; or additional uses of recorded tapes may surface later which were not included in either the project or the video recording consent statements. Abuse of the rights of participants is more likely to occur out of such situations than in connection with the original procedures. The recorded video tape extension consent statement in Table 1 was developed to help cover this situation. It includes requests for extension of time and for viewing by additional persons or for further purposes. It also specifies any limiting conditions. It is helpful to include this extension statement on the same form as the video recording informed consent statement.

The National Commission (1978) stipulates the procedures to follow for obtaining informed consent. According to the Commission, 'Provision should be made to obtain assent from children, consent or permission from adults and to monitor the solicitation of both.' Furthermore, 'A child's objections should be binding unless there is a prospect of direct benefit to the child.' In the spirit of this guideline, provision can be made on the consent statements for signatures by several prospective participants and a witness. In the family projects it is typical to expect parents and their children above the age of six years to arrive at their participation decision together and, if they choose to participate and agree to being video recorded, to sign the consent forms witnessed by a neutral party. This witness monitors all proceedings and testifies to the voluntary nature of their decisions.

Another consideration is whether to permit participants to view their own recorded videotapes. This decision is not always a straightforward one. There may be a strong negative impact on some persons from observing themselves or significant others on videotape. Discerning who is likely to experience a negative reaction or how intense the experience may be for a given individual can be a risky venture. When effects of viewing are even doubtful, it is wise to include a clause on the consent document waiving the right of participants to see their videotapes. With this strategy, participants would not expect to see the tapes; but a decision to permit viewing on a selective basis could be made later by project personnel. Participants should never enter a project believing that they might view their tapes when, in fact, they may not, and possibly should not, see them.

The last ethical consideration to be presented here involves producing or making use of distorted information extracted from recorded videotapes. These may be instances in which interpretations are taken out of context or where a context imposed on the recording situation results in distortion. When such information leads to erroneous conclusions which are used to support an opinion or theory, there are serious practical and ethical implications. Failing to observe the context of specific responses under study accounts for most distorted information extracted from video recordings. An example of such a distortion could result from a parent directing a child into solitary play activity when the video recorded behaviour (which omits the parent's instructions) will be scored later on some social adjustment scale. A more serious problem arises if the erroneous scores are used to support an hypothesis that the youngster is socially deficient.

Obviously, as with other ethical considerations discussed above, this problem is not unique to the video recording method; nor is the production or use of distorted information necessarily deliberate. However, the video recording method approaches an ideal by permitting careful information processing and accurate scoring with an advantage over other methods in producing more complete information. Therefore, it becomes that much more important for personnel using video recording methods to take all possible precautions to avoid or to correct distortions, however they are produced.

Video representation and reality

Our concern is whether video recordings accurately reflect the naturally occurring behaviour of participants. Are they representative of participants' responses outside of the video sessions? The remainder of this chapter will deal with identifying and minimizing factors which produce atypicalities in recording.

Video recorded behaviours may be unrepresentative in terms of their form, intensity, duration or frequency of occurrence. The more common distortions are: (1) the increased or decreased rate of focal behaviours; (2) changes in response magnitude, such as increases or decreases in severity or duration, of focal behaviours; (3) the appearance of behaviours which interfere with the activity under study; (4) the introduction of new, unrepresentative responses. The sources of such distortion are diverse, but we will concentrate on effects caused by the participants' reactions to the recording situation.

Participant reactivity Johnson and Bolstadt (1972) defined reactivity simply as 'the effect of the observation process on the observee'. While they were referring to the presence of a live observer, this definition and its implications appear to have relevance for all observation methods, including video recording. However, the specific effects on participants will vary depending upon the observation or recording method used, in combination with the context at the time and the individual differences of the participants. For example, reactivity may be noted in such diverse ways as changes in personal grooming and housekeeping practices, changes in voice tone or level, gestures and direct references to the camera and changes in the amount of focal behaviour.

The occurrence of participant reactivity has been described in the literature. Carmichael (1966) found strong evidence of client awareness of being video recorded across a set of notes and tapes from 19 therapy sessions, although the therapist was unaware of this reactivity at the time. In another project, increases occurred in the 'socially desirable' behaviour of aids on a ward for retarded clients during periods of video recording, which did not generalize to their unrecorded work on other wards or at other times (Spencer and coauthors, 1974). Gelso (1973) reported that video in contrast to audio recording inhibited self-exploration and diminished counselling satisfaction of clients with personal problems, and claimed that some of these effects interfered with therapy. Furthermore, there was no decrease in reactivity from the first to the second session.

That Gelso found greater reactivity to video than to audio recording is not surprising since such factors as bright lighting, operator movements and equipment sounds are usually prominent with video recording. Also, the participant's awareness that a greater amount of personal information is being collected and preserved would further heighten reactivity to video recording. In other comparison studies, clients in video recording conditions rated counselling as less stimulating (Tanney and Gelso, 1972), emitted fewer verbal statements per minute and showed decreases in the average physical distance between each other when in groups (Decker, 1976) than they did in conditions using other forms of observation.

There are apparently some generalizations within sub-populations. Our own observations lead us to believe that children adapt more quickly than adults when being video recorded. Possibly they forget the camera more readily and become absorbed in the activities at hand; certainly they are far less critical of physical characteristics if they later have an opportunity to review their tapes. Also, there appears to be less obvious reactivity from persons in larger groups than from individuals in smaller groups—perhaps because of some feeling of anonymity connected with membership in larger groups. There is also some indication that group differences in reactivity to video recording may occur as a result of social economic status (SES). Randall (1976) found that working class mothers verbalized significantly less to their infants during an obtrusive, live observer condition than did middle class mothers who showed no changes in their verbalizations across the same conditions. It seems likely that a similar or even greater effect would be found on this SES dimension with video recording.

Results reported by other investigators support the belief that there are differences in participant reactivity among therapy clients. Gelso and Tanney (1972) found that a group of subjects with compulsive traits were more likely to report inhibition when being audio recorded than were persons who were without these traits. Clients in counselling for personal problems as distinct from those in vocational counselling reported less satisfaction with the counselling experience while being video recorded (Gelso, 1972, 1973), and Decker (1976) found a positive correlation between counselling readiness and the number of therapeutically useful statements made by clients while being recorded on video.

Reactivity to being observed does not always occur. Stempf (1977), for example, claims that self-disclosure of patients in group therapy was not adversely affected by video recording. Kogan (1950) reported that caseworkers judged their clients to be low in reactivity to audio recording during therapy and concluded that this minimal reactivity dissipated within a few sessions. Purcell and Brady (1965) found little evidence of reactivity, reporting that adolescents adapted quickly to monitoring via a radio telemetry procedure.

How do we account for these conclusions, given the significant reactivity found in other studies? Perhaps some of the discrepancy may be explained by differences in the source of information, specifically information derived from subjective judgements versus more objective data. In projects that obtained both objective and subjective data, the results indicated that reactivity was present; whereas subjective judgements, whether from participants (Decker, 1976; Gelso, 1973) or from project personnel (Carmichael, 1966; Gelso, 1973; Tanney and Gelso, 1972), provided little or no evidence of a reactive effect. These results call into question the validity of judgements in this regard, particularly from persons with vested interests in the projects. Another possible explanation is that the manifestation of reactivity can take different forms and may therefore be inappropriately monitored. For example, where a specific reactive response is expected to be observed across a group of participants, but where the actual form of expression varies widely, the reactivity could be missed. In other words, although group differences in participant reactivity may abound, individual differences in participant reactivity are even greater. Nervousness is perhaps most commonly reported. Yet, even nervousness can vary radically—from pacing the floor to an indiscernible stomach quiver—and attempting to document its existence by observing too specific a response across a group of individuals will probably not be fruitful.

Although participant reactivity is highly individual, specific reactive responses are often clustered together and labelled with some commonly used blanket construct, e.g. nervousness. Typically, nervous responses are seen as being temporary reactions to change or to new situations, whereas other forms of reactivity are perceived more as expressions of human traits or intrinsic characteristics. Participants who are shy, suspicious, delusional or destructive belong to the latter category. Their reaction will most likely intensify the characteristics they bring to the video recording situation. The question may arise of whether to preclude an entire subgroup of individuals (e.g. in extremes, such as those labelled paranoid or brain damaged) from participation in video recording projects. In our opinion the participation decision should not be based on some generalized concept, but on an individual basis. With advance information about the idiosyncrasies of each participant's responses and with careful preparation, even potentially severe reactivity can be prevented. The final decision to include a potentially reactive participant in a project will depend on the expected degree of reactivity, the participant's level of cooperation, and the capability of project personnel to provide the required support.

Most reactivity reducing efforts can be grouped under one of two classifications: general routines and personalised routines. General routines are subdivided into five strategies: *preparation, familiarization, adaptation, minimization* and *programming*. Personalised routines are organized under two sets of strategies: *attention management* and *direct influence*.

Preparation of all prospective participants should begin with efforts to obtain their informed consent. In conjunction with educating participants about the project (thereby reducing some of the reactivity) this provides an opportunity to obtain information about their potential reactivity to video recording.

Familiarization activities acquaint participants with the video recording setting, the video tape processing and storage system, equipment and key personnel prior to the start of the project. This may include handling the equipment and observing it in operation. However, familiarization should not automatically include participant viewing of recorded tapes since, in some cases, the viewing may actually increase reactivity by interacting negatively with specific personal problems, increasing self-consciousness or simply heightening awareness of being recorded.

Adaptation is a strategy which can be implemented after recording has begun, but it may not be necessary to use the approach in all projects. A certain amount of time is set aside to allow the participant to get used to project conditions, contingent upon individual differences in reactivity and interaction with the objectives of the project. One method for determining the adaptation period involves taking baseline measures of specific reactive responses (e.g. verbal references to video or number of verbal interactions) until they reach specified criteria of occurrence. A change in the level of responding may occur simply as a function of time or with the opportunity to experience the situation. In two experimental demonstrations of this phenomenon, Bretherton (1978) found increased cooperation from one-year-old children over successive two-minute intervals and showed that, with repeated sequences of interactions between mothers and their children, the bouts became longer and more intensive (Bretherton, Stollberg and Kreye, 1981). However, a dilemma may exist when adaptation exposure may exacerbate other reactivity. Keeping hyperactive children within a small room for adaptation and videotaping may present an example of this dilemma in that the longer they are confined, the greater the risk of losing their interest and increasing their activity level. The increased activity is likely, in turn, to result in greater difficulty in keeping them confined to the video recording area.

Minimization of the contextual influence is an extremely important strategy for limiting reactivity. Placing the camera, microphone and operator out of direct view of participants and keeping the camera noise, required lighting and operator movement to a minimum are important to this endeavour. All equipment and controls should be out of the reach of children, not only to avoid harm (to them and the equipment) but also to avoid unnecessary disciplining and other disruptions. When possible, the camera should be operated from behind a one-way screen with a lens sensitive enough to produce good recording under normal lighting conditions; this avoids a build-up of heat as well as bright light. Ideally, microphones should be out of view or at least inconspicuous (e.g. suspended from the ceiling above the participants or attached to the camera). When the presence of the camera and operator cannot be avoided, additional precautions are necessary to minimize their influence. Operators' appearance and interactions should be as unobtrusive and neutral as possible at all times. Any movements with the camera ought to be performed smoothly and quietly, with changes in location of the operator and camera minimized through advance planning. Finally, it is advisable to avoid involving participants in any responsibility for organizing the recording situation, operating the equipment or even turning on the lights.

The *programming* strategies are planned in the design stages of a project. There are two commonly employed strategies. One involves either delaying video recording for some while after the time that participants believe they are being recorded or discarding beginning video segments. The decision of when to start recording or to stop eliminating tape segments should be based on some preestablished criteria of elapsed time or diminished reactivity. The second programming strategy is that of arranging the experimental design to equal out any effects resulting from participant reactivity. These programming strategies, together with the adaptation strategies, often help to achieve greater control over the influence of participant reactivity in research projects.

Any combination of these strategies may be applicable to any one project. For example, when the primary concern is nervousness, ordinarily a transitory effect, one or two of these general strategies may be sufficient to avoid the problem. However, when reactivity is severe it may be necessary to include several strategies, with perhaps some individualized assistance. In practice, the actual strategies chosen will be determined by the cost-benefits to the project.

Individual assistance can be personalised using two basic strategies: *attention management*, which indirectly influences a reduction in reactivity by increasing competing, non-reactive behaviour, and *direct influence* which focuses squarely on the participant's experience in attempting to reduce or eliminate reactivity.

Baiting the situation with items of interest to participants, such as table games, is an effective attention management procedure, particularly with children or with others having problems related to confinement. The procedure seems to work because the items help to divert attention from the video recording situation. As reactivity wanes, it should be possible to phase out unrelated items.

The altered states procedure, ordinarily administered outside the video session itself, is another attention management strategy. Through hypnosis or psychotropic medications, attention can be diverted from the video recording and focused on some other aspect of the situation. For example, Hall, LeCoun and Schoolar (1978) used a combination of amobarbital and structured interviewing with video recording and playback to treat a patient with multiple personality. The amobarbital not only aided the memory but also the verbalization of it, while reducing participant reactivity to the video recording.

Other attention management strategies include: scripting, which provides a complete, overall structure for participant responding in video sessions; instructing, which gives somewhat looser direction for participants to follow during the sessions; and prompting, for occasioning competing behaviours.

The direct influence strategies attempt to reduce the reactivity of participants through such procedures as active listening, discussion or providing reassurance and feedback. These procedures are especially useful in quelling anxiety made worse by the video recording situation, although occasionally more intensive psychological intervention, vis-à-vis counselling or psychotherapy, is required. A careful preassessment may help to identify high-risk individuals whose inclusion in the video recording project can then be accompanied by assurance of the available support.

References

Bretherton, I. (1978). Making friends with one-year-olds: an experimental study of infant–stranger interaction, *Merrill-Palmer Quarterly*, **24**, 29–51.

Bretherton, I., Stollberg, U., and Kreye, M. (1981). Engaging strangers in proximal interaction: infants social initiative, *Developmental Psychology*, **17**, 746–755.

Carmichael, H. (1966). Sound-film recording of psychoanalytic therapy, in *Research Methods in Psychotherapy* (Eds. L. Gottschalk and A. Overboch), Appleton-Century-Croft, New York.

Cohen, H. (1980). *Equal Rights for Children*, Rowman and Littlefield, Totowa, New Jersey.

Decker, R. E. (1976). The effects of visual observation, videotape and audio recording on verbal and nonverbal behavior in group psychotherapy, *Dissertation Abstracts*, **37**, 1428–B.

Gelso, C. J. (1972). Inhibition due to recording and clients' evaluation of counseling, *Psychological Reports*, **31**, 675–677.

Gelso, C. J. (1973). Effect of audiorecording and videorecording on client satisfaction and self-expression, *Journal of Consulting and Clinical Psychology*, **40**, 455–461.

Gelso, C. J., and Tanney, M. F. (1972). Client personality as a mediator of the effects of recording, *Counselor Education and Supervision*, **12**, 109–114.

Hall, R. C., LeCoun, A. F., and Schoolar, J. C. (1978). Amobarbital treatment of multiple personality: use of structured video tape interviewing as a basis for intensive psychotherapy, *The Journal of Nervous and Mental Diseases*, **166**, 666–670.

Hannah, G. T., Christian, W. P., and Clark, H. B. (1981). *Preservation of Client Rights*, The Free Press, New York.

Johnson, S. M., and Bolstadt, O. D. (1972). Methodological issues in naturalistic observation: some problems and solutions for field research, *Proceedings of the Banff Conference*, Research Press, Champaign, Illinois.

Kogan, L. S. (1950). The electrical recording of social casework interviews, *Social Casework*, **31**, 371–378.

National Commission (1978). *The Belmont Report: Ethical Principles and Guidelines for the Protection of Human Subjects of Research*, HEW Publication No. (05) 78-0013.

National Commission for the Protection of Human Subjects of Biomedical and Behavioral Research (1978). Protection of human subjects: research involving children, *Federal Register*, July 1978, 43 (No. 141).

Purcell, K., and Brady, K. (1965). Adaptation to the invasion of privacy: monitoring behavior with a miniature radio transmitter, *Merrill Palmer Quarterly*, **12**, 242–254.

Randall, T. A. (1976). An analysis of observer influence on sex and social class differences in mother–infant interaction, *ERIC Reports*, ED. No. 114204, March 1976.

Spencer, F. W., Corcoran, C. A., Allen, G. J., Chinsky, J. M., and Veit, S. W. (1974). Reliability and reactivity of the videotape technique on a ward for retarded children, *Journal of Community Psychology*, **2**, 71–74.

Stempf, C. R. (1977). The effects of the presence of video-recording on self disclosure in a group therapy setting as a function of repression and sensitization defensive styles, *Dissertation Abstracts*, **37**, 5380.

Tanney, M. F., and Gelso, C. J. (1972). Effect of recording on clients, *Journal of Counseling Psychology*, **19**, 349–350.

Using Video
Edited by P. W. Dowrick and S. J. Biggs
© 1983 John Wiley & Sons Ltd

Chapter 4

The Analysis of Video Records

Gabrielle M. Maxwell

and

Judith K. Pringle

University of Otago, Dunedin, New Zealand

This chapter contains some of the issues of concern in making decisions about the analysis of video records. The perspective is largely that of the student of social interaction concerned either to measure behaviour, to obtain judgemental ratings or to obtain behavioural judgements which use normative anchor points. While there are disadvantages to the use of video, its advantages in potentially increasing the reliability and validity of measurement are considerable.

Some techniques for covering the novel ethical issues are offered. Issues that determine choices about methods of analysis are discussed, including the use of continuous versus time sampling techniques. Finally, a sequence for decision-making strategies about choice of camera technique and method of analysis is briefly outlined to include the above considerations.

Measurements

In the sixties and early seventies, many people including ourselves believed that with the advent of video recording systems, computerized analysis of records and advanced multivariate statistical techniques it would be possible to reconstruct from the analysis of specific behaviour, the judgements we make about other people and about the situations in which we find ourselves. We believed that the analysis of social performance would be possible in a similar manner to the analysis of motor skills that could be made by the microanalysis of physical movement (Welford, 1980). Such a conceptualization led to a focus on *behavioural measurement*, which can be defined as the attempt to assess accurately the observable and objectively definable aspects of a record, such as the amount of gaze, postural configuration and other aspects of behaviour. At the same time, researchers often attempted to obtain *judgemental ratings* such as friendly/unfriendly, dominant/submissive which were the dependent variables that could be predicted by the *behavioural measures* (cf. Argyle, 1975; Mehrabian, 1972).

At first, researchers were content to explain some of the variance in social judgements by measuring behaviour. As techniques improved, researchers became dissatisfied with their failure to account for more of the variance. This failure is partly because it is difficult to measure enough of the behaviour, many of the behavioural measures are simplistically coded and the sequence and timing of events are almost certainly critical in determining human judgements. This is also true when using video records. Consequently, there has been a shift in research orientation so that increasingly more of the research has been concerned with analysing the sequence of behavioural events (Argyle, 1979) while other research has tended to use *behavioural judgements*.

We are using the term 'behavioural judgements' to cover instances where the rater's attention is focused on specific behaviour but the rater is expected not to measure it. The rater has to make a judgement about the level of the behaviour compared to norms which are established partly by his or her own experience and partly by experience in training sessions on a representative set of records. Examples of *behavioural judgements* would be instances where after viewing a record, raters are asked to use a seven-point scale with such labels as: looks a lot/looks very little, voice loud/soft, moves a lot/very still. Provided that raters are reliable, several behavioural judgements can be made after a single viewing of a research tape. An advantage of using behavioural judgements rather than behavioural measures is that the rater can adjust ratings for the effects of different contexts according to his or her understanding of social norms so that direct comparisons can be made of records obtained from slightly different applied or public settings.

A third type of measurement used with video records is to obtain a *judgemental rating* where the researcher is concerned with measuring the impression created by a subject. Frequently judgemental ratings will be obtained in studies of person perception where the effects of various experimental manipulations on the impression are being assessed (cf. studies of the effects of warmth or physical attractiveness). In social interaction research the problem has often been defined as one of explaining the impression by the variation in non-verbal behaviour (Mehrabian's 1968 studies of the concomitants of warmth and interest and Argyle, Alkema and Gilmour's 1972 study of the effects of variation in style and content on judgements of friendliness).

This chapter pursues three objectives. It discusses the advantages and disadvantages of using videotape and in particular issues in reliability and validity which can be tackled when the original record of behaviour can be readily re-examined as often as the researcher wishes. There is a short discussion on ethics relating to video analysis followed by a discussion of the basic methods of analysing the record. Finally, we suggest decisions that need to be made in analysing a video record and a sequence in which the decisions could be made. Throughout, distinctions are made between *behavioural measurement, behavioural judgements* and *judgemental ratings*.

Advantages and disadvantages

The event of videotaping has added an entirely new dimension to the study of human behaviour. Previously those who wished to study interaction behaviour were limited to measuring or judging what was occurring in real-time and limited to using only the number of observers that could be hidden unobtrusively in a crowded public thoroughfare or could be huddled behind a one-way vision screen. Reliability of such recording was a continual problem as the use of additional raters to check reliability meant further reducing what could be observed. The inability to slow the speed of events limited measurement to easily codable categories and the effects on raters of such variables as time of day, order of episodes rated, time elapsed since training sessions and extraneous cues were difficult to control or to eliminate.

A few researchers were fortunate enough to be able to afford film. The extra information thus obtained often made such studies classics (cf. Gesell and Halverson, 1942; Lewin, Lippitt and White, 1939), but these pioneer studies could rarely be replicated. The low cost of videotape, its reusability, the ease with which an amateur can record, the control over playback speed, the relative simplicity of editing records and the ability fairly simply to separate and recombine the image are all important features over film. The use of videotape enables a novice researcher to obtain data that previously required large research grants and highly trained support personnel. Furthermore, the ability to replay in a single room scenes filmed in a variety of locations enables the use of computers for immediate analysis of ratings and so eliminates the time that would otherwise be spent in coding, checking and transcribing scores.

However, the use of video is not without dangers and disadvantages. Once the available research facilities include video, it is tempting to use it on almost every occasion where behaviour is to be analysed. Even where the initial analysis is simple, there is a tendency to make a recording, 'just in case' later analysis is desirable. Similarly, it is tempting to overanalyse records simply because they are available, in a manner analogous to the survey researcher who asks questions that are not germane to the principle goals of enquiry. The decision to record should not, however, be taken lightly as there are a number of distinct disadvantages to the use of video. Behaviour can become less spontaneous because the subjects are concerned with being recorded. The recording itself is almost always more poorly defined than the observer's view of the original behaviour. Shadows interfere with the recorded image more than they do with the naked eye and the high light levels needed for clear records can produce discomfort. The unselective lens often focuses attention differently so that various behaviours appear more or less important; for instance gesturing usually seems more noticeable on a videotape than during an on-line observation. Three-dimensional cues are absent from the video record and since the two-dimensional image is lacking in cues of depth, movement towards the camera produce an enlarged image on the video in a way that is not apparent to the naked eye. The person observing a video record will often feel more remote from the situation whereas watching an actual scene increases the sense of involvement which may improve motivation and hence make for more accurate judgements when the raters are being required to take an interactional perspective, e.g. judging Mary's liking for Bruce. Fixed angles of observation imposed by the placement of the camera do not allow the same flexibility as the on-line situation, where observers may position themselves in order to obtain the best angle from which to view the behaviour of concern.

Thus on-line analysis, i.e. observing and recording behaviour while it is occurring, may often produce optimal results. However, video has some very specific additional advantages which have tended to make it the method of choice for a wide variety of research problems.

The specific advantages of using videotape for the analysis of data can be summarized under the two headings of reliability and validity.

Reliability of measurement from video records

The ability to replay all or part of a record makes it possible to develop scoring techniques that are highly reliable and to ensure that this is maintained throughout rating procedures. Such reliability can be achieved if the researcher is alert to the potential sources of unreliability and designs the recording procedure to eliminate the most common sources of bias.

When judgemental ratings are being made, unreliability can occur because of the responses of a particular judge or set of judges who are not representative of the possible population of judges. We have experienced this problem when using graduate students to rate self-disclosure. We found that New Zealand born and educated students made substantially different judgements from the original judge who was born and educated in the United States. Different judgements were also made by two other judges who were born and educated in Switzerland and England respectively. Similarly, the time at which the judgement is made and, in particular, the amount of time that has elapsed since training or since the last judging session are also factors that can alter reliability.

Judgements may also vary as a function of other judge characteristics; for instance whether the judges are male or female, well or poorly educated, trained or untrained, experienced or naive about psychological theories, similar or dissimilar from the subject in terms of culture. Judgements of the characteristics of others have often showed projection effects (cf. ratings of friendliness by Darnbusch and coauthors, 1965, and well-being by Irwin, Kammann and Dixon, 1978). In judgements of physical attractiveness we have found significantly lower reliability coefficients between male and female judges than within male or within female judges (Burr, 1977).

Interference from the behaviour of the judges themselves sometimes occurs in on-line studies. Sudden laughter from behind a one-way vision screen or a loud sneeze may be audible to the subjects, while in a public place the visibility of the judges and any failure to record unobtrusively may affect the subject's behaviour. Similarly, particular behaviour of the subjects may affect the judge's ratings unduly. For instance a casual remark may alert the judges to the nature of an experimental manipulation about which you wish them to remain naive (e.g. that the recording is being made after an intervention programme or that this is the second occasion they have gone through this procedure). These remarks can be easily eliminated from a video record.

Aspects of the situation in which judgements are made, or additional information possessed by the judges, can also affect reliability. We recently carried out a study to determine whether a group of judges who have made judgemental ratings (e.g. warm, proud, submissive, anxious) of subjects in interaction make the same judgements as judges who rate not only judgemental ratings but have been trained to make reliable behavioural judgements (e.g. speech frequency, voice volume, postural tension). It is possible that the training of judges to make behavioural judgements may also change their attentional focus in such a way that biases judgemental ratings.

Changes in the judging standards used by raters from the start to the end of a set of records may also be a possible source of unreliability. Kazdin (1977) describes this movement by raters away from original definitions of categories as 'observer drift'. He suggests a variety of ways for which this might be controlled, such as training all raters together as a unit, giving intermittent feedback on their accuracy, rating the videotapes in random order. These suggestions have been incorporated into our procedure for analysing video records.

Changes in a judge's frame of reference can also change as a function of the type of training material used and the amount of practice given in the use of the scales. We standardly obtain repeated judgements of the first rated records at the end of our rating sessions. If there is evidence of change in scores we continue to obtain repeated ratings until we are convinced that the judges can reproduce their ratings.

The actual order of presentation of the records is another possible source of unreliability. A preceding record may create a set that affects the ratings of the subsequent record. Although we have never found this with any of the studies we have made using video records, we have found that changing the order of a set of slides designed to measure accuracy in the recognition of facial emotion has changed the probability with which individual slides will be recognized (Harrison, 1979).

When measuring behaviour, other common sources of unreliability are fatigue from lengthy sessions, asking a rater to use too many categories, the difficulty of maintaining reliability at real-time speed, in addition to the well-recognized problem of the inadequate definition of behavioural categories. Pilot testing should always be carried out prior to assessing records to ensure that reliability cannot only be achieved but also maintained. This is a relatively simple task when the records are on videotape.

Access to the experimental hypotheses and background information on the subjects are well known as possible sources of unreliability in judgements, and on occasion we have suspected that such information can affect behavioural measures also. Thus a wise precaution is to always use raters who are blind to the experimental hypotheses and discard any results obtained when a rater is acquainted with a subject.

Another possible source of unreliability is the effect of any earlier impressions of a subject on the judgement of subsequent records of the same subject. We have found that judges are quite unable to recall accurately their earlier impressions of a subject whose record was judged at least 30 records previously. Furthermore, the judgements of other fresh judges of the later record seem to be consistent with that of the judges who were exposed to the same subject previously. However, the nature of the ratings and the conditions under which the judgements are made may create bias when raters judge the same subject repeatedly.

In summary, there are many possible sources of unreliability in the analysis of video records but all these are able to be overcome provided the researcher carries out adequate pilot testing of the rating methodology and is careful to eliminate or control for the most common sources of bias. Unreliability may arise from selecting judges who are not representative of the relevant population of judges, from specific characteristics of judges such as age, sex or education that may lead to differences in ratings, from information on the records that alerts judges to experimental conditions, from the effect of the measures themselves in changing the attentional focus of judges and hence altering ratings, from changes in the subjective definition of judges' anchor points over time, from the effects of the order of presentation of records, from fatigue, from the number of categories used, from the speed of replay, from inadequate definitions of behavioural categories, from knowledge of the experimental hypothesis and from the effects of previous exposure to the same subject. The ability to check and control all these potential sources of bias is an advantage available to the user of video records which is often not available when on-line analysis is used.

Validity of measurement from video records

Analysis of video records enables checks on a number of issues relating to validity. One problem with judgemental ratings is the effects of context on judgements. This is particularly critical when judgements are made of people in interaction situations where the judgements made of a particular subject may reflect the behaviour of others who are present in that situation. Attribution processes may lead to more favourable judgements of the subject if others are judged negatively, and vice versa. While these possibilities can be controlled by experimental designs, ensuring that others behave consistently, such designs may result in relatively artificial situations. An alternative way of coping with this problem is to capitalize upon another advantage of video recording. We have, with considerable success, recorded on two separate video recorders the two participants in a dyadic interaction. We then had the participants judged separately from the original records and also obtained judgements on a recombined replay using a split screen. In this way, we have been able to examine the interactive effects on judgements.

Similarly, differences in judgements can arise from the judges' attention to different cues from the same person. Separate judgements can be obtained from sound only and video only records. The video record can be further subdivided by the use of a split screen to allow separate judgement of facial or postural cues only. Facial cues can be made more salient by providing a zoom close-up of the face in addition to the total body shot on another part of the screen. Audio records can of course also be filtered to delete the content.

The validity of judgemental ratings is by no means simple. At one level the judgement has face validity to the extent that it is the impression itself that is likely to affect the future behaviour of others towards the subject. On another level, it has been the increasing concern of social psychologists to understand the cues that lead to such judgements. The ability to subject the record to both global judgemental ratings and to microanalysis of behaviour has encouraged the rapid development of the study of non-verbal behaviour and added a new dimension to the general literature on impression formation.

Ethics

The ethics of video recording raise new problems. The following procedures are normally followed in our laboratory:

1. All subjects are informed that they will be recorded on all or some of the sessions, although the exact sessions in a multisession experiment are not necessarily specified. They are shown all the recording apparatus including the concealed microphones and cameras. As well as being ethically sound, such a practice has the advantage of avoiding the situation where the subject believes that recording is possible and therefore spends time trying to puzzle out where the cameras and microphones are hidden and hence behaves in an unusual fashion. On the other hand, we have found that unconcealed microphones and cameras will often produce more self-conscious behaviour than concealed or partly concealed recording apparatus, even when the subject knows that the session is being recorded.
2. All subjects are asked to sign a release form which specifies the purposes for which the records will be used and the categories of people who may possibly view them. Subjects are free to refuse to sign the release form or to modify it to exclude some categories (e.g. first year student classes). Normally subjects are encouraged to suggest the exclusion of any category which might include people who know them personally and some take advantage of this option.
3. All raters and senior students in special training courses who view restricted tapes are required to sign a confidentiality statement which requires a promise not to disclose any information obtained from the tapes to anyone outside the group who views the tape. With less restricted tapes shown to larger groups such as undergraduates, a general caution precedes replay.

When cameras are used in public areas, different ethical considerations arise, but the same procedures in ensuring the confidentiality of replays are followed.

Methods of analysis

Post-viewing ratings

Judgemental ratings and behavioural judgements will usually be made by raters who view a selected segment of a record and then record their ratings. The procedure for replay is normally straightforward but the investigator must decide which segment to select and what rating scales to use. The issues of concern will be:

1. The reliability of the judges' ratings
2. The validity of the judges' ratings

3. The demand characteristics of the situation in which the ratings are made
4. The characteristics and past experience of the raters themselves
5. The training given to the raters
6. The nature of the scales to be used

Reliability and validity of ratings Many standard issues in experimental design will in principle be no different when video is used. (For example, see the excellent article on interjudge reliability by Strout and Fleiss, 1979.)

Generalizability theory (Cronbach and coauthors, 1973) offers an interesting alternative to classical reliability theory. In place of assuming a specific true score and a single set of conditions, generalizability theory accepts a universe of conditions involving differences in scales, judges and occasions (Wiggins, 1973). Therefore Cronbach and coauthors (1973) focus not on the stability of a set of scores, but rather on the generalizability of one set of observations to another. For example, it may be useful to generalize from self-ratings of social competence to observations of the subject in a social setting. In this way generalizability theory blurs the traditional distinction between reliability and validity. Examples of this approach may be found in studies by Farrell and coauthors (1979) and Weider and Weiss (1980).

Demand characteristics The hypothesis under investigation can be readily concealed when using video records. Records can be shown in random order, regardless of when they were recorded, and interspersed with dummy records. The investigator is encouraged to view the raters themselves as if they were subjects in an experiment by using counterbalanced experimental designs both to test for and to control the effects of such extraneous variables as sex of person rated, nature of topic, experimental condition and time of day.

Rater characteristics The effects on data of rater differences have already been discussed as part of the reliability issue (see page 36). Analysis of variance designs can be readily adapted to test differences between judges with respect to specific variables. If records are stored on video, they can easily be used for such methodological studies both prior to deciding on selection of raters and after the main analysis has been conducted.

Training issues Raters need to be familiarized with the video medium as well as the experimental task. A common feature of raters of social interactions, unfamiliar with using videotape, is the tendency to get involved in the conversational content at the expense of objectivity. Training should include the review of video records similar to the experimental set to provide stable anchor points for subsequent ratings. It is often useful to allow the raters to discuss the basis for their individual judgements until a consensus is reached.

The length of training will vary depending on such features as the degree of inference required of the raters, their prior expertise, the number of categories to be used and the variety of videotapes to be rated. Training sessions need to continue until raters are confident in their ability to make ratings and until they have reached an acceptable level of objectively measured reliability.

Example of experimental design to test for effects of training and content on judgemental ratings

Question   Does training raters to make 'behavioural judgements' reliably affect 'judgemental ratings' of impressions?

Background Ratings had been obtained from six judges on 120 tapes of Ss interacting with another. Seven-point judgemental ratings were used, e.g. friendly/unfriendly, warm/cold, tense/relaxed. In addition judges were trained to record reliably on such scales as averted gaze, excessive handing over, slow voice speed, blank face. Reliability coefficients assessing agreement between judges were greater than 0.65 on both the behavioural judgements on which they were trained and on the judgemental ratings where no training was given.

Design   Six additional judges were used to rate a random sample of 30 tapes using judgemental ratings only. No specific training in reliability was given and raters were not instructed to attend to any particular features of behaviour, although before starting the rating they were shown a variety of tapes chosen as being representative of the experimental set of tapes. This was to enable raters to adjust to the nature of the task and to provide an experience of the range of behaviour likely to be seen in the experimental set. These data represent an 'untrained' condition; these can be compared with the earlier data which represent a 'trained' condition. Correlations were calculated by correlating the average Ss scores for each judge in each condition and calculating the average interjudge correlation for all Ss within each condition for each judgemental rating. The correlations were normalized and compared using an analysis of variance design. Results showed that untrained raters did not differ significantly from raters trained on the use of behavioural judgement scales. ($F = 1.21$; df 1, 67; $p = 0.28$)

Choice of scales *Judgemental ratings* have been most commonly made using seven-point bipolar adjective scales anchored at both ends (cf. Argyle, Alkema and Gilmour, 1972). However, there is no reason that Q-sort or checklist techniques should not be used. The selection of scales for judgemental ratings can be guided by an already extensive literature. For example, Triandis (1977) reviews the basic parameters of person perception measures that have emerged in many studies. Almost all report a factor of love/hostility and a factor of dominance/submission, and some also report a factor of respect which does not coincide exactly with factors of liking or status. The investigator can choose scales from researched sources.

Behavioural judgement scales are, on the other hand, a relatively unexplored area of psychological assessment. Trower, Bryant and Argyle (1978) have developed a set of such scales for use in assessment and research in social skills. These provide descriptive labels for each scale point. There is no reason, in principle, why an investigator should not develop new scales or use magnitude estimation techniques to quantify observed behaviour.

Behavioural measurements are normally made in discrete operationally defined categories. The basic criteria for successful category coding systems are that the categories are exclusive of one another, cover all possibilities and can be reliably scored.

The simplest form of behavioural measure is to count the occurrence versus non-occurrence of a particular event (such as 'speaking', 'looking at other'). More complex systems depend on the observer grouping behaviours into categories. Examples include: FACS technique for coding facial expression (Ekman & Friesen, 1978), the kinegraph technique for postural coding (Birdwhistell, 1973) and Mehrabian's (1972) non-verbal behaviour coding schedules. Less specific coding schedules are well represented in the ethological literature (e.g. Hinde, 1973, Hutt and Hutt, 1970, McGrew, 1972) and can be readily developed by the investigator for a specific purpose.

The context of the measurement may be made within either a continuous or a segmented time sequence. The researcher can also choose an appropriate speed of playback in conjunction with the degree of analysis detail required. (See McDowell, 1973, for a comparison of time-sampling and continuous recording techniques.)

Continuous recording is used when the investigator is interested in a sequential description of events rather than inferred judgements of unitary behaviour (Kendon, 1979). Continuous recording is also desirable when the behaviour or its absence is very infrequent or highly variable across subjects (e.g. question-asking, gaze direction when handing over speech). It is especially valuable when the records represent only a small sample and when the subject numbers are small.

Time-sampling will be preferred when an extensive amount of material is available, subject numbers are large and the behaviour is relatively frequent (e.g. using personal pronouns). Time-sampling will also be favoured if the behaviour is difficult to classify on a continuous record, even when played at slow speeds (e.g. using a complex coding schedule to code leg, arm, head and trunk positions). The sampling interval chosen will depend on the frequency of the behaviour, its variability across subjects, the amount of data available and the method of analysis to be used. An extreme example is provided in frame-by-frame analysis most commonly used with film (Condon and Ogston, 1966; Kendon, 1972).

The ideal method of analysis will be determined by interacting factors, including numbers of subjects, length of records, number of comparisons being made, type of statistics contemplated, variance among subjects and probability of occurrence of target behaviours. The following guidelines should be useful:

1. Use either continuous recording or frequent time-sampling intervals when the subjects vary markedly in their behaviour.
2. Obtain a larger number of subjects in preference to increasing the number of samples of the behaviour per subject.
3. When behaviour has a probability of about 0.5 fewer samples are needed than when the probability of occurrence approaches 0.0 or 1.0.
4. When there is error in measurement, reliability is normally improved by using additional raters.
5. For economy, use multiple raters scoring continuously in real-time or in

time-samples at infrequent intervals, rather than one or two raters scoring continuously at quarter-speed or frequent time-sampling.

Sequence of making decisions about methods of analysis

Before making any records, the researcher will need to decide on the main hypotheses, the main comparisons to be made and the number of subjects to be used. This will provide the context for more specific decisions about the length of time of the video recording, the order in which the library will be compiled, camera angles, any use of split screen techniques and whether one or more records will be made of each session.

Pilot studies of recording and analysis techniques are then used to determine the clarity of the image, the optimal recording circumstances for easy measurement of the behaviour and whether these choices may affect the ratings of judges. The researchers should, at this stage, determine whether all or some of the data could be obtained more reliably by on-line analysis. These decisions will depend on:

1. The need for editing. Camera angle and gaze contact may be more accurately judged on-line while postural congruence may be more accurate on a split screen using two or three different camera angles.
2. Clarity of record. Gaze direction and small facial movements may be more reliable on-line while gestures may be easier off-line using slower speed replay.

After data collection the researcher can determine empirically the number of raters needed to establish the required level of reliability (cf. Cohen, 1977). This decision is likely to interact with decisions about continuous or time-sampling methods, speed of playback and the nature of any judgemental scales that are being chosen. The researcher is also advised to investigate the effects of rater characteristics (e.g. gender) and any demand characteristics that might affect ratings (e.g. order, training, time of day).

Finally, the researcher can proceed with the complete analysis of the experimental set of records. He or she may find that these same records are useful in later studies or for post hoc analysis that may elucidate the original findings.

Concluding remarks

The technology of video recording provides a permanent record at relatively low cost that has the additional advantages of being relatively simple to operate, edit and play back. This gives the researcher far greater flexibility in the analysis of data 'after the event'. The potential uses of videotape in research are many (Hutt and Hutt, 1970). However, the benefits may be emphasized when: the action of interest is very fast (e.g. onset of aggression) or very complex (e.g. facial display of mixed emotions); the changes in behaviour are subtle (e.g. gaze behaviour at turn-taking); sequential changes in behaviour occur (e.g. the emergence of postural congruence); specific parameters of complex behavioural events are being measured (e.g. greeting and parting behaviour); unobtrusive measurement is required (e.g. monitoring the development of mutuality between two people); and where the reliability of measurement is a problem.

References

Argyle, M. (1975). *Bodily Communication*, Methuen, London.

Argyle, M. (1979). Sequences in social behaviour as a function of the situation, in *Emerging Strategies in Social Psychological Research* (Ed. G. P. Ginsberg), pp. 11–38, Wiley. Chichester.

Argyle, M., Alkema, F., and Gilmour, R. (1972). The communication of friendly and hostile attitudes by verbal and non-verbal signals, *European Journal of Social Psychology*, **1**, 385–402.

Birdwhistell, R. L. (1973). *Kinesics and Context: Essays on Body-Motion Communication*, Penguin, London.

Burr, R. (1977). *An Investigation of the Factors Influencing Judgements of Physical Attractiveness*, Unpublished project report, University of Otago.

Cohen, J. (1977). *Statistical Power Analysis for the Behavioural Sciences*, Rev. Ed., Academic Press, New York.

Condon, W. S., and Ogston, W. P. (1966). Sound film analysis of normal and pathological behaviour patterns, *Journal of Nervous and Mental Diseases*, **143** (4), 338–341.

Cronbach, L. J., Gleser, G. C., Nader, H., and Rajaratnam, N. (1973). *The Dependability of Behavioural Measurements: Theory of Generalizability for Scores for Profiles*, Wiley, Chichester.

Darnbusch, S. M., Hastorf, A. M., Richardson, S. A., Muzzy, R. E., and Vreeland, R. S. (1965). The perceiver and the perceived: their relative influence on categories of interpersonal cognition, *Journal of Personal and Social Psychology*, **1**, 434–440.

Ekman, P., and Friesen, W. V. (1978). *Facial Action Coding System: Investigators Guide*, Consulting Psychologists Press, Palo Alto, California.

Farrell, A. D., Mariotto, M. J., Conger, A. J., Curran, J. P., and Wallander, J. L. (1979). Self-ratings and judges ratings of heterosexual social anxiety and skill: a generalizability study, *Journal of Consulting and Clinical Psychology*, **47** (1), 164–175.

Gesell, A., and Halverson, H. M. (1942). The daily maturation of infant behaviour: a cinema study of postures, movements, and laterality, *Journal of Genetic Psychology*, **61**, 3–32.

Harrison, P. (1979). *Recognition of emotions*, Unpublished thesis, University of Otago.

Hinde, R. A. (1973). On the design of check-sheets, *Primates*, **14** (4), 393–406.

Hutt, S. J., and Hutt, C. (1970). *Direct Observation and Measurement of Behaviour*, Charles C. Thomas, Springfield, Illinois.

Irwin, R., Kammann, R., and Dixon, G. (1978). 'If you want to know how happy I am you'll have to ask me', *N.Z. Psychologist*, **8**, 10–12.

Kazdin, A. E. (1977). Artifact, bias and complexity of assessment: the ABC's of reliability, *Journal of Applied Behavior Analysis*, **10**, 141–150.

Kendon, A. (1972). Some relationships between body motion and speech: an analysis of an example, in *Studies in Dyadic Communication* (Eds. A. W. Siegman and B. Pope), pp. 177–210, Pergamon, Oxford.

Kendon, A. (1979). Some theoretical and methodological aspects of the use of film in the study of social interaction, in *Emerging Strategies in Social Psychological Research* (Ed. G. P. Ginsberg), pp. 67–92, Wiley, Chichester.

Lewin, K., Lippitt, R., and White, R. (1939). Patterns of aggressive behaviour in experimentally created social climate, *Journal of Social Psychology*, **10**, 271–298.

McDowell, E. E. (1973). Comparison of time-sampling and continuous recording techniques for observing developmental changes in caretaker and infant behaviours, *Journal of Genetic Behaviour*, **123**, 99–105.

McGrew, W. C. (1972). *An Ethological Study of Childrens Behaviour*, Academic Press, New York.

Mehrabian, A. (1968). The inference of attitudes from the posture, orientation and distance of a communicator, *Journal of Consulting and Clinical Psychology*, **32**, 296–308.

Mehrabian, A. (1972). *Non-verbal Communication*, Aldine, Atherton.

Shrout, P. E., and Fleiss, J. L. (1979). Intra-class correlations; uses in assessing rater reliability, *Psychology Bulletin*, **86** (2), 420–428.

Triandis, H. C. (1977). *Interpersonal Behaviour*, Brooks/Cole, Monterey.

Trower, P., Bryant, B., and Argyle, M. (1978). *Social Skills and Mental Health*, Methuen.

Welford, A. T. (1980). The concept of skill and its application to social performance, in *The Analysis of Social Skill* (Eds. W. T. Singleton, P. Spurgeon and R. B. Stammers), pp. 11–22, Plenum Press, New York.

Weider, G. B., and Weiss, R. L. (1980). Generalizability theory and the coding of marital interactions, *Journal of Consulting and Clinical Psychology*, **48** (4), 469–477.

Wiggins, J. S. (1973). *Personality and Prediction: Principles of Personality Assessment*, pp. 277–328, Addison-Wesley, New York.

Using Video
Edited by P. W. Dowrick and S. J. Biggs
© 1983 John Wiley & Sons Ltd

Chapter 5

Computer-Aided Video

Andy Clarke

and

Heiner Ellgring

Max Planck Institute of Psychiatry, Munich

Gesell (1935) presented a 'cinemanalytic' approach to the analysis of behaviour, formulating five main features. These have remained essential to all methods in film and video research:

1. The film being propelled at a known speed minutely records time values and sequences.
2. Simultaneously and also minutely the film records space relationships and configurations.
3. The film records these spatial and temporal data in a series of discrete, instantaneous registrations.
4. These registrations can be serially reinstated at normal, retarded and accelerated rates.
5. Any single registration can be individually studied, in terms of time and space, as a delineation of a single phase of a behaviour pattern or a behaviour event.

These five propositions are extremely simple but their methodological implications for the objective study of behaviour are far-reaching. In addition to his work on cinematic studies on early infant behaviour, Gesell also proposed the use of film in clinical analysis and clinical training.

The history of film technology in scientific research has been reviewed exhaustively by Michaelis (1955) and in the human sciences by Reuch (1975), himself an early contributor to the development of the anthropological film. What follows in this chapter should demonstrate how present-day technology provides the video user with substantial improvements in many, if not all, aspects of behavioural analysis based on audiovisual recording. Thus qualitative improvements in accuracy and detail of observation can be achieved with the aid of sophisticated camera and optical systems, audio equipment and other recording features. Furthermore, the convenience and low cost of much necessary equipment free the user from many technical problems and permit concentration on the actual task at hand—observation and analysis.

In psychiatry, film recording was recognized and used by various workers as a medium for the storage and objective comprehensive presentation of examples of psychopathology, apparently by Kraeplin before 1920, and later by Page in 1938 and Lehmann in 1952 (see Michaelis, 1955). Despite the restrictive processing time involved with film, use of this medium in psychotherapy for self-confrontation was used 30 years ago by Carrere (1954).

Although the tube-based video screen for television had been invented during the thirties, its first applications in behavioural research and psychotherapy were reported after the development of the videotape recorder by Ampex in 1956 (Ginsburg, Anderson and Dolby, 1957). The advantage of the video medium led gradually to its establishment in many areas of psychiatric research and practice (Berger, 1970). To avoid confusion and repetition, the term video will be used here, although in many aspects the discussion also applies to film recording. For a comparison of video and film, see Utz (1980).

Parallel to the development of video technology, substantial improvements in behavioural data collection methods and technology have been made. An excellent review of this area has been presented by Hutt and Hutt (1970). Essentially, the data collection involves the recording of specified behavioural events and their times of onset and offset (Fitzpatrick, 1977).

Since the introduction of the interaction chronograph by Chapple (1949), many elaborations and variations have been reported (see Hutt and Hutt, 1970). Naturally, reported devices have increasingly included the computer analysis of behavioural data (e.g. Hoehne and Maurus, 1973; Tobach, Schreirla and Aronsen, 1962; White, 1970). Recently a series of portable event recorders have also been described (Fitzpatrick, 1977). The SSR (signals, senders and receivers) system described by Stephenson, Smith and Roberts (1975) (coincidental acronym?) is representative in that it allows the researcher freedom to define and score behavioural sequences and to store these data in a manner that permits troublefree transfer to the computer for permanent storage and analysis.

In the past few decades substantial advances have been made in observational methods, audiovisual technology and computerized event recording. More recently, the integration of these three aspects of behavioural analysis has become feasible.

Direct and indirect observation

The techniques for audiovisual recording on the one hand and data collection on the other, have often been applied independently. However, the availability of suitable equipment permits the researcher to design and implement systems which draw from both areas.

The issue as to whether direct or indirect observation be selected has been discussed ever since the widespread availability of film and sound recording. Here, direct observation is understood as observation in a natural or laboratory setting performed with the aid of notes, checklists or event recorders, and without the use of picture or sound recording. Indirect observation is understood as observation of such picture and/or sound recordings after the event or in some cases via video monitoring. These two alternative behaviour–observation–analysis paths are illustrated in Figure 1. In this figure, the lower path corresponds to the direct observation design. Thus, each behavioural phenomenon is observed once by the observer(s), the scored data being stored intermediately for later transfer to a processing computer. The upper path corresponds to the indirect observation design. Here, the behavioural analysis is recorded audiovisually by one or more cameras and one or more microphones. The resulting videotape can then be observed repeatedly and in as much detail as the technical quality (camera angle, sound clarity, separation, etc.) permits.

For most applications it can be seen that the indirect observation design permits much more flexibility and accuracy in the observational methods— provided the behaviour specimen of interest can be adequately 'captured' on videotape. Once recorded, it is possible to 'reproduce' the behaviour in the laboratory where the convenience of computer-aided observation and data collection is available. The various audiovisual recording media enable repeated observation at various speeds, comparison of observational methods and performance of reliability studies. To quote Barker (1978, p. 12) from his studies in ecological psychology: 'The advantages of the filmed record lie in the preservation of details that are lost in verbal accounts and the opportunity to go back and look again.' The proponents of direct observation, however, argue with some justification that the analysis of social behaviour in contrived situations is questionable (Conger and McLeod, 1977). Furthermore, the observation and recording of data from persons who are unaware, whether by direct observer or audiovisual means, brings up an ethical issue which as yet remains unresolved (see Fields, 1978, and Schaeffer, 1975).

It appears to us that for any analysis which is aimed at exploring the structural aspects of social interaction, an audiovisual recording is necessary. This was formulated by Gesell (1935) and has recently been emphasized by Kendon (1979), outlining the principles of context analysis and the role of filmed 'specimens of behaviour' for the researcher interested in the study of behavioural relationships.

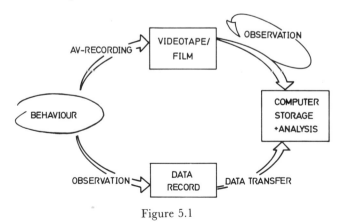

Figure 5.1

Video handling systems

For the behavioural scientist, the videotape serves as an intermediate storage medium for the behavioural phenomena or specimens which have been recorded. The advantages of video storage and current techniques employed in its applications in psychology are dealt with in some detail in the next two chapters of this volume. However, one disadvantage of the videotape as a storage medium is that the recorded information is not directly visible, as in film where a visual image is recorded on the carrier medium so that points of interest can be determined by direct examination or simple optical projection. With video, an electronic signal is recorded on magnetic tape and reproduction of the visual image requires a substantial amount of electronic circuitry. This can lead to considerable frustration, particularly when searching and evaluating recorded material.

This introduces us to the question of indexing the recorded material. The spectrum of possible systems for indexing tape reaches from the simple mechanical counters built into most machines through to computer-compatible coding and internationally transmitted radio time signals. In principle, the time-coding of magnetic tape may be likened to numbering the pages of a text. Considering that it would be unacceptable to neglect numbering the pages of a written text, it may be argued that a reliable indexing method for video frames should be included as a standard facility on video recording machines. The requirement of an adequate time-code is further endorsed because the time dimension plays an essential role in the examination of behavioural sequences. For applications such as role-playing and self-confrontation, it is likely that the mechanical counters built into most video recorders are adequate. However, for most observational work, the imprecision of such counters quickly becomes noticeable. Basically, this is because these counters display tape position as a measure derived from the tape length, rather than referring to the recorded video signal.

When measurement is made with direct reference to the video signal, the sync component of this signal, which is the electronic equivalent of the sprocket holes on a roll of film, can be used as an electronic trigger, so that frame accurate counting is achieved; i.e. the individual video frames are counted, rather than the tape length. Various 'video coders' using this technique have been developed for tape indexing. These generate an on-screen time display in hours, minutes, seconds and frames on each video frame. In principle, this technique is identical to that described by Van Vlack (1966) for the indexing of film in psychotherapy research. With video, however, this system has the disadvantage that it can be read only at play speed and in slow motion (and with some recorders in jogmode), but not in fast wind or rewind. A further disadvantage is that the time specification cannot be read automatically by an electronic decoder or computer.

Recently, however, a number of systems using computer-compatible time-coding have been developed which, among other things, overcome this problem. Such systems possess all of the advantages of the previously described indexing methods—above all, frame accurate coding and read capability at all tape speeds. Of greatest importance is the fact that these digitally recorded time-code signals can be read by the computer. This enables the constant monitoring of tape position and programmed control of the videotape machines.

The widely recognized difficulties arising from the collection of large amounts of video material, and the need to protocol and evaluate this efficiently, have played a major role in the recognition of the need—primarily in the professional television studio—for automatic techniques of indexing and controlling videotapes. In psychological research, these developments were foreseen by Ekman and Friesen (1969) and included in the design of their video information and retrieval systems VID-R and SCAN. As in Gesell's earlier system, such features as different viewing speeds, search and retrieval, temporal reorganization and access to a visual library collection are included in the concept. Of crucial importance, then, is the vastly improved user convenience made possible by currently available audiovisual and computer technologies.

An ambitious system which includes the possibility of transferring video images onto computer graphics was proposed by Futrelle (1973). This system, GALATEA, allows the user to produce animated line drawings of those aspects of the recording which interest him or her. A more modest system operating on the same principle has been implemented by Wallbott (1980) for the automatic measurement of hand movements.

A system for the protocolling and retrieval of audiovisual data (PRAVDA)

A system incorporating the advantages of computer-controlled video recorders and data collection equipment has been developed at the Max Planck Institute (MPI) of Psychiatry in Munich. The organization of the system is illustrated in Figure 2, where three basic levels of operation are represented.

Thus, at level 1, the user would work directly with the video machines, all control operations being performed by hand. At level 2, a wide range of instrumental aid may be introduced. This level includes the sophistication offered by the numerous remote control units and edit controllers available at this date. At such a level of integration, in principle, manual operation of the

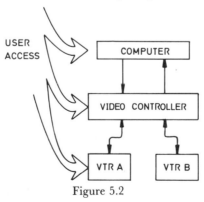

Figure 5.2

individual video recorders is no longer necessary. At the third, most complex level of organization, the remote control of the video recorders is performed by programmed routines; e.g. all search and edit functions may be performed automatically according to specified time entries. Further applications which capitalize on this level of sophistication include the collection of observational data and time-codes from video material, their storage and analysis. This corresponds to the integration of the event recorder, as described earlier, into a computer-supported video system.

In the remainder of this section we describe major aspects of the MPI facility, as applicable to other settings. In particular, we discuss video indexing, or time-coding—a prerequisite for accurate time specification and tape control, microprogrammed control routines and computer-aided operation on the MPI facility and observation and data collection techniques.

Video indexing

A central feature of the MPI facility is the synchronous recording of a time and control code in addition to the video and audio signals. The time-code is nothing more than a series of binary pulses which form a digital clock signal. One series or codeword is recorded per frame. The time-code signal is recorded on a separate track on the videotape and provides synchronous frame-accurate indexing of the video material. The time-code signal can be recorded either directly, in the case of a studio recording, or during transfer of material from a portable video recorder. Thus, it is possible to play back or 'reproduce' the behaviour in the laboratory where the convenience of computer-aided observation and acquisition is available.

The time-code used is the standard time and control code for videotape recording developed by the Society of Motion Picture and Television Engineers. It corresponds to the standard proposed by the International Electrical Commission (1974). Such a code is the key to efficient indexing and electronic control of videotape. Essentially, the time information is coded in binary coded decimal form, and can be recorded on the second audio channel of the videotape—if available (see Figure 3)—and/or inserted into the video signal during the so-called vertical blanking interval between frames. (Standard television systems do not use all lines for the transmission of picture content. In the vertical blanking interval several lines are free and can be used for inserting test signals, time-code and other identification information.)

The digital codeword for each video frame includes the following information:

> Hour, minute, second and frame count, an eight-position alphanumeric word for content coding and a sync word which indicates the end of frame and direction of tape motion

This enables reading of the time-code at all tape speeds from fast wind/rewind down to frame-by-frame step motion. The fundamental advantage with time-code is that any programmed routines (e.g. tape search, edit) are synchronized to the video signal and operate to frame accuracy. In order to perform such routines, those points in time (i.e. entrances and exits for each scene) at which the recorders have to be switched must be stored.

The definition of the stored points can be carried out in three ways:

1. The time information can be entered by hand via a keyboard. The entered data are then assigned to corresponding storage locations.
2. During observation at the video monitor an arbitrary number of points in time can be stored by push button. The time information thus selected is assigned to a data file in the process computer and may be complemented by content classification data.
3. The time information may be transferred from a data file which has been assembled earlier.

Microprogrammed control routines

Essentially, the handling of time-coded videotapes involves various combinations of three basic control routines:

1. Searching tape for a defined point in time
2. Presentation of a temporally defined scene
3. Frame-accurate editing of selected scenes from production tapes to the edited tape

These routines are controlled in the PRAVDA system by a hard-wired microprocessor (see Figure 4).

The search routine involves the controlling of one video recorder so that the videotape is positioned to any given point in time on the tape. The tape position is monitored by continuous reading of the recorded time-code, and the tape speed is program-controlled according to what might be termed a 'ballistic' curve, so that an optimum access time is achieved. The routine for the pres-

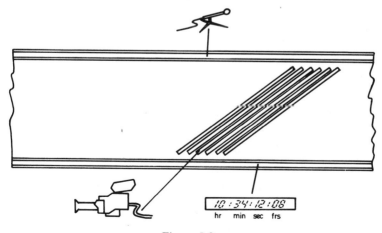

Figure 5.3

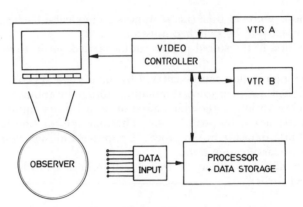

Figure 5.4

entation of a temporally defined scene involves, first of all, a search routine so that the tape is positioned shortly before the entrance to the scene. The recorder is then switched into play mode and after the cue-up time, during which the recorder stabilizes mechanically, the video and audio signals are switched to the monitor exactly at the selected entrance. The signals are then switched down at the exit time of the scene and the machine is halted. Since the beginning and ending points are stored, the scene can be presented repeatedly with negligible delay.

Editing of tapes involves essentially the same routines being carried out for two or more machines. Thus, the machines are positioned to their respective points in time for the edit. The edit can then be simulated or executed by switching the edit machine to record mode at the beginning of the scene. The configuration used in the PRAVDA system allows the transfer to and from the computer of time and content data, and enables high-level monitoring of the video functions. The program systems developed include procedures for the assembling and storage of protocols and edit lists as derived during an observation or analysis phase, associative search algorithms for the assembled data files and fully automatic editing procedures. All of these programmed routines derive their time reference from the time-codes recorded on the videotapes so that absolute synchronicity to the video content is maintained.

Observation and data collection

This mode of operation has been designed for the acquisition of binary states or events together with their time of occurrence and their duration. The essential features in this mode of operation are:

1. Multichannel input of observation data and their times of occurrence
2. Synchronicity of recorded data with videotape time-code

The binary channels can be driven by automatic speech detection circuity or by a human observer. Specifically, the system is equipped for two independent acoustic channels and up to eight observer channels which can be freely allocated (see Figure 4). The time reference is obtained from the synchronously recorded videotape time-code. Absolute synchronicity to the recorded behaviour is thus achieved with a resolution of 40 ms, corresponding to the individual addressing of each video frame.

The speech detector is designed to process two audio channels. It operates in the following fashion. In each channel, the envelope of the audio signal is derived and presented to a threshold detector. The presence or absence of a signal is determined by comparison of the signal envelope level with a selected threshold level. This threshold is set manually according to the dynamics of the incoming signal. The envelope signal is displayed on an analog meter and the output of the threshold detector by a LED diode. These enable the operator to establish the optimal setting for the threshold levels.

In this manner, the speech detector transforms speech into an on–off pattern. Since the detector was initially designed for the recognition of human speech during dyadic interaction, due consideration had to be given to the compensation of any cross-talk between channels. Lavalier microphones were selected for transducing the speech signals; this microphone type offers excellent directional characteristics and is therefore effective against acoustic cross-talk. In addition, electronic compensation was included so that, after envelope detection, the envelope level from either channel could be subtracted from that of the other channel, the attenuation factor of the subtracted envelope signal being manually adjustable. This factor is set for each channel to give optimal suppression of cross-talk. The resulting corrected signals are then presented to the threshold detectors, which in turn deliver the required binary signal.

Besides the two speech channels, the unit is equipped with an additional eight binary channels which are switched by observer keys. The input switching is processed together with the speech detector outputs, in buffer stages, for the interface to a PDP8F computer. The computer interface consists of a custom-wired module. The incoming binary signals are wired to the data lines through programmed buffer stages. The device and function selection facilities are programmed so that the data lines may be cleared, loaded and read into the central processor.

Observation may be performed in a number of modes; e.g. in real-time during recording, in real-time during playback, in slow (or fast) motion during playback. (Further possibilities include the synchronous, frame-accurate playback of two video recorders.) The video material presented for observation is accompanied by the synchronous time-code signal. The computer registers the behavioural states delivered by the observer keys and the speech detectors and allocates to these the corresponding videotape time-code.

More exactly, the detector and observer input lines are sampled repeatedly in a program loop; then, on the occurrence of a change in any input line, the time-code is read and stored together with the new input status. In this manner, the input channels are continuously monitored, the occurrence of events on any of the channels being stored for further processing. An excerpt from a typical four-channel data set is given in Figure 5; each behavioural state is listed with the point in time at which it commences. By using the recorded videotape time-code as reference, excerpts from the observed sequences may be exactly defined and analysed, and an identical time reference signal is allocated in the case of repeated observation. The resulting data set is initially stored in core; after termination of the observation phase, the data may be examined for plausibility and corrected as necessary before being written onto computer tape.

The temporal resolution for the chosen analysis can be set to any multiple of the basic video frame frequency. This is equivalent to setting a measurement resolution and may be considered as a high-frequency filtering of the data. By setting the resolution, for example, to five video frames (200 ms), any observed states which have a duration of less than five frames would be suppressed. The effect of varying the measurement resolution has been examined in connection with a general study of observer reliability (Wagner, Ellgring and Clarke, 1980). It was found that optimal validity and reliability is obtained from human observers of speech and gaze behaviour when a resolution of 280 ms is selected.

Application to single-case, longitudinal studies

The system described in the previous section has played an essential role in the recording, evaluation, and archiving of videotapes in connection with a long-term project involving single-case, longitudinal studies of depressive patients. The object of these studies has been to examine temporal changes in subjective mood and their relationship to observable changes in communicative behaviour (Ellgring and Clarke, 1978).

To date, 20 patients have been examined in this project. Each of these

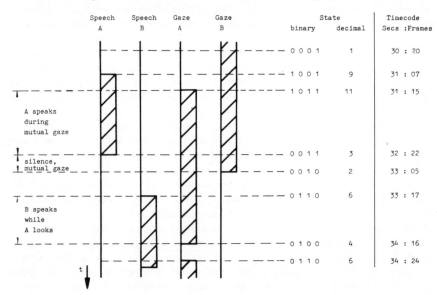

Figure 5.5

patients took part in clinical interviews which were performed twice weekly during hospitalization and during follow-up. This has yielded an average of approximately 18 interview recordings for each single case. The interviews have been scored and analysed for various verbal and non-verbal behaviours. This has included detailed observation of speech, gaze, gesture and facial expression, and rating of verbal content. In this section, the general strategy is demonstrated with the example of one single-case study.

The following brief results illustrate the different temporal courses of subjective and behavioural variables found in a 57-year-old female patient. As can be seen from Figure 6, the patient took part in 19 interviews over a period of 120 days during her clinical stay. Figure 6 shows the course of the patient's subjective mood rating. Initially this was good, showing a tendency to improve until the 25th day. During the next few days, a sudden lapse into a state of deep depression occurred. The subjective mood then appeared to improve again until the 80th day. A slight relapse occurred between the 100th and 120th day. The patient was treated from the 29th day with Amitriptylin.

For each of the interviews the speech and gaze of the patient and interviewer were observed as described in the previous section. This was carried out after each interview by four independent, neutral observers. In addition, a reduced number of interviews were selected for the analysis of gesture and facial expression. These were selected after the patient's remission when the course of the illness, as reflected in the subjectively rated mood and the measured speech and gaze, was known. Interviews were selected according to the extremes of subjective mood.

The analysis of gesture (Hiebinger, 1981) indicates that, among other things, a reduction of speech-accompanying hand movements and an increase in general manipulation are associated with depression. The results for the patient described here show that, as expected, worsening depression was accompanied by a continuous reduction in gestural behaviour. The analysis of facial expression is being carried out according to the facial action coding system (FACS) developed by Ekman and Friesen (1978). Initial results indicate that the samples from those interviews where the patient is more depressive contain fewer emotionally positive facial expressions (e.g. smiling) and more emotionally negative expressions.

The evaluation of gesture and facial expression, of course, involves more observer effort than the continuous coding of speech and gaze, some phases requiring frame-by-frame analysis. However, since all observational runs have as time reference the video time code recorded on tape with the audiovisual material, this enables the synchronization of the data during subsequent analysis phases. This possibility has been explored to some extent by Wagner (1981) and Hiebinger (1981) for the contingent relationships among speech, gaze and gesture. This technique is based on the concept of signal-averaging, which is suitable for the separation of weak, but systematic, event-related effects from ongoing activity. In the case of social interaction, its application yields information on the intensity and latency of intra- and interindividual coordination.

An approach to the analysis of behavioural sequences based on a structural model has been developed (Clarke, Wagner and Ellgring, 1980). The model is based on the theory of grammars developed for the description of natural and

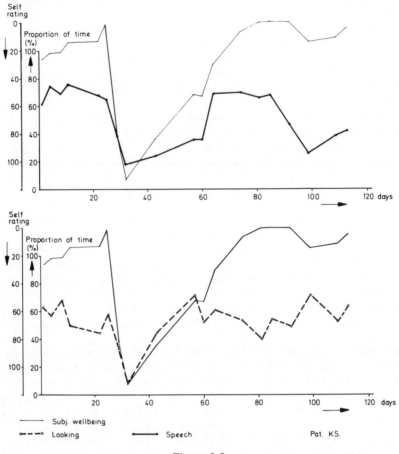

Figure 5.6

formal languages. Under the assumption that non-verbal communication consists largely of rule-governed behaviour it is proposed that a suitable grammar
can be derived using this theory. Some attempt has been made to construct
such a model and examine its usefulness for the examination of temporal
sequences of speech and gaze patterns. The results permit interpretation of
regularly occurring behavioural sequences which are governed by such factors
as situation, interaction and subjective mood. All the complex analyses mentioned rely on efficient observation techniques and, above all, temporal synchronization of data collected during different observational runs by means of
a computer-compatible time-code.

In addition to these formal analyses, editing strategies have been developed
for condensed video presentations of the observable behavioural changes. These
include the editing together of short sequences from each of the interviews with
one patient. For example, the first 15 to 20 seconds of the patient's answer to

a selected question are edited onto a second tape. Thus, the patient's response can be observed from interview to interview, and a general impression of the behavioural changes over the course of time can be obtained. Typically, these edited series involve excerpts from 20 to 30 interviews. In this way changes which have been found by statistical analysis of behavioural data can be collated and reviewed on video.

The single-case study outlined above indicates that there appears to be a systematic relationship between the temporal changes in the patient's subjective mood and the observed behaviour. Furthermore, the changes in gaze behaviour were found to occur in advance of the corresponding changes in subjective mood. Such temporal shifts may be explained as resulting from the existence of separate temporal systems governing the associated psychological levels (Ellgring, Wagner and Clarke, 1980).

Conclusion

The recent developments in microprocessor electronics and time-code equipment have vastly improved the efficiency of working with video material so that through the combination of data processing and video recording equipment a substantial rationalization of both data acquisition procedures and functional control of the recording machines may be achieved. Such a system, in which video editing and time-code control equipment is interfaced to a process computer, has been developed for the analysis of human communicative behaviour. The system provides exact indexing of the recorded material, automatic search and edit routines for the videotape machines and synchronicity of registered data. In summary, it can be maintained that given a sound theoretical basis, modern video and computer technologies can substantially increase the efficiency and accuracy of behavioural observation and analysis.

References

Barker, R. G., and Associates (1978). *Habitats, Environments, and Human Behavior*, Tossey-Boss, San Francisco.

Berger, M. M. (1970). *Videotape Techniques in Psychiatric Training*, Brunner/Mazel Inc, New York (New ed. 1980).

Carrere, J. (1954). Le psychocinematographie, *Ann. Medico Psychol.*, **112**, 240–245.

Chapple, E. D. (1949). The interaction chronograph: its evolution and present application, *Personnel*, **25**, 295–307.

Clarke, A. H., Wagner, H., and Ellgring, J. H. (1980). Eine syntaktische Analyse von Sprechen und Blickenbei dyadischer Interaktion, in: *Zeichenkonstruktion-Akten* (Ed. A. Lange-Seidl), De Gruyter, Berlin.

Conger, R. D., and McLeod, D. (1977). Describing behavior in small groups with the Datamyte event recorder, *Behavior Research Methods. and Instruments*, **9** (5), 418–424.

Ekman, P., and Friesen, W. V. (1969). A tool for the analysis of motion picture film or videotape, *American Psychologist*, **24** (3).

Ekman, P., and Friesen, W. V. (1978). *Facial Action Coding System*, Consulting Psychologists, Palo Alto.

Ellgring, J. H., and Clarke, A. H. (1978). Verlaufsbeobachtungen anhand standardisierter Videoaufzeichnungen bei depressiven Patienten, in *Fernsehen in der Psychiatrie* (Eds. H. Helmchen and E. Renfordt), pp. 68–77, Thieme, Stuttgart.

Ellgring, J. H., Wagner, H., and Clarke, A. H. (1980). Psychopathological states and their effects on speech and gaze behaviour, in *Language, Social Psychological Perspectives* (Eds. H. Giles and others), Pergamon, Oxford.

Fields, D. N. (1978). Legal implications and complications, in *Videotape Techniques in Psychiatric Training* (Ed. M. M. Berger), pp. 303–314, Brunner/Mazel Inc., New York.

Fitzpatrick, L. J. (1977). Automated data collection for observed events, *Behavior Research Methods and Instruments*, **9**, 447–451.

Futrelle, R. P. (1973). GALATEA, a proposed system for computer-aided analysis of movie films and videotape. *University of Chicago Institute for Computer Research Quarterly*, 37.

Gesell, A. (1935). Cinemanalysis: a method of behavior study, *Journal of Genetic Psychology*, **47**.

Ginsburg, P., Anderson, C. E., and Dolby, J. (1957). Video tape recorder design, *ISMPTE*, **66** (4).

Hiebinger, S. (1981). *Kommunikatives Verhalten im Verlauf der Depression*, Unpublished Dissertation, Salzburg.

Hoehne, A., and Maurus, M. (1973). Semiautomatic conversion of behavioral data from film to papertape for computer analysis, *Physiology and Behavior*, **13**, 317–319.

Hutt, S. J., and Hutt, C. (1970). *Direct Observation and Measurement of Behavior*, C. C. Thomas, Springfield, Illinois.

International Electrical Commission (1974). *Time and Control Code for Video Tape Recording*, Publication No. 461, Geneva.

Kendon, A. (1979). Some theoretical and methodological aspects of the use of film in the study of social interaction, in *Emerging Strategies in Social Psychological Research* (Ed. G. P. Ginsburg), Wiley, New York.

Michaelis, A. R. (1955). *Research Film in Biology, Anthropology, Psychology and Medicine*, Academic Press, New York.

Reuch, J. (1975). *The Camera and Man*, in *Principles of Visual Anthropology* (Ed. P. Hocking), pp. 83–102, Mouton, The Hague.

Schaeffer, J. H. (1975). Videotape: new techniques of observation and analysis in anthropology, in *Principles of Visual Anthropology* (Ed. P. Hocking), pp. 253–282, Mouton, The Hague.

Stephenson, G. R., Smith, D. P. B., and Roberts, T. W. (1975). The SSR system: an open fermat event recording system, *Behavior Research Methods and Instruments*, **7** (6), 497–515.

Tobach, E., Schreirla, T. C., Aronsen, L. R. (1962). The ATSL: an observer-to-computer system for a multivariate approach to behavioural study, *Nature*, **194** (4625), 257–258.

Utz, P. (1980). *Video User's Handbook*. Prentice Hall, Englewood Cliffs, New Jersey.

Van Vlack, J. (1966). Filming psychotherapy from the viewpoint of a research cinematographer, in *Methods of Research in Psychotherapy* (Eds. L. A. Gottschal and A. H. Auerbach), Appleton-Century-Crofts, New York.

Wagner, H. (1981). *Die Ermittlung sozialer Signale*, Unpublished Dissertation, Munich.

Wagner, H., Ellgring, J. H., and Clarke, A. H. (1980). Binaere Kodierung von Sprechen und Blicken: Validitaet, Reliabilitaet und ihre Abhaengigkeit von der zeitlichen Aufloesung, *Zeitschrift fuer experimentelle und angewandte Psychologie*, **21** (4), 670–687.

Wallbott, H. G. (1980). Ein System zur halbautomatischen, quantitativen Analyse von Handbewegungen, in *Aspekte der nonverbalen Kommunikation* (Ed. W. von Raffler-Engel), Fink, Munich.

White, R. E. C. (1970). WRATS: a computer compatible system for automatically recording and transcribing behavioural data, *Behaviour*, **40**, 137–161.

Using Video
Edited by P. W. Dowrick and S. J. Biggs
© 1983 John Wiley & Sons Ltd

Chapter 6

Developing a Videotape Library

Tim Betts

Department of Psychiatry, University of Birmingham

Chairman, Audiovisual Aids Sub-Committee, Royal College of Psychiatrists

Member, Working Party on the Uses of Television in Psychiatry of the Association of University Teachers of Psychiatry

Department of Psychiatry, Clinical Research Block, Queen Elizabeth Hospital, Birmingham

The facility to be able to show a lifelike audible moving picture of people, their conversations, feelings and behaviour and the events which affect them is an invaluable teaching aid in medicine and the allied clinical social sciences. Before the advent of educational video machines in the mid sixties the teacher had to rely on celluloid, with all its attendant disadvantages, to do this. Small wonder that the use of film as an educational aid was limited and those that were made often crammed far too many educational points into far too small a compass. Because film was expensive the building-up of experience in making educational material was limited as films could not be remade after they were launched on the market.

Video is so different that it would seem tailor-made for the educational world. Many people buy equipment; however, fewer use it regularly and to its full potential, or experiment with its use. One thing that 15 years of experience of using television in the teaching of psychiatry has taught me is that, judiciously used, television is one of the most powerful agents for change, without which, our teaching would be inestimably poorer. The use of television in psychiatric teaching can liberate the teacher from the drudgery of repetition, and can show his students things that even in a long clerkship they would not otherwise see. It also has an archival function—recordings we make today will show the clinicians of the future the problems we faced, how we tried to cope with them and how we felt about them.

There are many different uses for videotape systems in teaching psychiatry or any clinical, social or behavioural science. For many of these purposes a library of material, readily available, to illustrate problems of diagnosis or assessment, methods of examination or interview, techniques of treatment or management will be necessary. How does one set up such a library and use it to its best advantage?

One of the problems for the pioneers of the use of television for this purpose was that library collections grew up haphazardly and were poorly catalogued so that as a result a great deal of excellent material was hardly ever used. One of the main reasons why newly bought equipment is little used stems from the fact that the problems of using it and providing ready access to material have not been thought out. This readily leads to loss of enthusiasm and, as we shall see, it is enthusiasm which is so necessary in the initial setting up of a library and teaching service.

Before attempting to set up a video library the potential user should ask himself certain questions, as the answer to them will determine how he sets up his library and what equipment he will need. These questions are:

1. What will I be using my library for?
2. Will I be using my own material or material made by others (or both)?
3. If I use my own material, how do I maintain confidentiality?
4. How will I store material?
5. How will I catalogue it, so as to provide ready access?
6. How will I evaluate whether the material I have made is successful as a teaching aid?

What will it be used for?

This question is of obvious importance, but in many departments that use television this question was not asked until after equipment had been purchased. This is often coupled with an unrealistic expectation of what cheap educational equipment can do, so a department that has bought one single-tube camera and a backpack recorder in the naive hope of making a *Horizon* style documentary about schizophrenia is in for a disappointment. However, simple apparatus used carefully and for the right purpose can be very effective. I want to look first, then, at the uses to which simple educational television equipment can be effectively put.

Library of case material

In most departments of psychiatry this was probably the original use for videotape equipment. Before the arrival of simple educational videotape one of the main problems is teaching psychiatry to medical students was showing them examples of the conditions which they would find described in their textbooks or in lectures. Psychiatry is a personal intimate subject: the sight of even half a dozen medical students sitting in on out-patient sessions while some unhappy person tells all to the interviewing doctor is as distressing as the sight of a hundred students in a large lecture theatre staring at a bewildered schizophrenic. Television helps protect patients from this kind of experience.

However, even in a three-month course students will probably not see all of the conditions that the teacher would like them to have seen. As an example, take schizophrenia: not only should the student have some knowledge of the abnormalities of thinking, feeling and behaviour that are subsumed under the diagnostic label of schizophrenia, but he should also be able to recognize the condition in the field.

If the teacher has a library of videotape material about schizophrenia available for the student to see which includes videotape demonstrations of people with schizophrenia so that the student learns what the condition looks like, how people with the condition talk and behave and what are the relevant questions to ask, then the student is much better prepared for his first clinical experience. The same videotape interview of a patient with schizophrenia could be used in several different ways during the course: to illustrate what the condition looks like, to illustrate the phenomenology of the condition and to get the student thinking about how he would approach such a patient. Most departments, therefore, will assemble libraries of case history material like this for use in teaching. As we will see later, unless careful attention is paid to storage, easy retrieval of material, and good cataloguing a lot of this patient material will not be used properly and issues of confidentiality also have to be kept in mind.

In making the material one should also have some idea of who the eventual audience will be, although I have often been surprised that television material made to a certain standard for one audience will actually serve another differently qualified audience equally well. There are many levels of understanding of the same clinical interview; for instance, junior medical students, social workers or senior medical postgraduates may all learn different things from it but it may be equally valuable to all of them.

We will assume that a library of case material has been assembled—the original purpose of videotape in teaching departments. Initially it was collected for the lecturer to use either in a lecture itself to illustrate what he was talking about or in small group teaching. However, television is more versatile than this: it does not actually need a lecturer to switch on the monitor and to put a cassette into the machine and press the start button. Students can do this themselves.

Self-teaching material

The advent of cassette recording and replay video systems which are simple to use has enabled development of self-teaching material. A room is provided with a simple replay machine and monitor and a library of video material for students to look at, as often as they want to, in their own time without a teacher being present. Originally compilations of case history material were used in self-teaching programmes with a teacher adding a linking commentary, but latterly in our department and others, this simple use has developed into full-scale programmes made specifically for self-teaching and employing the techniques available to a University Television and Film Unit. This development significantly reduces the problem (common to many small clinical departments) of repetitive teaching and thus helps maintain the teachers' interest. Good quality self-teaching video programmes are a way of doing this which is both economic and effective. Providing compilations of clinical material with a simple linking commentary is very useful as the student can view it at his leisure at several stages of his training, with a different emphasis each time as his knowledge grows. Such clinical material is, of course, confidential and cannot be shown outside the department. In my department we are fairly certain that the enthusiastic teaching of psychiatry to students like this results in increased recruitment into psychiatry at a postgraduate level.

Self-teaching material made with professional help should obviously be in a format where the intervention of a teacher (except in the programme itself) is not necessary, although all of our self-teaching programmes can be used in whole or part in a lecture or tutorial (Betts, 1980). Self-teaching television should amplify, illustrate, explain or provide a model. Viewers should be watching the screen, not making notes; programmes should be supplemented therefore by readily available handouts summarizing points made in the programme. Programmes should not be too long: 25 to 30 minutes should not be exceeded. If this is not long enough then the programme should be divided into self-contained parts which gradually build up into a complete series, each part, however, being capable of being viewed on its own. The television screen is not the place for endless captions of lists and conditions—it should be the place where the student *sees* the relevance and application of the information he is learning. One of the skills in making a good self-teaching programme is deciding what to leave out, rather than what to put in.

The programme maker should avoid undue passivity: there is a danger in the audience sitting open-mouthed in front of the screen without engaging its critical or learning faculties. Optional or compulsory pauses can be built into the programme which demand a response from the observer; brief pertinent summaries of information given to date in the programme and their relevance to what comes next is also a good idea. I have found a very useful device is to incorporate real students into the programme; the watching peer group can readily identify with them and compare their own response to a particular problem with that shown by the televizised student. Incorporating students into the production has other advantages, not least that they can view the programme as it is being made and by their on-the-spot criticism in the studio help to shape a better programme.

Self-teaching tapes in 'fringe' subjects, such as hypnosis, provide students with the opportunity to see models and gain information on topics which there is not time to deal with in the main course. These tapes can supplement basic 'core' teaching. All our students, for instance, have a two-hour teaching session on sexual problems and their treatment: for those students interested in developing this knowledge further there is a back-up series in the self-teaching library of ten videotapes on human sexuality and its problems. Self-teaching tapes are also useful to have available if the student encounters an unusual situation which he needs to know about quickly. Occasionally, for instance, the student may encounter a patient who will not or cannot talk; the student will have a little theoretical knowledge about what to do but if he can take out the videotape '*The Mute Patient*' and review it straight away it will provide him with a detailed model of what to do and will enrich and enhance his clinical experience. There may also be outside experts and authorities that one would particularly like one's students to see and hear who cannot possibly visit a department frequently; captured on videotape the students can meet them as often as needed. How much better to see and hear Dr X enthusiastically expanding on his theories of schizophrenia than to merely read it in print.

A self-teaching room with open student access has therefore become part of our teaching programme and has other advantages in that from time to time students other than medical students who are doing special projects that impinge on psychiatry can see some of our material. In addition, visiting academics can see very quickly what we are trying to teach our students about psychiatry. Most of our programmes adapt readily to use in intensive three-day training courses in counselling (Betts, 1980). It is important in an open access system not to use material of a confidential nature (which is why almost all of our-self teaching programmes use role-playing) and some physical security is necessary as otherwise equipment (and tapes) may disappear.

Interview training

This extremely important use of videotape facilities is dealt with elsewhere in this book, but the departmental video library should be available to assist interview training by providing models of particular interview techniques or of good examples of how a situation may be handled. Parts of training interviews can therefore be kept and added to the library if they illustrate important training points. Only good examples of technique should be stored. Television is such a powerful medium that bad examples used as a dreadful warning can rebound, be remembered and become an unintentional model.

Examinations

Compilations of clinical material can also be used in examining the student's skills at the end of the course. Extracts from the library can be shown followed by a multiple choice paper or can be used as 'short cases' for discussion in an oral examination. All candidates in the examination should have an equal opportunity to view the videotapes if the examination is to be fair.

A separate but related development of a videotape library is to use clinical material to make problem-solving exercises of a programmed learning nature in which the student sees a sequential videotape of a clinical interview and can only move on from one sequence to the next when he has correctly answered questions about the preceding sequence. Such a videotape is time-consuming to make (particularly if branches are introduced into the system) but some departments of psychiatry are enthusiastic about their use. If videotapes are to be used for examination or programmed learning purposes then a very large stock of library material will be necessary; if fresh material is shot for the examination each time then, of course, after use it can be placed in the ordinary library.

So far I have looked at the use of videotape libraries in undergraduate and postgraduate teaching, but there are other uses for television in a department, and therefore more uses for a library.

Patient education

A further use for a videotape library which we are developing fairly rapidly is in patient education and counselling. The same self-teaching room can be used for patients as well as students and surprisingly the same educational material can sometimes do for both. As an example we have a videotape on techniques of relaxation which was made to teach medical students and nurses how to teach relaxation to a patient. (We regard good relaxation techniques as an essential part of therapy and with a rapid turnover in both nurses and medical students a self-instructional tape is invaluable.)

The tape works very well for this purpose, but latterly we have found that an even more economical use for it is for student and patient to view it together: both therefore learn together, discuss what they have seen and then the patient rehearses the techniques under the student's supervision. Similarly, a detailed videotape giving step-by-step instruction to medical students in how to treat vaginismus (which is very successful) has been shown by some students to their patients so that they can see what is going to happen to them and why.

Material can also be made primarily for patients. For example, I am developing a series of videotapes about epilepsy for people with the condition and their relatives and friends. However good the medical treatment of epilepsy, all people who develop the condition and are given the diagnosis for the first time need careful counselling to help them come to terms with it, so that unnecessary self-imposed or parentally imposed handicap is avoided. Such counselling includes the provision of accurate understandable information about the condition, particularly so that the patient can understand what the doctor is trying to do and how he may help himself. It is difficult in a busy out-patients clinic to give such detailed information (and answering the question 'what is epilepsy' is actually quite difficult), and even if one could, the patient who has just been told the diagnosis is usually in a state of numbed shock unable to take in what is being said. So we provide a series of videotapes which the patient can look at at his leisure (and as often as he likes) with his family, or with a nurse or medical student, or on his own, or with a group of fellow sufferers, and gradually acquire at his own pace detailed information that will help him. There is open access to this library of material, which is role-played, and copies can be kept near the out-patients who are supplied with a small playback facility.

This self-instructional material for patients can also be used with health professionals and students. The tape *Epilepsy, What Exactly Is It?*, which was made purely for patients, has proved very useful in teaching nurses, social workers and psychologists. Even medical students benefit from it, particularly as they can learn something of how to explain things simply to patients and the importance of doing so.

Will I be using my own programmes?

A major consideration that determines what equipment you get is whether you will be wanting to make your own programmes (as most will) or whether you feel that the supply of ready-made material in your subject and distributed by others is enough for your purpose. If you are not certain what is available for distribution in your subject then the first thing to do is to consult the catalogues of the British Universities Film Council or the Mental Health Film Council (addresses at end of chapter). Both of these organizations are extremely helpful and the BUFC has viewing facilities in London and the MHFC has regular viewing days. It is worth approaching them even if you work outside the United Kingdom as they may be able to put you in touch with similar organizations in your own country. If you are only going to show other peoples' material then you can concentrate your attention on good replay facilities and a good monitor, without having to make the usual budgeting compromises that trying to buy both recording and replay equipment bring.

There are, however, many advantages to being able to make your own material. Real patients can be shown if one is teaching a clinical subject and one can tailor precisely the recording to the audience that will see it; gaps which occur in a teaching programme can be quickly filled by making a video programme. No other programme, however excellent, will entirely match your teaching requirements: I always hope that those departments that use my programmes will eventually use the ideas in them to make their own local programme, because all my programmes are made to satisfy my own local needs.

In psychiatry, collaboration is possible between departments to make programmes that can then be used by all: this is one of the functions of the Working Party on the Uses of Television in Psychiatry of the Association of University Teachers of Psychiatry (Secretary's address at end of chapter). Four departments of Psychiatry (Manchester, Birmingham, Edinburgh and Cardiff) collaborated, for instance, in making five complementary programmes on medical interviewing which each department now uses. Collaboration like this is to be encouraged, as the needs of several departments can be met at once and material is made in a planned way (and is therefore more likely to be useful to other departments).

Many departments will of course use a mixture of their own material and that from other sources; the needs of confidentiality (see later) must be respected and clinical material should not be lent to other departments.

How do I maintain confidentiality?

The answer is by having firm procedures concerning the showing of material which you do not deviate from. Any videotape of real people which discloses personal information about them should only be shown to members and students of your department unless you have the explicit and informed consent of the person involved to do otherwise. Most practitioners who use television take the view that videotapes of patients suffering from mental illness should not be shown outside the department of origin. Exchanges of clinical material do not take place (and special precautions need to be taken with examination material).

In all our-self teaching tapes which are used by many other departments, role-playing by amateur actors, staff and students is used. Role-playing works if the role-player is not over-rehearsed (i.e. a spontaneous performance is captured) and the role-player is portraying a patient or clinical situation he knows well. Role-playing is certainly good enough to illustrate the principle features of a condition or a method of management.

The Royal College of Psychiatrists (address at end of chapter) has developed ethical guidelines to its members concerning the use of television. These guidelines are concerned particularly with the ethical responsibility that the professional has towards his patient, particularly when that patient is mentally ill and temporarily incapable of giving valid consent to a recording. The Royal College takes the view that recordings must be made with prior knowledge of the person involved and that consent must be obtained formally, almost invariably in writing, and provides examples of model consent forms.

If a patient has consented to a recording being made it should be made absolutely clear to him the purpose for which the recording will be used afterwards. With *very* few exceptions patient material should not be shown outside the local department and only to bona fide professional students of the department. Patients must have the right to withdraw consent at all times and tapes must always be erased if patients wish it. If the patient cannot give valid consent then a relative or the responsible medical officer must do so; if the patient recovers, consent must be re-obtained. Patients must have the opportunity of seeing the recording before making a final decision.

Video recordings must be kept securely and unauthorized access rigorously prevented. In other words, recordings of patients must be treated with the same respect as clinical records and must be the ultimate responsibility of the appropriate medical officer: in a large department this responsibility might be taken on by one senior member of staff. Now that videotape recordings are more durable consideration should also be given to whether consent to use a clinical recording should become void after a certain number of years, after which the recording would be destroyed.

The basis of confidentiality, then, is secure storage—but storage of videotapes also has to be such that authorized users have ready access to it. This means that even edited material used in self-teaching must be kept securely so that only bona fida students have access to it: unrestricted access can only be to those programmes that are meant for universal distribution and which therefore contain no clinical material.

How do I store my material?

There are a few technical considerations. Videotapes should be stored away from extremes of temperature and dampness. The atmosphere should be as dust-free as possible and the room in which the videotapes are stored should be protected from strong magnetic or electrical fields (if you work in a hospital it is worth while checking what electrical equipment your immediate neighbours possess). Videotapes do not last for ever, even when stored under ideal conditions—picture deterioration will eventually occur even in tapes that are never played. If the tapes are frequently used noticeable loss of quality will occur some time after one hundred plays; 'precious' material which is likely to be extensively used should therefore be copied from the original tape (the 'master') before being used. If you have extremely 'precious' material which might have such historical importance that it is worth more permanent preservation, then copying onto celluloid should be considered. For a short tape it is not really expensive (currently about £20 per minute). If you need advice about preserving historial material the British Universities Film Council should be able to put you in touch with the relevant experts (see Oliver, 1981). Once material is stored, access is facilitated by keeping a careful record of usage (which helps in evaluation) and a strict control over borrowing. Access is also facilitated by a good cataloguing system.

Cataloguing

Many extensive collections of valuable and illustrative clinical material are practically useless because inadequate cataloguing leads to inadequate retrieval of material. The time to start a catalogue is the day you purchase your first blank videotape—not after several years of collecting material. The kind of catalogue you use will depend on your local needs and conditions, but there are certain general principles.

Each blank videotape you acquire should be given an individual tape number which it keeps until disposed of when worn out (remember to 'wipe' clinical tapes before disposing of them from your library). Each recording you make should also be given an individual number and each *completed* programme you edit from the recording should also be given an individual number.

Each tape should have its own record card stored in a central file (a duplicate can be kept with the tape). The record card should indicate what has been recorded on the tape (if certain phenomena are particularly important in the recording and the department lacks editing facilities the card should indicate what the important points are and whereabouts on the tape the points occur—elapsed time location being best). The tape card should also give the recording number and the programme number.

The recording should also have its own card, which indicates the date on which the recording was made, the tape number (and any subsequent programme number), the machine on which the recording was made and any comment about technical quality of recording and playback. A note should be made about the subject of the recording (important events being time-located). In a clinical recording there should be a note of the patient's name and hospital number and the name and status of the interviewer (in case follow-up enquiries of the patient's present condition are made). There should also be a note of the patient's consent and the restrictions that have been put on the showing of the tape. Finally, the name of the clinician responsible for the patient should be recorded.

Programmes should also have record cards which indicate the recording number (so that the master tape can be found easily), the number of the tape on which the programme is currently recorded and an indication of the title and content (important events being elapsed time-located again).

It may seem cumbersome having three record cards that need to be cross-referenced but it aids quick retrieval of information and is worth the trouble of starting and keeping them up to date (and amended as tapes are wiped or disposed of).

Having set up a system which is already cross-referenced it is comparatively easy then to build into it, as your collection increases, a cross-referenced subject index suitable for your own particular needs: a particular recording may end up being cross-referenced under several subject headings. If it was a recording, for instance, of a clinical interview of a patient with schizophrenia then it may well be indexed under 'schizophrenia', 'thought disorder', 'auditory hallucinations', 'first rank symptoms', 'delusional perceptions', etc. Cross-referencing enables one to answer quickly some very common questions asked of the video librarian, like 'What happened to the patient subsequently?' or 'That was an interesting extract—have you any more on that particular patient?' or 'Have you any short videotape illustrations for my lecture on phenomenology which starts in five minutes?'.

Another useful practice is to identify the teaching points in an interview, keep that interview as the master tape and edit onto a separate tape the bits that are wanted. This second-generation tape is a short (say 10 minutes) tape which is then put in the library so that the teacher finds a small section of short tapes in the library under the title, say, of 'visual hallucinations' and can use the material at once without the time-consuming exercise of finding the right point in the original tape. Heavy use of recorded original material demands the use of a second copy to preserve the master tape anyway. As the copy wears out, relevant editing is taken from the master again.

How do I evaluate it?

Whether you are making your own material or using outside programmes it is important that you try to evaluate whether these meet the educational objectives you have set them. For example, in our training courses using self-teaching programmes (Betts, 1980) participants are asked to rate each programme in terms of informational content and understandability. Programmes that get a consistently low score are looked at critically by the author and then remade.

In an unpublished evaluation of the self-teaching programmes on sexuality we were able to show that self-teaching videotapes used on their own by students without a teacher were not different from the tapes plus a teacher, in terms of how much information about human sexuality and its problems the students retained (as tested by a multiple choice examination). A teacher on his own without the tapes imparted significantly less information than the other two methods. Of the three methods of presenting information the students expressed a preference for the combination of live teacher plus videotapes.

If you set up a library of relevant material to your course, use it frequently and index and catalogue it well and evaluate it rigorously. Only by evaluating your material in this way will you gradually shape it into the powerful teaching medium that it is; the great advantage of videotape is the ease with which you can wipe a programme and remake it.

Acknowledgements

A great many people have helped me develop my interest in educational television and the programmes I have made. Particular thanks must go to my friend Paul Morby, Producer of the Birmingham University Television and Film Unit, whose skills I have admired for the last ten years. Professor Sir William Trethowan has been unfailing in his support since we started developing our television teaching. Many members of staff of our department and the University Television and Film Unit have given a great deal of their help and time, particularly Sally Pidd, Peter Harvey, Barbara Dodd, Tony Parsons, Judith Baron, Kerry Bluglass, Alan Wilkinson, Peter Whittaker and Keith Rodgers, as have members of the Association of University Teachers of Psychiatry Working Party, particularly David Goldberg and Peter Maguire.

I owe a special thanks to many of my former students (several now training in psychiatry) who have made major contributions to our programmes, particularly Alison Weissberg, Alison Blake, Virginia Lowe, David Malins, Pauline Skarrott, Jan Birtle, Richard Tudor and Angela Raffle.

References

Betts, T. A. (1980). Teaching counselling skills to undergraduates and postgraduates, *Bulletin of The Royal College of Psychiatrists*, **1980**, 186–189.
Oliver, Elizabeth (Ed.) (1981). *Researchers Guide to British Film and Television Collections*, British Universities Film Council, Pitman Press, Bath.

Useful addresses

1. For advice about available programmes:
    (a) British Universities Film Council, 81 Dean Street, London W1V 6AA
    (b) Mental Health Film Council, 22 Harley Street, London W1N 2D
    (c) Dr Peter Maguire, Secretary AUTP Working Party on the Uses of Television in Psychiatry, Department of Psychiatry, Withington Hospital, Manchester 20
2. For ethical guidelines:
    Secretary, Audiovisual Aides Sub-Committee, Royal College of Psychiatrists, 17 Belgrave Square, London SW1X 8PG
3. For advice about equipment:
    Dr Peter Whittaker, Director, Birmingham University Television and Film Unit, University of Birmingham, Edgbaston, Birmingham B15 2TT

Catalogues describing programmes mentioned in this chapter which are available for general use can be obtained from the author.

Using Video
Edited by P. W. Dowrick and S. J. Biggs
© 1983 John Wiley & Sons Ltd

Chapter 7

The Instrument

Harald G. Wallbott

University of Giessen, West Germany

This chapter will cover some basic technical topics in the use of the 'video instrument'. It will focus on lighting and sound recording problems. Furthermore, editing techniques, masking techniques and placement and usage of the video camera will be discussed. Finally, a short outlook to future developments in audiovisual recording will be presented, as for instance digital video recording or cameras with built-in recorders, and their possible implications for research and practice. (For special topics the reader is referred to the list of selected references on the technical aspects of video that is provided at the end of the chapter.)

Before we start discussing the aspects stressed, one thing has to be mentioned which is basically important in the use of video. Contrary to the worldwide standardization of cinema (Super 8, 16 mm, etc.) or audio tape and audio cassette recording, video is characterized by a remarkable *lack* of standardization. A lot of different systems, standards and norms exist, which in most cases are not compatible with each other. Older systems (like VCR) vanish from the market, while new systems appear. This is especially important for video users who have to exchange or circulate tapes for scientific or practical purposes.

Thus, it is important from the very beginning of video usage (when buying the equipment) to keep that point in mind. Figure 1 presents a short overview of the most important video systems available today, together with some information for each of the systems.

For further discussion of some special problems of the 'instrument video' we will start from hypothetical 'modal' equipment. After these initial remarks we will discuss some problems which probably everybody who has used video may have encountered from time to time.

Lighting

For video recordings appropriate lighting is essential. Two aspects have to be mentioned here: one is the amount of light necessary, the other is the optimal placement of the lights.

system	spread	selection	portable recorders	maximum tape length	tape costs	costs of equipment	technical possibilities	prospects of the future
VHS	very wide spread (on the home market 60 to 70%)	large selection of recorders and cameras	available	240 min.	medium	small	slow motion, frame-by-frame, quick motion, (stereo sound for some recorders)	large
BETAMAX	wide spread (a little less than VHS)	large selection of recorders and cameras	available	210 min.	medium	small	slow motion, frame-by-frame, quick motion	large
U-MATIC	semi-professional or professional system gaining popularity	large selection of recorders and cameras	available	80 min.	medium to large	large	slow motion, frame-by-frame, quick motion, stereo sound, triple standard (PAL-SECAM-NTSC) recorders, electronical editing	large
JAPAN EIAJ-STANDARD 1	a little antiquated, but frequently used in scientific research	robust openreel recorders, also available as a cartridge system	available	60 min.	medium	medium	slow motion, frame-by-frame	small
VCR and VCR (LONGPLAY)	production has been ceased in 1980.		not available	180 min.	medium	small	slow motion, frame-by-frame	small
VIDEO 2000	new system (cassette turning principle like in audio cassettes)	only a few recorders available yet	not available	480 min.	small	small	slow motion, frame-by-frame, quick motion	?
1" and 2" PROFESSIONAL SYSTEMS	wide spread in professional applications and institutions	large selection of recorders and cameras	available	120 min.	large	large	all technical possibilities given, but complicated technology that often necessitates a technician	?

Figure 7.1 A comparison of the most popular video systems

Video cameras are very light-sensitive. Even under poor lighting conditions acceptable black and white recordings are possible. In fact, too much light may result in 'flat' recordings with poor contrast. In low-light conditions it is possible to use a smaller f-stop, i.e. a larger opening of the camera iris and the 'normal/low-light' switch provided by most cameras. Unfortunately, both options have severe drawbacks.

When using the low-light switch, the light reaching the video tube inside the camera is electronically amplified. This often results in a grainy picture and, when recording in colour, in distorted colours. Small f-stops have problems too. The f-stop does not only affect the amount of light reaching the light-sensitive tube but also the depth of field and the depth of focus. Small f-stops result in a smaller depth of field, i.e. the range away from the camera, in which objects stay in sharp focus. If an object, for instance a child at play moves towards and away from the video camera, the distance it may move while staying in focus becomes smaller with smaller f-stops chosen. Moving out of this range the object will be out of focus and the picture will be blurred, unless the focus is constantly adjusted. This makes recordings more difficult because a lot of attention has to be concentrated on camera adjustments. Though generally the depth of field becomes larger with larger f-stops and smaller with smaller f-stops, no quantitative data can be given here, because this relation is furthermore determined by the focal length, the light sensitivity and other characteristics of the lens system used. Finally, large f-stops tend to reduce the contrast of the picture, which again is an effect not particularly satisfying for the user. Thus, in video it is advisable to adjust the amount of light in such a way that medium f-stops may be chosen and the low-light switch does not have to be used.

This is often not too difficult. Even without a well-equipped studio this may be achieved by using portable spotlights that can be arranged to produce the amount of light necessary. Furthermore, furniture may be rearranged to make the best possible use of the light available. Technically the utilization of the light available may be optimized by exchanging the Vidicon tubes, which are the standard option in most cameras available, with Newvicon, Plumbicon or Saticon tubes. These tubes are much more light sensitive than the standard ones and reduce the 'smearing' effects and ghost flags typical of Vidicon tubes when the camera is panned or the object to be recorded moves quickly. Finally, these tubes are less inert and more resistant against tube burns. Burns occur when the camera is exposed to the open sun or bright light-reflecting surfaces, and can result in black stationary spots on the picture which may be permanent. Nevertheless, even when using Newvicon or Saticon tubes the camera should not be exposed to very intense light, and the lens shield should be used every time the camera is not in operation.

Besides the amount of light the placement of the light sources is important in video recording. Lights placed wrongly may result in recordings in which important features, for instance the face of a person, are covered by shadows and are thus invisible. Too much light or too much shadow may be quite unsatisfactory, e.g. in video feedback, where a person is not able to recognize her- or himself because of bad lighting.

If a prepared room or even a studio is available, proper placement of lights is usually not a severe problem. If such a room has to be designed for video recording, care should be taken from the earliest planning stages that the room is equipped with appropriate lighting facilities—not with heavy studio spotlights, obviously, which are expensive, obtrusive, produce a lot of heat and are usually *not* necessary, but with moveable spotlights, carefully arranged ceiling lights and if possible with dimmers that allow one to control the amount of light at any one time.

Appropriate and well-balanced lighting does not only contribute to the researcher's personal satisfaction with the recording but also has considerable therapeutic implications. It is much more satisfying for a client to watch a successful recording than to be confronted with a dim 'shadow play'. Furthermore, appropriate lighting is important if further analysis of the recordings is planned, for instance analysis of facial expression or eye-contact.

Sound recording

Unfortunately, good sound recording is one of the most difficult tasks in video recording. Microphones tend to record sounds which later are disturbing such as moving furniture or street noise. As a first step towards good sound recording it is advisable whenever possible *not* to use the built-in camera microphone most cameras provide. To use these built-in microphones seems plausible at first glance, because no special equipment for sound recording has to be set up and no additional cables lie in the way, but built-in microphones tend to record noises that result when the focal length is manipulated on the camera itself. Furthermore, these microphones usually are not of superior quality. While it is possible to 'zoom' a faraway scene optically nearer to the viewer, this is obviously not possible with a microphone, at least not with a built-in microphone.

An external microphone may be placed near the sound source independent of the location of the video camera or the recording equipment. It is often better to use one if high sound quality is asked for. With external microphones a lot of different options are available, such as high or low impedance microphones, condenser or dynamic microphones, Lavalier or stationary microphones and ones with different direction characteristics.

Generally, low impedance microphones should be preferred, because they allow for long cable connections up to 200 m or more. They are usually of superior recording quality compared to high impedance microphones. With high impedance microphones, even when using very short cables (e.g. 5 m), humming within the sound signal may occur.

The decision between dynamic microphones, which work on a 'mechanical' basis for the transformation of sound energy into electrical signals, and condenser microphones, which use an electrical condenser for this transformation, is more difficult. Dynamic microphones are usually less expensive, but more robust than comparable condenser microphones. Condenser microphones, on the other hand, are more expensive, more sensitive to dust, humidity and dropping on the floor (!). However, sound quality and sound sensitivity is higher than in dynamic microphones. Unfortunately, this high sensitivity may lead to 'overload' when exposing the microphone to very intense sounds or noises, which in extreme cases may damage the condenser microphone. Finally, condenser microphones need an external power supply via a battery or an external power supply unit. (If you decide to use them, remember to check the batteries!) To sum up, dynamic microphones may be preferred in situations in which the microphone is exposed to problematic or extreme surroundings, while condenser microphones are more useful in situations where high sound quality is needed.

Dynamic as well as condenser microphones are available as Lavalier or 'collar' microphones and as stationary microphones. The decision as to which type to use will depend on the recording situation and the persons to be recorded, as well as on the purpose of the recording. Lavalier microphones are attached to the clothes of the person, near her or his mouth. If people are sitting somewhere for an interview or a discussion, sound quality is usually very good and to a large extent free of disturbances. However, some people have a tendency to fiddle with the microphone or the cable when speaking or listening, which may in turn result in a lot of distortions in the recording. This is sometimes a problem when working with 'nervous' persons. Further problems might arise if one tries to attach the microphone to the person when she or he is wearing a T-shirt, etc.

So far we have only discussed the case where people are sitting. But what can be done if they move around during the recording, walk, or if we want to record children at play? In these cases Lavalier microphones have the advantage that, whatever happens, the microphone is near the speaker, thus guaranteeing high quality sound. However, what about the cables the person has to carry around? Fortunately, portable transmitters exist which are identical in sound quality to microphones connected by cables to the recorder. As many transmitters and receivers may be employed as there are persons to be recorded. Unfortunately, this transmitting process is quite sensitive to external influences. Nearby radio stations or unshielded cables may distort the transmitted signal and result in humming. These 'wireless' facilities pose the additional problem that the transmitter also has to be attached to the person. This may lead to severe problems of obtrusiveness, i.e. people are made very aware of the fact that they are being recorded.

Thus, in many situations a stationary microphone would be preferred. Stationary microphones may be placed quite unobtrusively somewhere in a corner and can even be hidden. The directional characteristics of the microphone then become very important. Directional characteristics influence the sensitivity of the microphone to sounds coming from different directions. A distinction can be made between 'spheric', 'cardioid', 'super-cardioid', 'eight' and 'super-unidirectional' characteristics. Figure 2 represents these different directional characteristics, together with a schematic situation showing where these types might be employed.

A microphone with an 'eight' characteristic can be used, if two speakers facing each other in an interview situation have to be recorded, thus guaranteeing that the utterances of both speakers are caught. If it is possible to place a microphone between or above the speakers so that all speakers are localized in the sphere or cardioid of highest sensitivity, one with 'spheric' or 'cardioid' characteristics might be used for group discussions. 'Cardioid' or 'super-cardioid' may be selected if a single speaker is to be recorded who is not too far away from the microphone. If the speaker is further away (e.g. more than 5 m), a 'unidirectional' microphone may be used. These microphones have to be used with considerable care. They have the major advantage that high quality recordings are possible, even when the speaker is quite far away from the microphone. However, a severe drawback results if the speaker moves around, thus eventually getting 'lost' by the microphone. Unidirectional microphones should only be employed, then, if one can be sure that the speaker will not move around much or if an assistant is available who 'follows' the speaker with the microphone all the time.

Some practical precautions for high sound quality may be taken, independent of the choice of microphones, especially when doing field recordings. Generally, microphones should be placed as near as possible to a sound source. When recording in the open air, a wind shield is mandatory. Furthermore, whenever possible a solid tripod should carry the microphone or it should at least be placed on a felt pad or something similar to prevent vibrations or floor noise. Finally, whenever possible manual gain control should be preferred to an automatic gain control. Automatic gain control is not able to distinguish between noise and the signal to be recorded. In silent passages it therefore tries 'to do its job' and amplifies the arriving signal which, for instance, in speech pauses is pure noise or humming. In pauses, noise will become louder and louder, as the automatic control adjusts the amplification. If somebody starts to speak again, this will be 'too' loud for the automatic gain control level set during the pause. The signal is deamplified only after some seconds, which means that the speech will initially be recorded with too high a level. The result is the same the other way round: after loud sounds or noises, for instance sneezing, speech is recorded with too low a level! This characteristic of automatic gain control results in familiar problems: in pauses humming and noise become very loud, while speech after pauses is distorted and speech after loud noises is too low. If manual gain control is used, a test recording to obtain the optimal level is mandatory. Too low levels result in humming, while too high levels distort the signal to be recorded. Unfortunately some video recorders, especially most VHS and BETAMAX recorders, do not allow for manual gain control. Thus, if high sound quality is looked for it should be considered when purchasing a recorder.

Camera placement and camera usage

Whether a camera has to be hidden or not, it should always be positioned as unobtrusively as possible. Obviously this depends on the kind of recording needed. If facial expression is important, the camera *has* to face the person to be recorded, but tele or zoom lenses might be employed, which allow one to place the camera further away from the subject without losing important information.

In the case of a dyadic interaction or an interview, one needs to consider whether only the client is to be recorded. Should the client be recorded frontally or from the side? Should client and interviewer be recorded? If only one camera is available, not much choice is given, especially if both interactants are to be

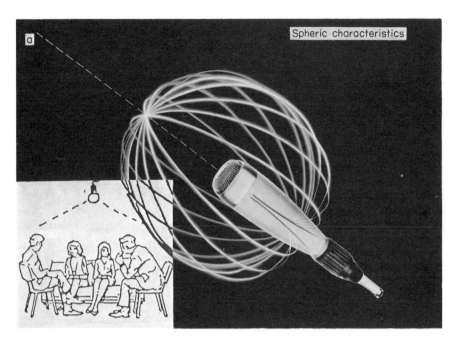

Spheric characteristics

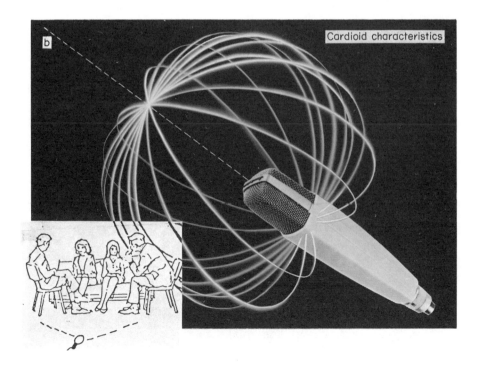

Cardioid characteristics

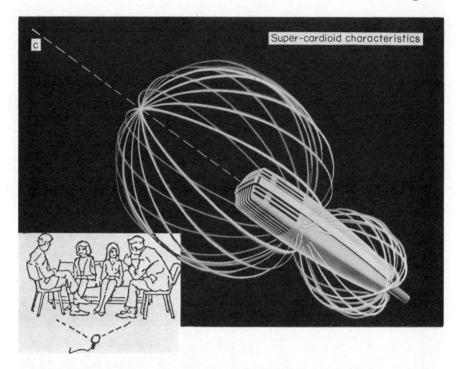

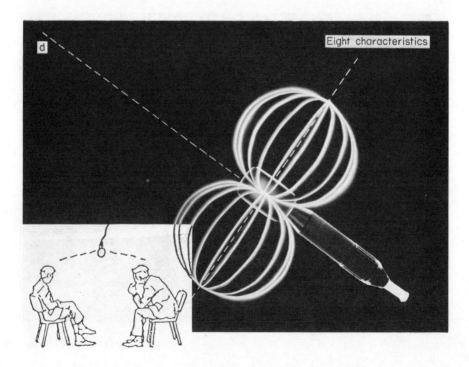

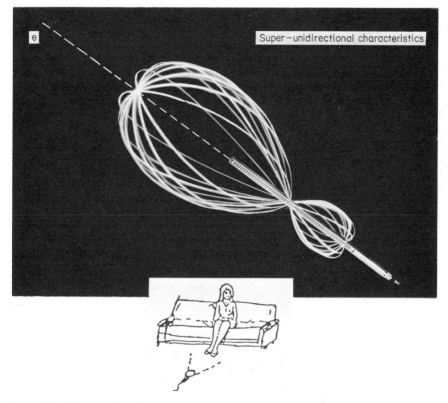

Figure 7.2 Different direction characteristics of microphones. (By courtesy of Sennheiser electronic, West Germany)
a. Spheric characteristics, b. Cardioid characteristics, c. Super-cardioid characteristics, d. Eight characteristics, e. Super-unidirectional characteristics.

recorded. In such cases the camera has to be located somewhere beside both persons. It may be placed on a tripod or less obtrusively be mounted on the wall in a corner of the room. For special purposes it may even be mounted at the room's ceiling to record from a 'bird's view'. Some of these possibilities obviously necessitate a remote control device for movements of the camera and/or the zoom lens. If this is too expensive, an appropriate lens (for instance a wide-angle lens) that covers the whole area where 'the action is' has to be chosen or an assistant has to be employed to control the necessary zoom lens and camera movements.

Usage of zoom lenses as well as camera movements is not without its problems. First of all, someone besides the interviewer is needed to operate the camera. However, the interviewer or therapist will be the person most interested in the recording and thus knowing best what and when to record. Normally this cannot be communicated to a camera assistant during the course of an interview or a clinical session. Thus, camera movements and zooming are often the arbitrary decisions of the camera assistant. Important information may be lost in this way if the camera does not focus on the person where 'the interesting things' are happening. Obviously each camera position or movement is practically a manipulation of the viewer, because certain features of the scene are accentuated and others negotiated. It should be kept in mind how readily changes in camera angle or zooming might negate, stress or adulterate incidents and events. To name just one example: it is very well known in cinema and television that a person appears larger, more important and more powerful when the camera looks 'up' to that person, instead of facing the person directly.

For some applications camera movements and zooming may be necessary. If, for instance, a child at play who moves around in a room is to be recorded, the camera certainly *has* to follow. If a certain 'dramaturgy' of a recording is asked for (cf. in video self-modelling), zooming on important features of the scene is necessary. In most other cases a fixed camera should be preferred because of the potential information loss and the manipulation tendencies of zooming and camera movement. This is especially true if scientific behaviour analysis from the recordings is planned. Then camera angle, type and succession of takes as well as the focal length of the zoom lens should be constant within and across persons whenever possible. If only one person is to be recorded this is usually no severe problem, especially if the person is sitting somewhere. If more than one person is to be recorded simultaneously, the optimal location of the camera has to be determined in pre-tests, making sure that the persons will not cover each other. Of course, in these types of recordings one has to be aware of the fact that the subjects will appear quite small on the video monitor, which implies that subtle movements like facial expression will hardly be recognized.

Finally, some technical possibilities for hiding a camera to produce unobtrusive recordings should be mentioned. Probably the most frequently used technique is the one-way mirror. In specially built studios one-way mirrors are often already part of the design. Light loss has to be considered when using one-way mirrors. That means that the cameras employed have to be quite light sensitive. As we have mentioned, this is especially important for colour recordings in order to prevent 'wrong colours' and colour distortions.

Even without one-way mirrors it is relatively easy to hide a camera in bookshelves, etc. When doing field recordings in the open air a lot of possibilities to hide camera and equipment may also be found, if powerful tele or zoom lenses are employed. Furthermore, specially designed angle lenses are available for certain purposes (cf. Eibl-Eibesfeldt, 1979). In these lenses the light reaches the camera tube through a hole in the side of the lens system via a mirror, the frontal part of the lens being a dummy. This allows recordings without pointing the camera at the persons to be recorded.

Split screen, special effects and editing techniques

Obviously the best solution is often to use more than one camera. If two cameras are used, a split screen technique is usually optimal, whereby the two interacting persons are recorded frontally with one camera each and these two pictures are then combined via a video mixer, resulting in a picture showing the two persons side by side. The two persons can be recorded as large as necessary for the purposes given, for instance head only, the upper body or the whole body. Technically split screen recording is fairly easy. Both cameras are connected to a video mixer. These mixers are nowadays not very expensive and are available even for the 'home standards' VHS or BETAMAX. If placement of the cameras and optimal split screen picture are pre-tested before the actual recording and camera angles and zoom or focal length are determined, the whole recording may be run without an assistant or further adjustments being necessary. Assistants will not need to run around creating an often unwanted and artifical 'studio atmosphere'. Furthermore, the researcher, interviewer or therapist may concentrate on his primary task and *not* on the video technology. Video may be a quite unobtrusive and very helpful instrument if everything is planned and tested carefully in advance of the actual recording.

More sophisticated mixers and even effect generators may be employed that allow different combinations of two or more cameras, fading, wiping and other effects. Effect generators may be especially useful where the identity of a person has to be protected. Some generators allow black and white reversal, thus presenting a 'negative' of the person from which she or he is fairly unrecognizable. Or black rafters may be superimposed over the person's eyes. With additional acoustical filters or distorters even the person's voice may be changed, thus making recognition of identity by voice cues impossible.

One special effect generator, the 'videotimer', has to be mentioned especially. For the scientific analysis of behaviour it is preferable to have an exact timebase inserted in the picture. These timers are connected to camera(s) and recorder(s) respectively and often allow one to superimpose running time information, consecutive frame numbers or even digital time-code marks for computer-controlled editing on the video picture. An easier but less accurate way to achieve this is to place a digital clock behind the subject and to record this clock together with the subject.

Editing of the recordings is often desirable, especially for demonstration tapes or for video self-modelling. Editing during the actual recording by starting and stopping the recorder selectively is often difficult or impossible. Thus, the tape usually has to be edited afterwards. Video editing is more difficult than audio editing, because it cannot be achieved with just scissors and splicing tape, and has to be carried out electronically via a copying process. Two recorders are thus the minimum necessary equipment for editing. The original recording has to be of good quality, because in the process of copying and editing some quality loss is unevitable. The most simple editing procedure (sometimes termed 'rough editing'; cf. Clarke, 1981) is characterized by just copying the selected scenes or takes onto a second recorder, without employing special editing facilities. The transitions between such rough edits appear on the video monitor as short breakdowns of the picture, because the recorder needs up to 5 s to reach operating speed and to properly record the video signal. Most recorders now provide the user with a facility that allows rough editing with visible quality comparable to electronic editing. When using the 'stop' button of these machines (U-MATIC, VHS, BETAMAX) the tape is rolled back a bit. When switched back into the 'record' mode, the edited scenes will follow one another quite smoothly with no apparent laps between two consecutive scenes. Rough edits with such machines therefore have about the same visual quality as an electronic edit. However, electronic editing is necessary if either very high quality edits with no breaks between consecutive scenes or edits at exactly defined points in time (i.e. to a certain defined video frame) are required.

Electronic editing devices also allow the opportunity to simulate an edit before actually performing it; thus the possible results can be pre-viewed and the edits can be corrected, which is often impossible once the edit has been performed. The editing devices available today especially for the semi-professional U-MATIC system are very sophisticated and user-orientated, though quite expensive.

Possible future developments

Video is a quite 'recent' medium. In 1956 Ampex introduced the first practical video recorder. In 1967 the first portable recorder appeared on the American market. In 1969 the famous EIAJ standards were decided upon that helped at least a bit to standardize the different video systems. In 1973 the first low-priced colour camera and finally in 1975 the now popular 'home systems' (BETAMAX and a little later VHS) were introduced. Now only 25 years after the dawn of the video era the market has exploded with a lot of different systems, cameras, recorders and auxiliary equipment. I will try to discuss some of these developments here, some of which may become important for video usage.

Most home recorders today have just one audio track, i.e. only mono recordings are possible. However, some semi-professional and professional recorders (U-MATIC, VHS, 1 in, 2 in) already provide *two audio tracks*. In some countries television is presently transmitting programmes with stereo sound; in the future some home recorders too will probably have the facility of stereo sound recording. It is known from audio recording that stereo recording has considerable advantages compared to mono recording. Especially when recording more persons or discussions, stereo is better able to 'separate' the different speakers, thus making what has been said more understandable. Furthermore, stereo sound video recording will allow the researcher to use the second audio track to record comments or remarks concerning the ongoing interaction, which may then be used in video feedback. Finally, it is possible to translate on the second audio track what has been said into other languages for demonstration in other countries.

Digital video recording is another prospect for the future. In digital video recording, either on digital magnetic tape or on magnetic disks, the video signal is not recorded as an analog, as in today's recorders, but instead after an analog-to-digital conversion as a digital code for each point in the video picture. As is known from digital audio recording, this process allows for much higher spatial and temporal resolution and thus superior recording quality. Furthermore, no drop-outs and other distortions are possible, because when replaying each digital code combination is checked to find out whether it is 'allowed' or not. By this process all 'noise' is filtered out. Digital video recorders are already available, but are out of the reach of most budgets.

The most important developments for the video user seem to happen in the area of *camera construction* and camera design. Video cameras are constantly constructed to be lighter, smaller, more light sensitive and comparatively less expensive than their bulky, heavy and expensive predecessors. This is especially important for field recordings when the cameras have to be carried around, and also in relation to obtrusiveness, because the small new cameras are easier to hide or to place unobtrusively. The same tendency towards lighter and smaller equipment holds true for portable recorders.

Other new camera developments include automatic light and colour adjustments for colour recording. Both are important because they free the user from a lot of manual adjustments on the camera. For special purposes, infrared video cameras have been developed which are sensitive only to infrared light but *not* to visible light. These cameras may become important for monitoring tasks, for instance of patients in a hospital during the night. Using these cameras and an invisible infrared light source will not disturb the patient but the camera will 'see' everything that happens.

A last major step that will be very important for the video user are *cameras with built-in recorders*. If these developments prove practical and successful, the user will be freed from the heavy recorder and the cables that need to be carried around today, especially when doing field recordings. Cameras with built-in recorders presented so far are not much larger than Super-8 film cameras, but obviously combine the advantage of ciné (i.e. small cameras with no additional equipment necessary for recording) with the major advantages of video (i.e. instant replay and reusable tape). Unfortunately, we will probably have to wait for some more years before these 'ultimate' video cameras/recorders will be commercially available.

Final remarks

Basically, video is not a 'difficult' medium to use if one is aware of technical basics, of the problems and of the technical and practical possibilities of the medium. Although video can be a powerful and important tool for research and practice, all too often the equipment is used without much thought or, after some time of 'playing around', is not used at all. Often in a first euphoria, video equipment is purchased without much awareness of the inherent demands, problems and possibilities. It is used for some short time and then vanishes into some dark, rarely opened 'video tomb' because of technical problems, lack of expertise and time or because of general disappointment or frustration. This implies that the potential user should get down to the problems as well as to the possibilities of video even *before* buying the equipment.

References

Clarke, A. H. (1981). Videoeditieren: Implikationen und Technik, in *Video und Medizin* (Ed. B. Kuegelgen), Perimed, Erlangen.
Eibl-Eibesfeldt, I. (1979). Similarities and differences between cultures in expressive

movements, in *Nonverbal Communication* (Ed. S. Weitz), 2nd ed., Oxford University Press, New York.

Technical aspects of video: Selected references

Books and articles

Bensinger, C. (1973). *Petersen's Guide to Video Tape Recording*, Petersen Publishing, Los Angeles.

Bensinger, C. (1979). *The Home Video Hand Book*, Esselte Video, Santa Barbara.

Bensinger, C. (1979). *The Video Guide*, Esselte Video, Santa Barbara.

Berger, M. M. (Ed.) (1978). *Videotape Techniques in Psychiatric Training and Treatment*, Revised Edition. Brunner-Mazel, New York.

Cary, M. S. (1979). Comparing film and videotape, *Environmental Psychology and Nonverbal Behavior*, **3**, 243–247.

Ekman, P., and Friesen, W. V. (1969). A tool for the analysis of motion picture film or videotape, *American Psychologist*, **44**, 240–243.

Fahry, D., and Palme, K. (1979). *VideoTechnik*, 2 vols, Oldenbourg, Munich.

Fleischer, D. (1974). *Praxis der Video-Aufzeichung*, Siemens AG, Berlin.

Harwood, D. (1973). *Video as a Second Language: How to Make a Video Documentary*, VTR Publishing, Syosset, New York.

Harwood, D. (1978) *Everything you Always Wanted to Know about Portable Videotape Recording*, VTR Publishing, Syosset, New York.

La Bruzzo, R. (1970). The what and how of video hardware and tape, in *Videotape Techniques in Psychiatric Training and Treatment* (Ed. M. M. Berger), pp. 244–250, Brunner-Mazel, New York.

Lachenbruch, D. (1979). *Videocassette Recorders: The Complete Home Guide*, Everest House, New York.

Lechenauer, G. (1979). *Videomachen*, Rowohlt, Hamburg.

Marsh, K. (1973). *Independent Video*, Straight Arrow, San Francisco.

Murray, M. (1975). *The Videotape Book*, Taplinger, New York.

Oliver, W. (1971). *Introduction to Video-recording*, Foulsham, London.

Onder, J. J. (1970). *The Manual of Psychiatric Television: Theory, Practice, Imagination*, Maynard House, Ann Arbor.

Price, J. (1979). *Video Visions*, New American Library, New York.

Robinson, J. F., and Beards, P. H. (1976). *Using Video Tape*, London.

Robinson, R. (1974). *The Video Primer: Equipment, Production, and Concepts*, Link Books, New York.

Scheflen, A. E., Kendon, A., and Schaeffer, J. (1970). On the choice of audiovisual media, in *Videotape Techniques in Psychiatric Training and Treatment* (Ed. M. M. Berger), pp. 233–243, Brunner-Mazel, New York.

United Business Publications (1977). *The Video Handbook*, 3rd ed., United Business Publications, New York.

Utz, P. (1980). *Video Users Handbook*, Englewood Cliffs, New Jersey.

Video CCWG (1975). *Video Handbuch*, Büro der Off-Kudamm-Kinos, Berlin.

Video Freex (1973). *The Spagetti City Video Manual*, Praeger Publications, New York.

Wallbott, H. G. (1982). Audiovisual recording: procedures, equipment, and trouble-shooting, in *Handbook of Methods in Nonverbal Behaviour Research* (Eds. K. R. Scherer and P. Ekman), Cambridge University Press, New York.

Weiner, P. (1973). *Making the Media Revolution*, MacMillan, New York.

Williams, R. L. (1976). *Television Production: A Vocational Approach*, Vision Co., Salt Lake City.

Wilmer, H. A. (1967). Technical and artistic aspects of videotape in psychiatric teaching, *Journal of Nervous and Mental Disease*, **144**, 207–223.
Zettl, H. (1977). *Television Production Handbook*, Wadsworth Publishing, Belmont, California.

Journals and newsletters

Audiovision. Das Medienmagazin, Monthly journal, Trimedia, Hamburg, West Germany.
Audiovision in Psychiatrie and Psychotherapie, Dr G. Romahn, Abt. Psychiatrie—Neurologie des Kindes- und Jugendalters, Planetenallee 33, D-1000 Berlin 19, West Germany.
Human Ethology, Cheril Travis, Department of Psychology, University of Texas, Knoxville, Tennesee 37916, U.S.A.
Kinesis, Institute for Nonverbal Communication Research, 25 West 86th Street, New York 10024, U.S.A.
Nonverbal Components of Communication, Rosalyn Lindner, Department of Geography/ Sociology, State University College at Buffalo, 1300 Elmwood Ave, Buffalo, New York 14222, U.S.A.
TV in Psychiatry, Dr L. Thyhurst, University of British Columbia, Department of Psychiatry, 2075 Westbrook Mall, Vancouver, B.C., Canada V6T 1W5.
Video, Quarterly journal, Vereinigte Motor Verlage, Stuttgart, West Germany.
Videography, Monthly journal, United Business Publications, New York, U.S.A.
Video-Informationen, Dr Heiner Ellgring, Max-Planck Institut für Psychiatrie, Kraepelinstrasse 10, D-8000 München, West Germany; Harald Wallbott, Justus-Liebig Universität, Fachbereich 06, Otto-Behaghelstrasse 10F, D-6300 Giessen, West Germany.
Video for Interaction Research and Training Users Group (VIRTUG), Dr Angela Summerfield, Department of Psychology, Birkbeck College, Malet Street, London WC1E 7HX, Great Britain.

Editor's Note on Ethical Uses of Video

Simon J. Biggs.

The view expressed by Tim Betts (Chapter 6) on a patient's right to view potential teaching material in which they appear differ from those of Renne and others (Chapter 3), when they discuss the use of videofeedback in therapy. In the latter case videofeedback may be judged to be anti-theraputic in the eyes of the clinician, examples of which can be found in chapter thirteen (Trower and Kiely). In order to reduce confusion on this important ethical matter it may be useful to point to some differences between the two situations.

In the theraputic situation a contract has been made by the first party (the client) with the clinician (the second party) about the first party's right to view themselves. Traditionally clinicians have been very careful when giving verbal feedback to a client. Much of the effectiveness of counselling and psychotherapy would seem to depend upon the clinicians ability to judge whether a client would benefit from insight at a particular point in time. Video may, for these general purposes, be seen as one of many tools in the clinician's arsenal and feedback be negotiated within the context of the theraputic relationship. A 'non-viewing' clause could be added to the consent statement if one suspects that viewing may damage the client.

When video is being shown to third parties, it is to a large extent removed from the original context in which it was made. Mistakes in the third party's interpretations of the client's intentions are thus more likely to be made. Further, third parties are more liable to interpret the client's behaviour in terms of 'set', the context within which it is shown (rather than recorded) and the labels given to the video in this new situation. Any replay to third parties, I feel, should therefore include an opportunity for clients to explain their intentions as well as a recognition that consent has been given. This is par-ticularly important in view of experience indicating that those being taped are often concerned that they can explain what has happened to others who might see the tape outside its original context. However, although the clinician is the gatekeeper to viewing in both Betts and Renne and others, Betts points out that the first person should also see the tape before it is shown to others. It seems that difficulties arise primarily when one wishes to show a video for teaching purposes as an example of when *not* to use it as feedback. Two competing solutions suggest themselves here, firstly one may wait until the client would not be damaged by seeing themselves on video and then continue with the vetting procedure. A second solution may be to use a video which shows a role-play of the original situation and which does not betray the confidentiality of the clients themselves.

Using Video
Edited by P. W. Dowrick and S. J. Biggs
© 1983 John Wiley & Sons Ltd

PART II

INTRODUCTION (PRACTICE)

Simon J. Biggs

As the previous section has shown, video can be very useful as a record of events and an aid to detailed observation. We now turn to its use as an agent of change, where video has been used in therapy and training to show clients how they are seen 'from the outside'. Now, whereas the skilled observer often only has the information caught on tape plus standard techniques for coding material, viewers (who see themselves) also have immediate access to their personal history and their feelings while the taped events were taking place. The interplay between one's perception of this context, its consistency with past events and the difference between one's intentions and how one actually performed have now become more important. It is this interplay between personal perceptions of self and external information about the self which marks the value of video as a therapeutic medium.

Thus, historically speaking, video has been used in both training and therapy primarily because it allows clients to reflect upon themselves and their relationships with others. In the heady days of the sixties the medium was subject to exuberant claims and many workers expected that video would do for psychology and the social sciences what the microscope has done for medicine. This growth of interest prompted the *Journal of Nervous and Mental Deseases* (1969) to publish a series of articles which catalogued the many ways in which video was being used by particular practitioners. Here, it seemed, was a way of reducing the inequalities of the theraputic relationship which also gave access to the complexities of interpersonal behaviour and self-perception. The feel of these papers can best be expressed by quoting from Alger's contribution entitled 'Therapeutic use of videotape playback', in which he says: 'It would seem then, that the ways in which videotape can be utilised are probably limited only by ingenuity' (p. 433).

There followed a series of attempts to make video the central feature of an intervention. Higgins, Ivey and Uhleman (1970) published a paper entitled 'Media-therapy' which addressed methods of training in behavioural skills used in day-to-day interaction, while Brooks (1976) labelled her use of video in groupwork 'teletherapy'. At the same time a group of sociologists at the University of Lausanne (Willener, Milliard and Ganty, 1976) gave birth to 'videology', a central feature of which was the user of video as a catalyst for the analysis and transformation of both the self and social groups. However, so far as many practitioners were concerned, the medium was best seen as a tool at the disposal of a therapist already skilled in understanding complex psychological phenomena and not as a theraputic modality in its own right (see Alger and Hogan, 1969). This last point might help to explain a repeated criticism by reviewers (Bailey and Sowder, 1970; Griffiths, 1974) that video has not been subject to controlled study, its use often being contaminated by other therapeutic interventions. As a consequence of this, little is still known about the particular qualities of video itself.

At this time differences in the use of video were becoming more clear. Firstly, it could be used as a means of confronting clients with aspects of themselves that might otherwise be subject to intellectualization and denial. This technique, broadly labelled 'self-confrontation', was based on the therapeutic value of insight and aimed at the elaboration of existing modes of behaviour. A second, behavioural use capitalized on the value of video as a source of feedback. Trainers using this approach were concerned with the process of skill-learning, the analysis of particular instances of behaviour, the recording and elaboration of progress made and the modelling of appropriate alternative patterns of social interaction. In both cases, which of course reflect well-known divisions within the helping professions, video was seen to give a concrete reflection of an event with any intervening biases reduced to a minimum. Clients could easily view their behaviour from a distance, repeatedly if necessary, until progress had been made. This new source of information was not usually available and might otherwise be easily lost in the vagaries of normal social comment and when the natural consequences of action were often lost or difficult to see. In short, access could be gained to the process as well as the results of one's social and individual 'style'.

In this section we have tried to explore the state of the art by looking at current uses being made of video, where it has been integrated as a central element in the process of change and where it has been shown to be effective. The reader is invited to consider Caplan's model of social psychiatry, as elaborated by Bender (1976), as a guide to the section. Broadly speaking, these workers have claimed that one must be effective on at least three levels to achieve change. Firstly, practitioners can look at their interventions in terms of how far they are working directly with clients; secondly, by reaching a larger number of clients by passing skills on to other workers such as trainee psychologists, social workers, nurses and day-care and residential workers; and finally, by influencing the wider social milieu within which events are taking place. Direct work with clients has been represented here by McRea's chapter on body- and self-image, Dowrick's work on self-modelling techniques and a chapter by Hosford and Mills who look at video in social skills training. The transmission of skills to other professionals can be found in Hargie and Saunders' chapter. Finally, Henny has written about existing European work which has often been overlooked by trainers and therapists. His chapter explores the ways in which video can be used as an agent of social change.

References

Alger, I. (1969). Therapeutic use of videotape playback, *Journal of Nervous and Mental Disease*, **148**, 430–436.

Alger, I., and Hogan, P. (1969). Enduring effects of videotape playback experience on family and marital relationships, *American Journal of Orthopsychiatry*, **39**, 86–98.

Bailey, K. G., and Sowder, W. T. (1970). Audiotape and videotape self-confrontation in psychotherapy, *Psychological Bulletin*, **74**, 153–181.

Bender, M. P. (1976). *Community Psychology*, Methuen, London.

Brooks, D. D. (1976). Teletherapy, *Perspectives in Psychiatric Care*, **14**, 83–87.

Griffiths, R. D. P. (1974). Videotape feedback as a therapeutic technique: retrospect and prospect, *Behaviour Research and Therapy*, **12**, 1–8.

Higgins, W. H., Ivey, A. E., and Uhleman, M. R. (1970). Media-therapy: a programmed approach to teaching behavioural skills, *Journal of Counselling Psychology*, **17**, 20–26.

Willener, A., Milliard, G., and Ganty, A. (1976). *Videology and Utopia*, Routledge and Kegan Paul, London.

Using Video
Edited by P. W. Dowrick and S. J. Biggs
© 1983 John Wiley & Sons Ltd

Chapter 8

Impact on Body-Image

Celia McRea

Queens University, Belfast

A very strong factor, possibly the most influential, affecting a person's view of the world and his behaviour is his self-image, or his awareness and perception of himself as a separate, objective being. The self-viewing experience has attained wide popularity as a method for inducing self-awareness and control, reducing defensiveness and distortion, and developing interpersonal understanding and skill. In relation to the study of body-image as a component of self-image, videotape recordings are liable to be a great asset. However, as yet few investigators have harnessed the full potential of this technique. In this chapter, after attempting to define the rather nebulous concept of 'body-image', distortions in this sphere are examined. In addition to the more extreme cases, usually found in the psychotic, particular attention is given to a more 'normal' sample, namely the obese.

In relation to this latter population three main topics are addressed:

1. The existing evidence which suggests that the obese suffer from a distorted body-image.
2. Explanations for the unrealistic self-images manifest in the overweight.
3. The question as to whether or not the attainment of a realistic body-image is therapeutically important for the obese.

As these issues are examined, areas in which video techniques could, and do already, assist progress are illustrated.

Video confrontation

Confrontation, the reflection of information about the self from outside sources, has long been used as a technique in psychological intervention. Videotape recordings provide patients with a rare opportunity to observe how they appear to others, and many investigators express enthusiasm about the therapeutic potential of this self-image confrontation technique. The wide variety in the clinical use of feedback techniques is apparent in the surveys (Bailey and Sowder, 1970; Berger, 1978; Danet, 1968).

Most of the studies in the relatively new field of self-image confrontation have been conducted since 1960 and, with few exceptions, have been primarily exploratory. However, most authors report that the technique of confronting an individual with his own image or behaviour can produce marked changes in that behaviour (Cornelison and Arsenian, 1960; Miller, 1962; Walz and Johnston, 1963; Ward and Bendak, 1964). Berger (1978) notes that there is unanimity among investigators who utilize videotape confrontation that through this experience insight can be heightened. It seems that via this self-viewing experience people can learn more of what is unknown about themselves, but which is known to others. Attitudes, roles and behaviour patterns can be modified, and self-images and concepts altered as individuals achieve a clearer sense of their own identity.

Although the majority of research has been inconclusive, a few experimental studies have begun to provide clearer evidence about the effects of videotape feedback. One promising avenue of research has been the assessment of changes in self-conception following feedback.

Griffiths and Gillingham (1978) note that the cognitive accompaniments of behaviour, of which self-conception is one aspect, can be shown to exert some influence on overt actions (Bandura, 1969). Thus if videotape feedback can modify self-referent attitudes, it may be possible to facilitate the production of beneficial behavioural change. Investigators have therefore stressed the need for studies to assess whether or not videotape feedback can induce changes in an individual's cognitions about himself.

Griffiths and Hinkson (1973) assessed patients' self-concepts by means of two anxiety scales and a semantic differential. The semantic differential was factor-analysed and the resulting factor was labelled 'social ease'. A significant improvement in this 'social ease' score was observed in the patients who received videotape feedback, both in the way they rated themselves and in the way they thought others saw them. (The scores reverted to their original level 14 days later.)

Boyd and Sisney (1967) provide some evidence that videotape playback effects a change on an individual's distorted self-image. These investigators examined changes in self-concept and concepts of interpersonal behaviour following self-image confrontation via videotape. In-patients on a psychiatric ward were rated by Leary's interpersonal checklist and it was found that, compared with a control group, interpersonal concepts of the self, the ideal self and the public self became less pathological and less discrepant with one another following the self-image confrontation. Similarly, Braucht (1970), within the context of assessing immediate effects of videotape self-confrontation on the self-concepts of psychiatric patients, reports that such patients increase in self-concept accuracy significantly more than a control group.

Gottheil, Backup and Cornelison (1969) were among the first to draw attention to the fact that if self-image confrontation is a useful therapeutic tool in combating denial, it should be effective in a condition such as anorexia nervosa where, in addition to disturbances in body concept, visible changes in body structure are clearly evident. In this single case study, the female patient was confronted with an image of her body on the monitor. This was inconsistent with her own body image, so she had three options: (1) to deny the screen image; (2) to change her self-image; or (3) to become disorganized. Initially she tenaciously denied the evidence on the screen, just as she had previously denied mirror evidence, and resisted information from her family and physicians. Finally, however, after repeated self-confrontation, it became more difficult for her to maintain this denial, and a change in her body image occurred so that thinness became ugly rather than comforting.

In a more recent study, Biggs, Rosen and Summerfield (1980) have found that anorexic clients attributed more negative qualities to their body-image following video feedback when compared with normal viewers. A serious disruption in their self-image was seen to have taken place.

Body-image

In its most literal sense body-image refers to the body as a psychological experience and focuses on the individual's feelings and attitudes towards his own body. It is concerned with the individual's subjective experiences with his body and the manner in which he has organized these experiences. Schilder (1935) defines the body-image as: 'the picture of our own body which we form in our mind, that is to say the way in which the body appears to ourselves'.

Researchers are increasingly turning to the analysis of the normal individual's body as a psychological phenomenon. As Fisher (1972) states: 'A man's body is, after all, synonymous with his existence. It should come as no surprise that his perception of its attitudes colours his experience of life.'

However, despite the importance which individuals afford to their body-image, it appears that they have surprisingly inaccurate perceptions of it. For example, Fisher (1973) has pointed out that if you walk into a room and are unexpectedly confronted with your own mirror image, you may momentarily feel that you are face to face with an unknown, somehow alien person.

Clinically, distortions of body-image are seen in different neurological conditions as phantom limbs, Gerstmann syndrome and others, but these distortions are limited and specific. Fisher and Cleveland (1968) review the bizarre bodily perceptions reported by schizophrenics. Confusion relating to masculinity and femininity, disintegration, deterioration, depersonalization or a sense of loss of body boundaries have all been reported in the psychotic. Even 'normal' populations can suffer adverse consequences due to their possessing inaccurate body-images. Numerous investigators have stressed the importance of this variable for the obese (Bruch, 1973; Garner and coauthors, 1976; and Stunkard and Mendelson, 1967).

The existing evidence which suggests that the obese suffer from a distorted body-image

In contemporary Western society, fat is stigmatized. The prevailing attitude attached to obesity is one of rejection and disgrace. The condition is regarded by most as ugly, sinful, self-indulgent, immoral, unhealthy and anti-social (Allon, 1973). The impact that this rejection has can be irreversible. Such attitudes, learnt in childhood, can form the basis for self-hatred in later years.

Anxiety and self-doubt may ensue in those who become obese or who are fearful lest they become overweight.

Bruch (1973) notes that ideally there should be no discrepancy between body structure, the body-image and social acceptance. However, because the obese live under the pressure of such a derogatory social environment, this continuous insult to their physical personality may result in a distortion of body-image. The studies dealing with body-image and behavioural correlations of weight reduction are difficult to compare, but generally the evidence suggests that a relation exists between obesity and disturbed body-image. Traditionally, attempts to quantify and objectify body-image have concentrated upon projective techniques, such as 'draw-a-person' tests, questionnaires to assess satisfaction with the body and scores derived from projective responses to inkblots. However, these measurements have been severely criticized (Fisher and Cleveland 1968; Wylie, 1961). One component of body-image that offers an opportunity for more objective measurement is perception of body size. Slade and Russell (1973) designed an instrument for the direct measurement of perceived body size which is employed in numerous body-image studies. The visual size estimation apparatus consists of two lights mounted on a horizontal bar, attached in such a way that they can be moved to indicate perceived widths of specific regions.

Mirror images and other self-representations are increasingly being employed by investigators attempting to measure feelings and attitudes towards the body. For example, studies employing mirrors consisting of flexible sheets of Plexiglass, which can be curved to produce different distortion settings, draw attention to the fact that subjects are extremely vague concerning their mirror images, despite infinite experiences of such confrontation (Orbach, Traub and Olsen, 1966; Schneiderman, 1956; Traub and Orbach, 1964). Distorting lenses are also employed in the investigation of body-image phenomena (Glucksman and Hirsch, 1969). This procedure involves projecting slides of subjects and systematically distorting them. Subjects are then requested to make the distorted screen images correspond to their body size. Results from Glucksman and Hirsch's study indicate that the obese increasingly overestimate their own body size during and following weight loss.

Schontz (1969) has noted that if so many different procedures all have legitimate claims to validity, it would certainly seem that the body-image is a ubiquitous phenomenon. However, it would seem to be a reasonable assumption that people do not normally mentally compare the size of various body parts with the distance between inanimate objects such as moving lights (Slade and Russell, 1973). Photographs or drawings, although providing a greater degree of realism, are never, to the author's knowledge, life-sized. It is left to the subject to translate from the scale of the representation into their 'true' body dimensions. In addition to ignoring the fact that the body is three dimensional, such instruments ignore the importance of movement. Schilder (1935) emphasizes the importance of mobility. Mobility plays an essential role, not only in defining the boundaries of the self but in differentiating one's self from the total perceptual environment. We would not know much about our bodies unless we moved them. The inactivity so characteristic of obese people may well be related to their often disturbed body concept.

The video self-image confrontation technique obviates these criticisms and offers unique advantages as a tool for body-image study:

1. Video feedback provides a more realistic measurement than those which have been used in the past.
2. Body parts can be represented on the same scale as the subject.
3. Movement can be incorporated in the assessment.
4. It can be argued that the monitor presents subjects with a more vivid sense of the three dimensions than does any existing two-dimensional apparatus which attempts to measure perceived body size.

At present the author is investigating the potential of video techniques in the treatment of obesity (Summerfield, 1980). One pilot study was with a relatively small group of patients who had a long history of unsuccessful treatment from family doctors and other medical specialists, including some unsuccessful psychotherapy and behaviour modification. All were female volunteers with no history of any primary metabolic disorder. Of these 20 severely obese adults, 11 were assigned to a video condition and 9 attended sessions at a specialist obesity clinic giving advice on diet and personal problems. The video group were taped individually during a structured interview and each then watched her tape while being asked to comment on how she perceived her body. (They attended three to eight sessions over a maximum period of 18 weeks.) Data were also collected on perceived body size and self-concept.

Seven of the eleven video patients lost weight, but none of the controls did so. The range of weight loss over the treatment period was 1 to 6 kilos. This is a modest but noticeable amount, given the patients' previous histories. It was also interesting to note that for the video condition the number of sessions attended was positively correlated with the amount of weight lost. To begin with they did not want to look at the video image of their whole bodies, and this could only be overcome by getting them to describe one part of the body at a time. However, these initial reactions developed into interest, and 10 of the 11 ladies in the video condition eventually made changes in their hairstyles and dress. Thus video feedback appeared to exert some influence on the self-perceptions and behaviour of these people who had long histories of resistance to other forms of intervention.

Although some other investigators have administered paper-and-pencil tests after video confrontation (Griffiths and Gillingham, 1978; Paredes and coauthors, 1969a, 1969b), such measurement techniques detract from the objectivity afforded by the video. A study by Allebeck, Hallberg and Espmark (1976) indicates the significance of the television system for body-image research. These investigators modified a television monitor so that subjects could adjust the size and height/width proportions of the picture. Deviations from correct measures were read directly by means of electrical instruments. It was found that, when adjustments made by a group of obese people were compared to those made by a control group, the obese differed significantly in the adjustments of body proportions, tending to underestimate the height of their picture in relation to the width. The fact that a group difference was found for adjustments of body proportions and not for ones of an external object (a cube) indicated that the difference referred to the body-image and not to general perceptual disturbances. These investigators suggest ways in which their apparatus could be improved. A screen could be used for whole body studies (this experiment concentrated only upon the faces of the subjects) or colour could be introduced.

Fisher (1973) suggests that there are two main reasons which account for inaccuracy in relation to body-image. Bodies are constantly changing and there is often a time-lag in bringing body concepts up to date. Thus when the obese are dieting, and successfully losing weight, they underestimate the actual decline in their bulk. Their concept of their reduction in size as a result of the weight loss lags behind the real state of affairs.

Practical difficulties also hinder individuals from attaining accurate mental images of their physical form. In addition to the fact that clothing conceals the body for most of the time, it is literally not easy for a person to get a good look at his own body. Even an intricate assembly of mirrors does not permit a good examination of the rear view. These factors lead to the slightly surprising conclusion that the majority of the population does not get an opportunity to scrutinize their physical images. Although confrontations with images in mirrors and photographs are frequent, diverting attention to a mirror or camera interrupts the continuity of expressive behaviour. The videotape appears to be the most comprehensive form of objective confrontation. Not only does it present information about the self more completely, directly and concretely than any other media, but it also permits easy, repeatable verification of information through immediate replay.

Is the attainment of a realistic body-image therapeutically important?

The obese evaluate their bodies negatively and are extremely self-denigratory. They appear to have unconsciously given up the struggle to preserve a non-derogatory attitude towards themselves. Stunkard and Mendelson (1967) suggest that a circular relationship develops between body-image disturbance which predisposes to esteem-lowering experiences and depressive moods, which in their turn reinforce the disturbed body-image. Our own self-regard largely reflects what others think of us. However, the converse is also true, and until the obese come to terms with their bodies in a realistic manner there is little hope of breaking the vicious circle. In the light of these observations it appears that the achievement of a realistic body-image is therapeutically important for weight loss. While the obese devalue themselves, they will fail to attain a high self-regard, and this is one of the most significant factors in the battle to lose weight.

Paredes and Cornelison (1968) have used audiovisual self-confrontation to help alcoholics understand the self-deceiving and self-defeating mechanisms they use to deny or conceal their conflicts and low self-esteem. They argue that following such understanding the alcoholic may be motivated to work towards finding ways of coping with or solving conflicts, other than through drinking. Many investigators have noted the similarities between compulsive overeating and alcoholism (Glatt 1974), and Bruch (1973) has emphasized that any approach to losing weight should attempt to effect a change in the person himself so that he no longer abuses the eating function in futile efforts to solve other problems of living. Storms (1973) has demonstrated that self-observation can change the causal interpretation a person gives to his own behaviour. The self-viewing individual is more likely to accept personal, dispositional responsibility for his behaviour and is less likely to deflect responsibility to the situation. No doubt successful therapy usually involves making a patient aware of his own behaviour and convincing him to accept personal responsibility for that behaviour. Self-observation apparently aids this process and, to that extent, should be therapeutic.

Apart from the studies of Gottheil, Backup and Cornelison (1969) and of Biggs, Rosen and Summerfield (1980), which dealt with the other extreme in the eating disorders, namely anorexia nervosa, only a minority of investigators have attempted to assist patients attain a realistic awareness of their body-image. Stunkard and Mendelson (1967) note that the relatively intractable nature of the disturbance in body-image highlights one form of treatment which has ameliorated it, namely long-term psychotherapy. Cappon and Banks (1968) suggest that the obese should look at themselves in the nude daily, in front of full-length angled mirrors. They found that the obese overestimate their body size. However, even after casual confrontation with their mirror images, these errors diminish significantly, at least for a short period.

There is an important difference between just superficially looking at yourself and really doing so. It would appear that the average person probably 'keeps his distance' when casually viewing himself, whereas the videotape presents an 'uncensored' confrontation. For example, Fisher (1958) describes the case of a badly crippled woman who had made an adequate adjustment to her distorted body until she saw a film of herself. Although she had frequently seen her image in mirrors, the picture that was conveyed by the non-censoring camera appeared to her as overwhelmingly ugly and grotesque. She was deeply shocked and depressed by the experience. Thus some writers have warned against the negative effects possible from self-viewing, which range in seriousness from a reduction in the favourability of self-descriptions (Geertsma and Reivich, 1965; Walz and Johnston, 1963) to the onset of gross anxiety (Cornelison, 1966) and even suicide (Alkire and Brunse, 1974).

Nevertheless, feedback is important. Attempts to learn new behaviour in the absence of feedback usually result in a lack of change, or even deterioration, and yet behaviour often continues on the basis of rather unreliable feedback from other people's responses, or 'internal' feedback from self-evaluations and attitudes. Such self-generated feedback may be both inaccurate and unjustifiably negative.

One of the main aims of feedback should be to provide information regarding the discrepancy between actual and ideal performance, and towards this end the video confrontation technique is ideal. A new apparatus for measuring perceived body size and shape might incorporate the ideas of Allebeck, Hallberg and Espmark (1976) and Dowrick (1978). Life-sized body representations could be made amenable to adjustment by subjects, and edited tapes projected as the basis for self-modelling. Thus, for example, in addition to acquiring objective measurements of obese subjects' perceived body size and shape, they might be shown tapes of how they would look at normal weight, or the discrepancy between their image of themselves and reality could be highlighted.

References

Alkire, A. A., and Brunse, A. J. (1974). Impact and possible casualty from videotape feedback in marital therapy, *Journal of Consulting and Clinical Psychology*, **39**, 203–210.

Allebeck, P., Hallberg, D., and Espmark, S. (1976). Body-image—an apparatus for measuring disturbances in estimation of size and shape, *Journal of Psychosomatic Research*, **20**, 583–589.

Allon, N. (1973). The stigma of overweight in everyday life, in *Obesity in Perspective* (Ed. G. A. Bray), Vol. 2, Parts 1 and 2, Fogarty International Centre Series on Preventive Medicine.

Bailey, K. G., and Sowder, W. T. (1970). Self-confrontation in psychotherapy, *Psychological Bulletin*, **74**, 127–137.

Bandura, A. (1969). *Principles of Behaviour Modification*, Holt, Rinehart and Winston, New York.

Berger, M. M. (Ed.) (1978). *Videotape Techniques In Psychiatric Training and Treatment*, Rev. ed., Brunner/Mazel, New York.

Biggs, S. J., Rosen, B., and Summerfield, A. B. (1980). Videofeedback and personal attribution in anorexic, depressed and normal viewers, *British Journal of Medical Psychology*, **53**, 249–254.

Boyd, H., and Sisney, V. (1967). Immediate self-image confrontation and changes in self-concept, *Journal of Consulting Psychology*, **31**, 291–296.

Braucht, G. N. (1970). Immediate effects of self-confrontation on the self-concept, *Journal of Consulting and Clinical Psychology*, **35**, 95–101.

Bruch, H. (1973). *Eating Disorders*, Basic Books, New York.

Cappon, D., and Banks, R. (1968). Distorted body perception in obesity, *Journal of Nervous and Mental Disease*, **146**, 465–467.

Cornelison, F. S. Jr. (1966). Learning about behaviour—a new technique: self-image experience, *Mental Hygiene*, **50**, 584–587.

Cornelison, F. S., and Arsenian, J. (1960). A study of the response of psychotic patients to photographing self-image experience, *Psychiatry Quarterly*, **34**, 1–8.

Danet, B. N. (1968). Self confrontation in psychotherapy reviewed, *American Journal of Psychotherapy*, **22**, 245–258.

Dowrick, P. W. (1978). Suggestions for the use of edited video replay in training behavioural skills, *J. Pract. appr. dev. Handicap*, **2** (2), 21–24.

Fisher, S. H. (1958). Mechanisms of denial in physical disabilities, *Archives of Neurology and Psychiatry*, **80**, 782–784.

Fisher, S. (1972). *Body Experience in Fantasy and Behaviour*, Appleton-Century-Crofts, New York.

Fisher, S. (1973). *Body Consciousness*, Calder and Boyars, London.

Fisher, S., and Cleveland, S. E. (1968). *Body Image and Personality*, Dover, New York.

Garner, D. M., Garfinkel, P. E., Stancer, H. C., and Moldofsky, H. (1976). Body image disturbances in anorexia nervosa and obesity, *Psychosomic Medicine*, **38**, 327–336.

Geertsma, R. H., and Reivich, R. S. (1965). Repetitive self-observation by videotape playback, *Journal of Nervous and Mental Disease*, **141**, 29–41.

Glatt, M. M. (1974). *Drugs, Society and Man. A Guide to Addiction and Its Treatment*, Medical and Technical Publishing Co. Ltd.

Glucksman, M. L., and Hirsch, J. (1969). The response of obese patients to weight reduction. II: The perception of body size, *Psychosomic Medicine*, **31** (1), 1–7.

Gottheil, E., Backup, C. E., and Cornelison, F. S. (1969). Denial and self-image confrontation in a case of anorexia nervosa, *Journal of Nervous and Mental Disease*, **148**, 238–250.

Griffiths, R. D. P., and Gillingham, P. (1978). The influence of videotape feedback on the self-assessments of psychiatric patients, *British Journal of Psychiatry*, **183**, 156–161.

Griffiths, R. D. P., and Hinkson, J. (1973). The effects of videotape feedback on the self-assessment of psychiatric patients, *British Journal of Psychiatry*, **123**, 223–224.

Miller, M. F. (1962). Responses of psychiatric patients to their photographed images, *Diseases of the Nervous System*, **23**, 296–298.

Orbach, J., Traub, A. C., and Olson, R. (1966). Psychophysical studies of body image. II: Normative data on the adjustable body-distorting mirror, *Arch. gen. Psych.*, **14**, 41–47.

Paredes, A., and Cornelison, F. S. (1968). Development of an audiovisual technique for the rehabilitation of alcoholics, *Quart. J. Stud. Alcohol.*, **29**, 84–92.

Paredes, A., Gottheil, E., Tausig, T. N., and Cornelison, F. S. (1969a). Behavioural changes as a function of repeated self-observation, *Journal of Nervous and Mental Disease*, **148**, 287–299.

Paredes, A., Ludwig, K. D., Hassenfeld, I. N., and Cornelison, F. S. Jr. (1969b). A clinical study of alcoholics using audiovisual self-image feedback, *Journal of Nervous and Mental Disease*, **148**, 449–456.

Schilder, P. (1935). *The Image and Appearance of the Human Body*, Kegan, Paul, Trench, and Trubner, London.

Schneiderman, L. (1956). The estimation of one's own bodily traits, *Journal of Social Psychology*, **44**, 89–99.

Schontz, F. C. (1969). *Perceptual and Cognitive Aspects of Body Experience*, Academic Press, New York.

Slade, P. D., and Russell, G. F. M. (1973). Awareness of body dimension in anorexia nervosa: cross sectional and longitudinal studies, *Psychology Medicine*, **3**, 188–199.

Storms, M. D. (1973). Videotape and the attribution process: reversing actors' and observers' points of view, *Journal of Personality and Social Psychology*, **27** (2), 165–175.

Stunkard, A. S., and Mendelson, M. (1967). Obesity and the body-image. I. Characteristics of disturbances in the body image of some obese persons, *American Journal of Psychiatry*, **123**, 1296.

Summerfield, A. B. (1980). *Videofeedback as a Method of Modifying Behaviour*, Invited paper presented to the Twenty-second International Congress of Psychology, Leipzig.

Traub, A. C., and Orbach, J. (1964). Psychophysical studies of body image. 1. The adjustable body-distorting mirror, *Archives of General Psychiatry*, **11**, 53–66.

Walz, G. R., and Johnston, J. A. (1963). Counselors look at themselves on videotape, *Journal of Counseling Psychology*, **10**, 232–236.

Ward, W. D., and Bendak, S. (1964). The response of psychiatric patients to photographic self-image experience, Newsletter for research in psychology, *Veterans Administration*, **6** (4), 29–30.

Wylie, R. C. (1961). *The Self-Concept*. University of Nebraska Press, Lincoln.

Using Video
Edited by P. W. Dowrick and S. J. Biggs
© 1983 John Wiley & Sons Ltd

Chapter 9

Self-Modelling

Peter W. Dowrick

Department of Psychology, University of Alaska, Anchorage

Self-modelling is defined as the behavioural change that results from the observation of oneself on videotapes that show only desired target behaviours. Theoretical support for the procedure derives from three major sources. Firstly, observational learning studies indicate that behaviour change is enhanced by model similarity. Secondly, research in video replay indicates that feedback of mistakes can be deleterious. Finally, self-image and self-efficacy propositions are evidently supportive of the self-modelling paradigm. The applicability to visible skill training is clear. The general technique involves creating a short self-model videotape and allowing the trainee to observe it repeatedly. It is unclear thus far what are the relative contributions of motivation (simply seeing success where failure has previously been a frequent experience) and information (new data on specific behaviours and their payoffs).

Methods for creating self-model tapes either capitalize on existing behaviours (usually inducing short-term superior performances, e.g. using role-play) or make use of illusory techniques (e.g. a camera angle which obscures essential support). Either approach is enhanced with simple editing. Numerous case studies and a limited number of more extensive investigations have been reported in a wide variety of applications. These include motor, classroom, workshop, recreational, and daily living skills for physically handicapped and able-bodied people. They also include social skills and other behavioural change for therapeutic benefit (e.g. hyperactivity, aggression, sexual problems). In addition to single case studies, efficacy of the procedure has been found in disparate settings in favourable contrast to contingency contracting, peer modelling, error replays and no treatment controls. A major thrust of future research will be towards understanding the mechanisms of self-modelling.

Structured video replay

Self-modelling is a structured form of video replay. Attempts to tamper purposefully with structure are relatively new in the evolution of videotape usage, and reasonably so. There has not been time since the recent and rapid advances in technology that made video readily available for human endeavour to discover which of so many avenues of refinement might be worth following.

In the sixties it was generally and perhaps simplistically assumed that the more self-information that people could derive from videotape the better off they would be. The earliest questions were 'What kind of psychological processes does video replay help?' and 'What existing techniques does it supplement or replace?'. As it became apparent that video did not help all people in all situations, it was asked 'What specific populations will benefit (most)?' and 'How can the technology be improved?'. So essentially the focus (no pun intended) was on the subject/viewer; discover the appropriate referring conditions, ensure receptivity during the reviewing process and the video replay technology will produce beneficial changes. If these questions had been answered rapidly the direction of further refinements would have been clear. Given the equivocation of the answers, we are pressed to ask some very different questions.

Clearly a whole new set of questions will be generated by shifting the emphasis away from the viewer to what is being viewed. Perhaps there exists some *form* of video replay which is efficacious, possibly in a way which cuts across subject populations and referring conditions.

Self-modelling is part of an approach to video technology which asks 'What kinds of recorded episodes will help a person to change?'. Specifically it addresses the possibility that video replay of exclusively successful and adaptive behaviours leads to behaviour change and therapeutic benefits. In more formal terms, self-modelling is defined as '*the behavioural change that results from the observation of oneself on videotapes that show only desired behaviours*'. Subjects see recordings, therefore, which have been selected, edited or otherwise contrived to show their adaptive functioning rather than their typical inadequacies.

Because self-modelling diverges from the philosophical mainstream of video replay it seems valuable to devote a few pages to some theoretical rationale. Those readers who need no such reassurance will find the later sections, descriptive of practice and outcome, to be autonomously readable. Some may find the interconnections with other techniques, proposed below, to be helpful in generalizing their own knowledge and skills.

Origins in theory

The technique of self-modelling has developed, with promise, on a pragmatic basis. It may eventually warrant its own theoretical analysis; in the meantime, however, it is clear that the principles of self-modelling can be supported by arguments from existing lines of research. These are observational learning, video feedback and self-image studies, and I will briefly discuss them in turn before describing the early self-modelling applications of the seventies.

Observational learning

By its very ubiquity observational learning (Bandura, 1969) is undeniably one of the most important influences on personality development. Whether labelled as modelling, imitation, matching behaviour, identification or contagion, and whether used therapeutically or occurring spontaneously, the process refers to behavioural change which takes place subsequent to the observation of similar behaviours. Clearly, the number of potential observational learning situations (live, filmed or otherwise) far exceeds the amount of learning that takes place, so that issues concerning what makes a model potent are foremost. A large number of factors have been extensively but incompletely investigated (Bandura, 1977b), many of which are irrelevant to self-modelling—the case where the model is the same person as the observer. However, some factors have an important if indirect bearing.

The major factors to be considered here are those which are relevant to attention processes and to observer–model similarity. The ability of a model to gain the observer's attention is an obvious prerequisite for learning to take place (Bandura, 1969). Just as people appear more interested in photographs of themselves than those of others, they demonstrate greater arousal at the sign of their own moving pictures on videotape (Fuller and Manning, 1973). It seems likely that recordings of oneself have greater attention gaining power than images of any other person, except perhaps for one recently and richly enamoured, although the evidence for this is not documented. Specific attributes of both the model and the observer have been studied, but most often, unfortunately, in isolation. Some of these may have an effect on attention and on other learning processes. For example, status (Lefkowitz, Blake, and Mouton, 1955), social power and attractiveness (Mischel and Grusec, 1966) may be attention-catching. If the learning process depends on these attributes being considerably greater in the model than in the observer, one would predict that a self-model could not be effective. However, there are data which indicate that a large discrepancy between observer and model leads to failure, as, for example, in Muzekari and Kamis' (1973) work with a large sample of chronic schizophrenics. Therefore, effective self-modelling could be predicted if the status, power and attractiveness of the self were enhanced.

On the basis of their study, Muzekari and Kamis advocated the use of models whose behaviour and apparent potential were similar enough to allow the subjects to identify with them. The theme of identification has often been referred to and, were it backed adequately by research, would lead to a compelling prediction for the efficacy of self-modelling. Unfortunately, 'identification' can be a loosely specified term; e.g. Stotland, Zander and Natsoulas (1961) *told* a group of their subjects that they were similar to their model. However, the related concepts of perceived similarity (Rosekrans, 1967), age (Kornhaber and Schroeder, 1975) and behavioural similarity (Kazdin, 1974) are amenable to more rigorous scientific investigation. All the studies cited above and many others support the proposal that an effective model would be similar to the observer except for an added degree of competency.

Video feedback

The second major area of research with importance for self-modelling is that of video feedback or self-confrontation—unstructured video replay. After the initial wave of exuberance, it began to emerge that obtaining positive results was not as simple as letting loose a camera crew in a psychiatric ward. Nor was it a case of choosing the appropriate setting or subjects. Stoller's (1967, 1969) claims for video replay enhancements to group therapy were in direct conflict with a controlled study by Danet (1969); Carrere (1958) was an early enthusiast for the treatment of alcohol abuse, but Schaefer, Sobell and Sobell (1972) found this type of confrontation could drive their clients to drink even more. The studies which indicated negative results were always better designed (Bailey and Sowder, 1970; Griffiths, 1974), but perhaps they needed to be to get published. Results reported by Martin (1971) bear mentioning briefly. In a controlled study of group psychotherapy he found replay effects to be beneficial with one group, detrimental with another and equivocal with a third, without his being able to make causal inferences. However, given that other variables were controlled, the discrepant outcomes presumably reflect differences in the content of the video recordings.

All the studies which found negative results used total replay without any other adjunctive procedure, whereas reports claiming efficacy often included descriptions of therapists' commentaries which would alter the client's perceptual focus (in particular, see Stoller, 1969). Applications which are directed towards specific skills and avoid emotional confrontations also show more promise in controlled studies (e.g. social skills and professional skills training— see Hosford and Mills in Chapter 10 and Hargie and Saunders in Chapter 11 of this volume). The generally discrepant findings do not fit well with a feedback model which implies that the more information people have about themselves the better they will operate. It is more cogent to propose that videotape replay is efficacious when it provides the conditions that make modelling effective. At least two theoretical models have proposed this view (Dowrick, 1977; Hung and Rosenthal, 1978). In essence these proposals imply that error identification is not useful in itself—it must carry with it information about what to do adaptively. If we choose to structure video replay the indicators are that effective client performances should be retained and emphasized. Does this also suggest that enhancing self-esteem is important if not essential to video training and therapy?

Self-image

One difference between self-modelling and other forms of video replay is that self-modelling shows no errors. It could be argued that any self-scrutiny (via videotape or otherwise) would alter one's self-esteem as a function of perceived success and error rates. At least with respect to trying to achieve certain outcomes, self-modelling would therefore predictably increase self-esteem. While the suggestion that a boost to the self-esteem provides necessary and sufficient conditions for improved functioning is highly controversial, there are some important findings which deserve close scrutiny.

At one extreme there are claims that extreme devestation to self-esteem can result in virtually complete loss of adaptive functioning. For example, Bettelheim (1960) has referred to 'walking corpses' in Nazi concentration camps, explaining their condition to result from such a total loss of self-esteem that they had given themselves over entirely to environmental factors. The concepts of self-image and self-esteem are difficult to define (see McRae in Chapter 8 of this volume), but some people who 'give up' may see themselves not so much as worthless but as powerless. Indeed, there have been several empirically supported theories which have emphasized the importance of perceived control as a personality variable (e.g. Perlmuter and Monty, 1980; Phares, 1976; Rotter, 1966), including that of 'learned helplessness' (Abramson, Seligman and Teasdale, 1978). Briefly, this proposes that a perception of lost effectiveness in events that a person tries repeatedly to control results first in anxiety, then in depression characterized by apathy—a giving up of trying that generalizes to other facets of life. Such theories point strongly to the dangers that are inherent in any video replay which might undermine a person's self-belief.

On the positive side, there is the implication that replay which enhances self-belief would improve psychological functioning. Strongest support comes from Bandura's proposal that perception of self-efficacy is essential to acquiring new skills and to coping with failures or other aversive events (Bandura, 1977a, 1982b). He goes beyond the theories cited above by claiming that adaptive responding to our environment (as a result of therapeutic change or otherwise) critically hinges on a self-belief system that enables relevant skills to be put into action; the acquisition and integration of cognitive and behavioural skills are necessary but not sufficient in themselves for behavioural change. Bandura's proposal is highly suggestive of the potential efficacy of a 'feed forward' mechanism such as self-modelling which may provide both the skills information and a positive impact on the self-expectancy mechanism. Indeed, Bandura (1982a) himself has made this observation.

Although an emphasis on self-belief seems far from radical behaviourism, Skinner too has predicted the value of structuring video replay to show adaptive-only responses. In his personal notebooks he recorded his advice to a baseball coach against showing players their poor strikes. Instead, a batter in a slump should 'be shown a short film of himself hitting home runs'; of players generally who have been making errors 'let them see themselves playing brilliantly' (cited in 'Notebooks: B. F. Skinner,' 1981, p. 64). Such a strategy is not substantially different from some of the examples of self-modelling described below.

Origins in practice

Reports of self-modelling have been appearing from various sources intermittently over the past decade or so. It appears that different people developed the same or similar techniques independently.

An early case study which attracted considerable attention was that by Creer and Miklich (1970) of the National Asthma Center in Denver, Colorado. In their case self-modelling was the daughter of necessity in place of peer-modelling which was considered desirable but impractical. They described a ten-year-old boy, 'Chuck', with a history of social problems currently proving disquieting in a residential treatment programme for asthmatic children. He had found himself the target for taunts and aggression by other children, he would not cooperate with reasonable institutional routine and his behaviour around adults was frequently not appropriate for his age (e.g. giggling, tickling and, during interviews, leaping into the interviewer's lap). After identifying suitable target behaviours and taking baseline observations, the investigators made two videotape recordings. Both recordings were rehearsed role-plays starring Chuck, two other boys and one adult in a series of familiar settings. The crucial difference between the two recordings was that one showed Chuck's *typical* (described as 'inappropriate') actions while the other showed *adaptive* ('appropriate') behaviour.

After a two-week non-intervention period to allow any effect of the role-play to dissipate Chuck watched his adaptive self-model tape, 5 minutes daily for two weeks. During this period his behaviour abruptly improved. By contrast these changes sharply reversed during the next two-week interval when he watched his typical behaviour on videotape (also 5 minutes daily). Finally, after another two weeks of viewing the appropriate self-model, Chuck's behaviour stabilized and he apparently coped well for the remaining 6 months of his stay in the institution. These results appeared very promising and their publication was received with much enthusiastic correspondence. However, for what appeared to be such a simple but efficacious technique, reports of new applications were strangely slow to appear. Miklich and Creer (1974) themselves reported a few more case studies.

At the University of California at Santa Barbara, Hosford independently noted success with essentially the same strategy but which he referred to as 'self-as-a-model'. He worked with very different populations (e.g. prison inmates) indicating that success was not dependent on childhood naivety towards the content of the videotape. In an early study (Hosford and Brown, 1975) he treated stuttering using a self-model audiotape (see page 114).

These early applications were limited by the available technology. Role-plays for videotaping were planned and then executed in front of a camera with a wide-angle stationary lens. Unsuitable 'performances' were simply discarded and re-recorded *in toto*. While this approach was simple it had distinct limitations. In particular, it became readily evident that in many cases target behaviours simply could not be role-played. The very actions and reactions which needed to be demonstrated by the (self) model were the same ones which the subject had difficulty in producing. More creative methods of making self-model tapes were called for.

Fortunately, by the mid seventies the technology had improved to the extent that hand-held cameras with zoom lenses were readily available, and general equipment prices were low enough that it became a reasonable proposition to own a second recording machine. This enabled a far greater flexibility in the creation of self-model tapes. For example, in 1975 my first use of self-modelling was made with a four-year-old boy who had been referred as 'hyperactive' (Dowrick and Raeburn, 1977). Indeed, under observation he showed very poor concentration, he whined to gain attention and he very readily threw temper tantrums when attention was not received. His concentration span was virtually non-existent when he was provided items to play with by himself, whereas he attended quite well in the presence of others. We therefore decided to train his independent play behaviour. It proved relatively simple to create a self-model tape by encouraging his play across a table from his mother but excluding her from the picture. It was also necessary to edit out off-target behaviour and occasionally visible adult interactions. We then measured the effects of the self-model tape relative to a recording of typical behaviour under different conditions of medication. Essentially, we found that independent playing improved during self-modelling, but remained stable under all other conditions. The study was seen as a useful verification of the self-modelling effect, but perhaps more importantly it broadened the methodology of self-model tape creation by not requiring the subject to role-play the target behaviours.

Implementation of self-modelling

Self-modelling functions more like feed-forward than feedback; subjects see themselves not so much as they were but *as they might be*. There are a number of different ways that this may effect be achieved.

The foremost ways to create self-model tapes, role-play, camera work and editing have been briefly touched upon and will be described in more detail later in this section. One further method bears mentioning for its tantalizing potential. Psychotropic medication may have specific behavioural effects which can be captured by a video camera. This fortuitous possibility was capitalized upon in the case of a socially withdrawn five-year-old boy (Dowrick, 1979). Self-modelling using previously proven methods was successfully used to a stage where the boy would join a group of other children and play alongside them. However, his rate of interaction was so low that making further self-model tapes seemed formidable until we chanced upon a suitable disinhibitor. A chance remark of his mother to the effect that his usually taciturn father became positively garrulous upon drinking alcohol led us to speculate that young 'Charles' might respond to a single moderate dose of diazepam (Valium). This indeed proved to be the case, the acute effects being sufficient to provide ample footage of self-modelling material. We were able to separate the verbal and non-verbal interactions and subsequently measure distinct self-modelling effects in multiple baseline treatment. Socialization changes for Charles were large and far-reaching, as measured by observations during intervention and at follow-up.

Unfortunately, the effects of psychotropic medication are seldom as specific or as readily observable, so less dramatic methods are generally used to create self-model recordings. There are two guiding principles to be followed. Firstly, maximize the subject's performance while recording. Secondly, extract the best value subsequent to the recording. These two principles and other practical considerations are best illustrated by discussing one case example in reasonable detail.

Case study

At the time of this study, 'Shirley' was nearly six years old, with mild congenital cerebral palsy. She experienced some loss of motor control resulting from dysfunction of the central nervous system. One of her specific difficulties was related to walking over irregular surfaces. She walked with apparent fluency across floors or pathways, but she was intimidated by obstacles such as ropes or sticks even as much as 1 or 2 cm thick. She would typically grasp manual support and slide her foot over the irregular surface. Curbs and stairs seemed out of the question. The occupational therapist who identified and estimated the severity of this problem had worked with Shirley over some months as opportunity had allowed. This patient coaching and coaxing had produced few changes in Shirley, so the rapid progress subsequently achieved with self-modelling was very dramatic. The process and outcome were documented and made into a film (Dowrick, 1978a).

Outline of procedures

Maximize subject's performance while recording, by any of:
- incentive
- verbal encouragement
- physical support (out of view)
- flattering camera work
- rehearsed role-play
- medication
- patience

Collect sufficient recording (probably 10 to 20 min) to create a self-model.
Extract the best value by editing to:
- remove mistakes
- enhance aesthetics
- repeat adaptive sequences
- resequence events
- insert from other material

Finalize the self-modelling tape to be 2 to 5 min, depending on the age of subject and complexity of behaviour.
Present tape to the subject at regular, spaced intervals (e.g. 6 times over 2 weeks). Monitor progress, and repeat with new recordings as necessary, involving the subject as much as possible. Combine with other intervention strategies.

After an assessment of Shirley's abilities on developmental criteria, she was videotaped in her attempts to negotiate surfaces just beyond the limits of her capacity. The situation was maximized in two ways. Firstly, Shirley was given ample incentives and reinforcements to produce a command performance. Clearly, role-play was not possible, but in other situations it would be used at this point. Shirley was simply set an 'obstacle course', made aware that she was on camera and told that if she did well she would be able to see herself 'on TV'. This incentive is generally highly motivating for both children and adults. Shirley's obstacles were plastic tubes and wooden blocks no more that 2 cm thick. Her enthusiasm was mixed with trepidation, resulting in much hesitation followed on occasions by a clear step but most often a foot sliding across the object. Meanwhile, she received encouragement and verbal praise for her attempts. Certain blocks she would not step over and here we introduced a second means of maximizing the recording. We allowed her the support of grasping the occupational therapist's hand; at the same time the camera's zoom lens was focused towards her feet. This manoeuvre resulted in an impression of Shirley walking up to a wooden block and stepping over it. The videotaping served the dual purpose of recording an assessment and of providing material from which to make a self-model tape for intervention.

The next stage involved extraction of the best material now available. This was done by editing in a very simple, almost crude fashion. *In vivo* recordings had been made on portable equipment (National high-density $^1/_2$ inch Porta-pak, now superseded by BETAMAX, U-MATIC and other colour portables at comparable prices). The recorder was simply connected to another (National video cassette recorder) by suitable cables so that copying could take place. A machine with editing capabilities is, of course, preferable. However, this arrangement was inexpensive and permitted the copying of appropriate sequences onto another tape. Sequences of action in which Shirley functioned poorly, or in which the prompts and support to her efforts were evident, were omitted in the creation of her self-model film. Only those sequences which showed her 'as she might be' at a more adaptive stage of her development were copied. On the basis of this criterion only a fraction of the original recording was suitable, but the best segments were repeatedly copied to provide two minutes of self-model tape.

This procedure requires some initial patience in the acquisition of the mechanics, and thereafter is very easy to perform. Shirley's tape took less than half an hour to finalize. It contained various unaesthetic picture disturbances, but these apparently did not detract from the subsequent learning. More investment in editing facilities can make the procedure easier and also much more exact. For example, with suitable equipment extremely short sequences of action, maybe a few frames in length (i.e. a fraction of a second in duration), may be captured without visual disturbance in the final recording (see Clarke and Ellgring in Chapter 5 and Wallbott in Chapter 7 of this volume).

The two minute edition of self-model tape was then shown to Shirley three times a week for two weeks. These time parameters were arrived at on the basis of other studies and they appear to work well for a variety of subjects in different situations. However, meeting the major concerns of maximizing exposure and minimizing boredom through repetition may be achieved in other ways. While Shirley watched her tapes, she was given no comments about her performance because of a desire to avoid contamination of the effects of simply watching the videotape. Nonetheless, it can be assumed that endorsing comments to the subject on their effective behaviour can prove to be valuable (see Schwarz and Hawkins, 1970).

Following the intervention period, Shirley was reassessed. Her progress in the time period was remarkable, notwithstanding the fact that she had effectively only 12 minutes of intervention over the time span. Her progress was assessed more exactly as part of a larger study described below in the *Efficacy* section of this chapter. Generally, she was able, without assistance, to step over all of her original obstacles. Furthermore, she could step over the wooden blocks stacked three high. Most encouragingly, her skills generalized. When taken outside, she stepped up curbs in a bold fashion, although the surfaces were quite different from those seen on her videotape.

The above case exemplifies an application of self-modelling. In particular, it demonstrates that thoughtful camera work followed by simple editing can make a self-model film readily available, even when role-play was simply out of the question. These techniques appear to have widespread application.

Editing

Hosford has also found editing to be both simple and useful. For example, in his earliest empirical evaluation (Hosford and Brown, 1975), he resourcefully treated stuttering in a setting where no speech therapist was available. As a principal part of a counselling package he used a recording in which he edited out speech hesitations to produce a self-model. He reported a reduction of stuttering frequency from 8.7 to 0.8 times per minute over 12 weeks.

A particularly useful innovation introduced by Hosford in his work with adults has been to involve them in the process of editing (Hosford, 1981). In effect, subjects are required to examine recordings and identify 'This is the me I want to be'. Such a procedure not only strengthens the 'feed-forward' concept, but seems especially desirable on ethical grounds. Some studies (e.g. Creer and Miklich, 1970; Dowrick and Raeburn, 1977) have shown that subjects have a stronger tendency to imitate their own behaviour when it is adaptive than when it is not. A comparable tendency seems to apply in observational learning from others (Rosenbaum and Tucker, 1962). Therefore the client has some built-in safeguard, but to involve the subject so explicitly in what is in effect both the goal determination and the content of treatment procedure seems to be the ultimate in consumer protection.

Applications

Over the past ten years, self-modelling has been used as the major component, sometimes the sole component, in a wide variety of training and treatment applications. Physical skills range from walking with French sticks (prosthetic device) to playing billiards and pool. Vocational skills range from professional teaching to writing in a left-to-right orientation. The area of communication includes selective mutism and anger control; personal and social adjustments vary from aggression to cross-gender behaviour. Examples of applications are listed in this section under four general classifications. Because the depth of interest of each topic will vary for different readers, I include only brief descriptions and refer to original sources.

Physical skill

The visible nature of most physical skills makes them a natural target for video intervention. Often physical skills add to the quality of life for the trainee, sometimes at a very basic level, providing a modicum of independence, say for a severely spastic child learning to feed her- or himself. Sometimes the change is a sophisticated one, such as in learning a recreational sport. Self-modelling has been applied at both extremes.

The case of Shirley described in some detail above provides an example of daily living skills useful to a handicapped person. Other children in similar settings have been trained with the same methodology in therapeutic exercises, maintaining posture, walking with or without prosthetic devices, feeding and dressing themselves (Dowrick, 1976). These children were typically in the 5 to 12 years age group. Some children learned skills that were recreational, such as throwing and catching balls or bouncing on a trampoline, although these were chosen to improve general coordination and dexterity. Swimming is a recreation that has particular benefits for spina bifida children because they can more readily match their able-bodied age-mates in the water. Self-modelling proved beneficial to three such children whose severity of disability made them paralysed below the waist (Dowrick and Dove, 1980). In this case the children watched their tapes shortly before normally scheduled swimming lessons and one evident benefit was the great reduction in apprehensiveness (when the tape was a self-model) usually encountered at the beginning of the lesson. This study will be discussed more fully in the section below on efficacy.

Self-modelling applications

Physical and vocational skills (disabled, athletic and others)	*Communication skills*
walking	interviewing
swimming	job seeking
exercising	social skills
basketball	stuttering
trampoline	selective mutism
maintaining posture	public speaking
walking with sticks	
feeding	*Personal and social adjustment*
dressing	
workshop assemblies	resisting aggression
reading	thumb-sucking
writing	bed-making
billiards	hyperactivity
running	shyness
teaching	tantrums
	parenting
	class disruption
	cross-gender behaviour
	anxieties
	phobias
	sexual adjustment

At another extreme, self-modelling has proven helpful to able-bodied adults playing sports. One case involved a top class athlete who had been unable to correct an asymmetry in his running. When we asked him to 'overcorrect', the video recordings revealed an even stride, providing self-modelling material. Rather than come 60 kilometres several times a week (through London traffic) to view this recording, he was able to take a copy for use on a locally available recorder. Although we have no empirical data on this case, the athlete claimed a remarkably rapid recovery, indicating possibilities in this area of application. However, positive data are available for the training of pool table skills (billiards). In this case, all shots were recorded from directly in front of the player, with the whole table in view, and it was simply a case of editing to retain successful shots only. The study was undertaken primarily to compare two models of learning (self-modelling versus learning from mistakes, described on page 120), but it also demonstrates an effective procedure to train hand–eye coordination.

Vocational skills

Some physical skills serve a vocational purpose. For example, sheltered workshop employment may include a task such as assembling packing boxes which needs knowledge of the assembly itself and also requires dexterity. Both can be acquired through self-modelling, apparently more simply and effectively than a token incentive scheme (Dowrick and Hood, 1981). Again editing was used to remove errors and to increase apparent speed. In this case all self-model recordings were combined onto one longer tape so that workshop employees could watch as a group. This gives the opportunity, too, for peer modelling if tasks and abilities are not too disparate.

Classroom skills have also been improved with self-modelling, both for students and for teachers. Any visible skill should be amenable: orientation to the page in beginning writing and reading when the finger is used as a cursor; oral skills may be more suited to audiotape. Hosford (1981) reports the effective use of self-modelling for the training of teachers in the university setting, with both teaching assistants and professors. He also used similar techniques with counsellor trainees. The teachers and students individually chose the behaviours to be targeted for improvement. The videotapes were longer than those described above, viz. 10 minutes per target behaviour with two or three targets per subject. The method of tape creation was similar, with simple selection and editing where possible and coached rehearsal where necessary.

Communication skills

As with other skills, communication can be a matter of survival, or it can be a sophisticated enhancement. So far, self-modelling has been applied to the more basic end of the spectrum. As previously mentioned, Hosford used an audio self-model with a stutterer. His client was one of several prison inmates with communications deficits treated by Hosford. Others included those who had particular difficulty in maintaining verbal self-control during their pre-parole interviews (Hosford, Moss and Morrell, 1976). Role-play was the primary method used to create self-model recordings, but it was during this work that Hosford began involving subjects in self-selection of model sequences because the visual components of self-control under difficult questioning are so idiosyncratic.

Deficits in social conversation occur both as a result of inability and because of skill inhibition. The latter can occur in children such that the inhibition is strongly situation specific: termed 'selective mutism' (see Kratochwill, 1981). A slightly different application of self-modelling was used successfully with two children who spoke freely in their homes but nowhere else—most notably not at school (Dowrick and Hood, 1978). Selective mutism is very difficult to treat and a variety of procedures had been attempted in the 6 to 12 months that the

children had attended school. The intervention eventually f(
cessful involved videotaping the children at home, using mater
as a backdrop. After transcripts of those tapes had been made,
other recordings in the school to make possible a self-model that w
a Hollywood style 'fake'. That is, material from one setting was \
with that from the other to make it look as if each child was answerin⸌   ⸌ions
and making comments at school. Cuts from one scene to the other were very
crude, so it was obvious what had been done. However, both children subsequently responded to reviewing their own tape (but not the other's) with
improvements at least to a level of adaptive classroom functioning.

Self-modelling has also been used with adult conversation and job-seeking
skills. At the New Zealand Crippled Children's Society, Auckland Branch,
group training for basic social skills is available for young adults. It is a training
package including modelling, role-play, feedback and group discussions. Videotape is used for immediate replay, guided by self-modelling principles. That
is, it is assumed that trainees will improve by reviewing what they do better
than usual. If a recorded role-play does not go well, more modelling and
coaching is used. If it does go well, it is replayed, skipping over ineffective
sequences, and repeating, still framing, and commenting upon improvements.

Personal and social adjustment

Most of the skills training mentioned in this chapter can help a person's
psychological well-being—maybe even improving one's coordination at billiards can contribute to this. Improved well-being may not be the by-product
so much as the primary purpose of the training, as in the behaviour therapy
paradigm (see Lutzker and Martin, 1981; Rimm and Masters, 1979). In such
cases the target behaviour (which must be visible for videotaping) is chosen
not so much as an end in itself, but more particularly as one which leads to a
change in emotional well-being. Such cases described previously include children who were brought by their parents to a hospital psychiatric clinic, e.g.
the shy boy Charles and the boy who was 'hyperactive'. In another case in
which the child's boisterous behaviour (physical aggression and tantrums) was
unmanageable, both parent and child were trained by self-modelling adaptive
reactions towards each other (Dowrick, 1978b).

Davis (1979) reports successful self-modelling intervention with three disruptive school children. The children were capable of role-playing adaptive
behaviour enabling the construction of suitable videotapes. Although previous
contingency management efforts had proved ineffective, self-modelling replay
was reported to be quickly and dramatically successful. Adaptive behaviours
are not always obvious. One child, a four-year-old boy, was referred on the
basis of cross-gender behaviour, a problem with implications for personal and
social adjustment, but clouded with ethical concerns and potential value judgements. Careful observation of 'Jeremy' revealed that he was extremely enter-
taining with ironing boards and other stereotyped playthings, but simply at a
loss with junior engineers' kits. Self-modelling to become comparably enter-
taining with a wide range of toys proved possible, after a suitable peer had
been found to elicit sufficient target behaviours for editing (Dowrick, in press).

Self-modelling also seems to have potential in the treatment of anxieties. It suits graduated performance training by reiterative application and has proved relatively fast in a few cases of children with phobias (doctors, dentists, human biology), but this is my own clinical impression with insufficient evaluative data to make a comparison with systematic desensitization or participant modelling. Hosford (1981) also reports favourably of treatments for the diverse anxieties of public speaking and of flying. Sexual deficits are also frequently treated as anxiety problems, even when they occur in established marriages, and two cases reported by Hosford offer interesting promise. Both cases were clinically successful, and in one instance the couple not only did their own recording but carried out all editing with full privacy, receiving instructions only on the principles of self-modelling and the technical operation of the equipment. It is interesting that the procedure worked when previously used erotic films had not been arousing to the men in either case.

Efficacy

In spite of the recent beginnings of self-modelling applications, efficacy has been established at several levels. Some kind of positive effect (versus no treatment) has long been established. Subsequently, it appears that this effect is not a placebo type and there is increasing evidence about self-modelling relative to other forms of intervention.

In many of its applications, self-modelling has been used as part of a therapeutic package. Some adherents have made it the principal component with apparent success, but specific evaluation has been prevented by clinical priorities. Case studies using reversal (Creer and Miklich, 1970) or no treatment comparisons (Dowrick and Raeburn, 1977) provided the beginnings of real evidence for an active component. Interesting variations in case studies have been provided in which treatment has been compared across subjects—child and mother responding differentially to the same videotapes (Dowrick, 1978b)—or across different components of the same subject's behaviour—verbal and non-verbal interactions (Dowrick, 1979). These studies used sound observation techniques and reported good reliability on data collection. However, they suffer from the question that hangs over all single case reporting: 'What happens when numbers of subjects are assigned to this treatment?'

The first group study involved 18 physically handicapped children between 5 and 13 years of age (Dowrick, 1976). Physical disorders included spina bifida, cerebral palsy and muscular dystrophy. Shirley, described above, was one of these children. To provide a no-treatment comparison for self-modelling with this heterogeneous group of children, we selected, videotaped and assessed two target activities for each child, but created a self-model recording for only one of these activities. For example, Shirley's severe disabilities affected her ability to dress. On the same day as her obstacle course, she was also videotaped in her attempts to manipulate buttons, zippers and upper garments. Which of two target activities was to be self-modelled was randomly determined for each subject after videotaping. Assessment observations before and after intervention were made 'blind' to the procedure, using a magnitude estimation method which allowed comparison across dissimilar behaviours. The treatment effect using a one-tail t-test was highly significant ($p < 0.0005$).

Subsequently, Miklich, Chida and Danker-Brown (1977) reported a study which specifically indicated that self-modelling was not a placebo effect. They targeted bed-making in a children's residential asthma centre, but led the children to believe that they were simply part of a student's art project. Change in behaviour took place even without the subjects' awareness.

Further support was provided in the application to swimming with spina bifida children (Dowrick and Dove, 1980). In this study a multiple baseline across subjects was used. That is, all children began by seeing tapes of their normal behaviour in the water. After a few sessions, a self-model tape was shown to one subject only. The other children were introduced to their self-model tapes after successive intervals, and the pattern of change was clearly seen to be related to the timing of intervention. The children were not told the nature of the tapes, but were simply instructed to watch the screen on all occasions. Furthermore, one child was given successive self-modelling treatment. Three times he responded to a new videotape produced after he had reached a plateau.

Between-treatment comparisons are always difficult because of problems in controlling the quality of each intervention. Nonetheless, it is necessary somehow to make reasonable comparisons and several attempts have been made. An obvious target for comparison is with peer-modelling. The situation with the selectively mute children (Dowrick and Hood, 1978; summarized in Kratochwill, 1981) was fortuitous in this respect. Both children were, of course, surrounded by classmates who spoke freely but were not responded to as models. After the self-model tapes had been constructed both children watched one tape only: i.e. one subject saw her own tape while the other subject observed it too. This continued for a number of sessions (phase 1). The other self-model tape was then used (phase 2) and the procedure was repeated for two more phases. Effectively at each session one child saw a self-model while the other observed a peer-model. Systematic observations revealed that changes, maintained at a six-month follow-up, accrued during self-modelling only.

Hosford's applications with teacher training mentioned above also compared self- and peer-modelling, finding both equally effective. This would suggest that for some behaviours either self- or peer-modelling could be preferred on the basis of which was more easily implemented, whereas for others the self-component may be crucial. Agnes Murray at Fordham University, New York, is currently completing a doctoral study investigating self- versus peer-modelling for children with disruptive classroom behaviour, and Rita Sjunnessen at the University of Alaska, Anchorage, is making a similar type of comparison in training public speaking skills.

Another target for comparison is contingency management because of its established efficacy in many areas. The only reported study addressing this issue concerned productivity in a sheltered workshop (Dowrick and Hood, 1981). Fifteen subjects were randomly assigned (within their level of disability) to one of three groups: self-modelling, cash incentives and attention control. Attempts were made to make intervention time spent equivalent across groups.

In the case of the cash incentives, a daily points system with weekly back-up was provided at a level of elaborateness that required the same supervisory staff effort as the self-modelling. Improvements in productivity following brief intervention showed the active treatments to be statistically superior ($p <$ 0.05), the self-modelling group producing the greatest changes. These were maintained at a four-month follow-up.

Mechanisms

While the evidence is steadily growing that structured video replay of oneself is efficacious, it becomes increasingly important to investigate the parameters of this structure. The first consideration might be to test the assumption of self-modelling by a comparison with learning from one's errors. A study for this purpose has just been completed at the University of Alaska, Anchorage. The subjects were 18 evenly matched pairs of pool players who competed with each other twice. After the first round, losers only were assigned to either a self-modelling or an error-learning condition. Tapes were edited to show, in the first case, only successful shots and, in the second case, only the missed shots. Subjects then observed their edited tapes for 2 minutes on six occasions spread over approximately 2 weeks. After the rematch, it was simple to compare the subjects' performances both with their own earlier play and with that of their opponents. Results provided a clear vindication of self-modelling. In terms of the absolute number of successful shots, *all* subjects in the self-modelling group showed increases whereas less than half the other players improved their number. In terms of the absolute number of *un*successful shots (which varies somewhat independently of success), *all* and *only* subjects in the error-learning group seemed worse off relative to their opponents.

Another study recently completed at the University of Alaska was devised by Frank Gonzales to throw some light on whether self-modelling works by providing skills information or by boosting self-belief. Again using pool table skills to provide a simple dependent variable (number of balls pocketed) two forms of structured replay were devised. One was self-modelling as previously employed, which contains skills information: the tape shows the correct angle of the cue for a given alignment of billiard balls. In the other form of replay, skills *mis*information was shown but apparent efficacy was maintained (faked). This was achieved by retaining all shots that missed, but only as far as striking the cue ball and editing in a successful outcome from a 'data bank' of suitable recordings. The findings of a controlled study were primarily that reviewing either type of edited tape produced significant improvements (compared with a control condition), but that virtually identical improvements were achieved with either apparent or real efficacy on tape. Therefore it appears that motivation without skills information may at least in some conditions be sufficient for behavioural change using self-modelling.

Results so far tend to confirm some of the hypotheses drawn from data on observational learning, feedback and the impact of self-image, at the same time raising some new questions. But present conclusions are tenuous. We have made just a few steps towards a systematic analysis of what mechanisms are at work when we see part of our behaviour on the video screen.

The future

The rapid increases in both knowledge and technology promise further bold steps ahead. As more people become at ease with the medium, applications of self-modelling should multiply. Greater complexity and diversity of target areas, more intensive sessions and greater fluency with reiteration to accelerate development should eventuate.

Expansions in the clinical and training areas will need to be matched by further parametric research. Certain basic dimensions, such as the length of recording, the viewing frequency and intersession intervals, are obvious targets. While we have found some parameters that work, we have no real evidence that they are optimal. Less obvious (and less tangible) are the parameters of mastery. Adopting the 'feed-forward' concept, how far 'forward' can we go? We are presently guided by clinical judgement that performances should remain credible—but it remains a tantalizing prospect to quantify and test out that concept.

Other aspects of what to include in structured replay also need to be investigated. More work is needed on error learning as it may covary with the task to be learned or some other circumstance. Perhaps a judicious mix to approach a 'coping self-model' would prove sound. Is self-modelling a special case of vicarious learning or is peer-modelling an attenuated form of self-modelling? Testable hypotheses are called for. Apparent components of motivation by self-image enhancement and of information for skills acquisition also need to be elucidated further.

Self-modelling may not be confined to a recorded medium. Comparisons with live and mental practice could be fruitful. The advantage of self-modelling over live practice is that activities may be mastered that otherwise prove defeating. The advantage over mental rehearsal is that following the video image is far more compelling and requires no special imagery skills. However, the mental version is much cheaper and more flexible. Covert forms of behavioural training can be shown effective but tend to be weak (see Kazdin and Smith, 1979). Interestingly, what is reported in the literature as 'covert modelling' often turns out on closer inspection to refer to covert self-modelling (e.g. Harris and Johnson, 1980).

Does self-modelling deserve a revised, more coherent theoretical framework? Existing theories are clearly being stretched in interesting directions by the data coming to hand. Some answers may be found in Part III of this volume, but we are still at the stage of struggling to formulate better questions. I have a strong inner sense, however, that a better gestalt in which to place self-modelling as an agent of change is soon to be perceived.

References

Abramson, L. Y., Seligman, M. E. P., and Teasdale, J. D. (1978). Learned helplessness in humans: critique and reformulation, *Journal of Abnormal Psychology*, **87**, 49–74.

Bailey, K. G., and Sowder, W. T. (1970). Audiotape and videotape self-confrontation in psychotherapy, *Psychological Bulletin*, **74**, 127–137.

Bandura, A. (1969). *Principles of Behavior Modification*, Holt, Rinehart and Winston, New York.

Bandura, A. (1977a). Self-efficacy: towards a unifying theory of behavioral change, *Psychological Review*, **84**, 191–215.

Bandura, A. (1977b). *Social Learning Theory*, Prentice-Hall, Englewood Cliffs, New Jersey.

Bandura, A. (1982a). The self and mechanisms of agency, in *Social Psychological Perspectives on the Self* (Ed. J. Suls), Erlbaum, Hillsdale, New Jersey.

Bandura, A. (1982b). Self-efficacy mechanism in human agency, *American Psychologist*, **37**, 122–147.

Bettleheim, B. (1960). *The Informed Heart*, Free Press, New York.

Carrere, M. J. (1958). Psychogenic de l'alcoholism et attitude psychotherapique, *Annales Medico-psychologique*, **116**, 481–495.

Creer, T. L., and Miklich, D. R. (1970). The application of a self-modeling procedure to modify inappropriate behavior: a preliminary report, *Behaviour Research and Therapy*, **8**, 91–92.

Danet, B. N. (1969). Impact of audio-visual feedback on group psychotherapy, *Journal of Consulting and Clinical Psychology*, **33**, 632.

Davis, R. A. (1979). The impact of self-modeling on problem behaviors in school age children, *Social Psychology Digest*, **8**, 128–132.

Dowrick, P. W. (1976). *Self Modelling: A Videotape Training Technique for Disturbed and Disabled Children*, Unpublished doctoral dissertation, University of Auckland, New Zealand.

Dowrick, P. W. (1977). *Videotape Replay as Observational Learning from Oneself*, Unpublished manuscript, University of Auckland, New Zealand.

Dowrick, P. W. (Producer) (1978a). *How to Make a Self Model Film*, N.Z. Crippled Children Society, Auckland, New Zealand (Film).

Dowrick, P. W. (1978b). Suggestions for the use of edited video replay in training behavioral skills, *Journal of Practical Approaches to Developmental Handicap*, **2**, 21–24.

Dowrick, P. W. (1979). Single dose medication to create a self model film, *Child Behavior Therapy*, **1**, 193–198.

Dowrick, P. W. (in press). Video training of alternatives to cross gender behaviors in a 4-year old boy, *Child and Family Behavior Therapy*.

Dowrick, P. W., and Dove, C. (1980). The use of self-modeling to improve the swimming performance of spina bifida children, *Journal of Applied Behavior Analysis*, **13**, 51–56.

Dowrick, P. W., and Hood, M. (1978). Transfer of talking behaviors across settings using faked films, in *Proceedings of New Zealand Conference for Research in Applied Behaviour Analysis* (Eds. E. L. Glynn and S. S. McNaughton), Auckland University Press, Auckland, New Zealand.

Dowrick, P. W., and Hood, M. (1981). A comparison of self modeling and small cash incentives in a sheltered workshop, *Journal of Applied Psychology*, **66**, 394–397.

Dowrick, P. W., and Raeburn, J. M. (1977). Video-editing and medication to produce a therapeutic self model, *Journal of Consulting and Clinical Psychology*, **45**, 1156–1158.

Fuller, F. F., and Manning, B. A. (1973). Self-confrontation reviewed: a conceptualization for video playback in teacher education, *Review of Educational Research*, **43**, 469–528.

Griffiths, R. D. P. (1974). Videotape feedback as a therapeutic technique: retrospect and prospect, *Behaviour Research and Therapy*, **12**, 1–8.

Harris, G., and Johnson, S. B. (1980). Comparison of individualized covert modeling, self-control desensitization, and study skills training for alleviation of test anxiety, *Journal of Consulting and Clinical Psychology*, **48**, 186–194.

Hosford, R. E. (1981), Self-as-a-model: a cognitive social learning technique, *The Counseling Psychologist*, **9**, 45–62.

Hosford, R. E., and Brown, S. D. Innovations in behavioral approaches to counseling, *Focus on Guidance*, **8**, 1–11.

Hosford, R. E., Moss, C. S., and Morrell, G. (1976). The self-as-a-model technique: helping prison inmates change, in *Counseling Methods* (Eds. J. D. Krumboltz and C. E. Thoresen), Holt, Rinehart and Winston, New York.

Hung, J. H. F., and Rosenthal, T. L. (1978). Therapeutic videotaped playback: a critical review, *Advances in Behaviour Research and Therapy*, **1**, 103–135.

Kazdin, A. E. (1974). The effect of model identity and fear-relevant similarity on covert modeling, *Behavior Therapy*, **5**, 624–635.

Kazdin, A. E., and Smith, G. M. (1979). Covert conditioning: a review and evaluation, *Advances in Behaviour Research and Therapy*, **2**, 57–98.

Kornhaber, R. C., and Schroeder, H. E. (1975). Importance of model similarity on extinction of avoidance behavior in children, *Journal of Consulting and Clinical Psychology*, **43**, 601–607.

Kratochwill, T. R. (1981). *Selective Mutism: Implications for Research and Treatment*, Erlbaum, Hillsdale, New Jersey.

Lefkowitz, M. M., Blake, R. R., and Mouton, J. S. (1955). Status factors in pedestrian violation of traffic signals, *Journal of Abnormal and Social Psychology*, **51**, 704–706.

Lutzker, J. R., and Martin, J. A. (1981). *Behavior Change*, Brooks/Cole, Monterey, California.

Martin, R. D. (1971). Videotape self-confrontation in human relations training, *Journal of Counseling Psychology*, **18**, 341–347.

Miklich, D. R., Chida, T. L., and Danker-Brown, P. (1977). Behavior modification via self-modeling without subject awareness, *Journal of Behavior Therapy and Experimental Psychiatry*, **8**, 125–130.

Miklich, D. R., and Creer, T. L. (1974). Self modeling, in *Behavior Modification in Rehabilitation Settings: Applied Principles* (Eds. J. C. Cull and R. E. Hardy), Charles C. Thomas, Springfield, Illinois.

Mischel, W., and Grusec, J. (1966). Determinants of the rehearsal and transmission of neutral and aversive behaviors, *Journal of Personality and Social Psychology*, **3** 197–205.

Muzekari, L. H., and Kamis, E. (1973). The effects of videotape feedback and modeling on the behavior of chronic schizophrenics, *Journal of Clinical Psychology*, **29**, 313–316.

'Notebooks: B. F. Skinner' (1981). *Psychology Today*, **February 1981**, 63–70; 72.

Perlmuter, L. C., and Monty, R. A. (Eds.) (1980). *Choice and Perceived Control*, Erlbaum, Hillsdale, New Jersey.

Phares, E. J. (1976). *Locus of Control in Personality*, General Learning Press, Morristown, New Jersey.

Rimm, D. C., and Masters, J. C. (1979). *Behavior Therapy: Techniques and Empirical Findings*, Academic Press, New York.

Rosekrans, M. A. (1967). Imitation in children as a function of perceived similarity to a social model and vicarious reinforcement, *Journal of Personality and Social Psychology*, **7**, 307–315.

Rosenbaum, M. E., and Tucker, I. F. (1962). The competence of the model and the learning of imitation and non-imitation, *Journal of Experimental Psychology*, **63**, 183–190.

Rotter, J. B. (1966). Generalized expectancies for internal versus external control of reinforcements, *Psychological Monographs*, **80** (1, Whole No. 609).

Schaefer, H. H., Sobell, M. B., and Sobell, L. C. (1972). Twelve month follow-up of hospitalized alcoholics given self-confrontation experiences by videotape, *Behavior Therapy*, **3**, 283–285.

Schwarz, M. L., and Hawkins, R. P. (1970). Application of delayed reinforcement procedures to the behavior of an elementary school child, *Journal of Applied Behavior Analysis*, **3**, 85–96.

Stoller, F. H. (1967). Group psychotherapy on television: and innovation with hospi-
talized patients, *American Psychologist*, **22**, 158–162.
Stoller, F. H. (1969). Videotape feedback in the group setting, *Journal of Nervous and
Mental Disease*, **148**, 457–466.
Stotland, E., Zander, A., and Natsoulas, T. (1961). The generalization of interpersonal
similarity, *Journal of Abnormal and Social Psychology*, **62**, 250–256.

Using Video
Edited by P. W. Dowrick and S. J. Biggs
© 1983 John Wiley & Sons Ltd

Chapter 10

Video in Social Skills Training

Ray E. Hosford

and

Michael E. Mills

University of California, Santa Barbara

Over a decade ago, Del Vecchio and Dundas (1970) commented that the 'qualities of videotape make it the vanguard medium of the "communications revolution"' and that '. . . videotape is emerging as (the therapeutic) medium of choice' (pp. 253–254). Bailey and Sowder (1970) similarly stated that 'videotape recording represents a technological breakthrough with the kind of significance for psychiatry that the microscope has had for biology' (p. 1). Such comments not only have been enthusiastic but somewhat prophetic. Video-based interventions are being utilized in an increasing variety of therapeutic settings including client pre-therapy training (Strupp and Bloxom, 1973), microcounselling (Ivey, 1971; Saltmarsh and Hubele, 1974), therapist training (Danish, 1971; Hargie and Saunders in Chapter 11 of this volume), as well as in research settings in which video recordings have been used to standardize stimulus presentation to subjects (Mills, 1980; Myrick, 1969).

In psychological treatment settings, video-based or video-augmented interventions have also been used to treat alcoholism (Sarason and Ganzer, 1971), drug addiction (Reeder and Kunce, 1976), sexual dysfunction (Hosford, 1981; Serber, 1974), suicidal intent (Resnik and coauthors, 1973), disruptive behaviour of children (Goodwin and Mahoney, 1975), anorexia nervosa (Gottheil, Backup and Cornelison, 1969), anxiety (Melamed and Siegel, 1975), employment interviewing skill deficits (Barbee and Keil, 1973), assertion deficits (Galassi, Galassi and Litz, 1974), phobias (Bandura, Blanchard and Ritter, 1969), marital social skills deficiencies (Eisler, Hersen and Agras, 1973) as well as a number of other psychological and behavioural problems (see Curran and Monti, 1982; Wine and Smye, 1981).

Several unique characteristics of video technology have made it a valuable component of many behavioural and cognitive therapeutic interventions, particularly social skills training. In addition to producing a visual and auditory record which is essentially permanent and can be replayed conveniently again and again, Del Vecchio and Dundas (1970) note that video:

... is explicit in its communication, capable of carrying the simplest to the most complex ideas and information. In McLuhan's terminology, videotape is a 'mosaic', a multi-level, multi-perspective medium which engages all the senses, directly or indirectly, and thereby involves its audience totally. Thus, videotape is a highly personal medium for the individual viewer; it demands and obtains his participation. Videotape also communicates rapidly—with refined programming and editing an hour's worth of lectured information can be televised in 10 minutes and usually with improved understanding and retention by the audience . . . (p. 254).

Although Del Vecchio and Dundas may not have speculated about the reasons for the efficacy of videotape as a teaching technology, some evidence suggests it may be due to the functional structure of the human brain. Biopsychological research suggests that essentially separate sensory channels and information processing and storage systems characterize the brain (Gazzaniga, Steen and Volpe, 1979; Nauta and Feirtag, 1979). Unlike print, video can address each of these major, semi-independent systems of the brain *directly and simultaneously*. For example, video can present an apple visually while the word 'apple' is graphically superimposed on the screen and while the spoken word 'apple' is presented from the audio track. Limiting information flow to one brain information processing and storage system theoretically would require additional effort on the part of the learner to transfer and translate the information from one system to another, in much the same manner that cognitive knowledge must be translated into behavioural performance. With the unique properties of videotape to involve major brain systems simultaneously, therapists can develop very potent interventions which can be used effectively to help clients ameliorate a variety of problems for which they seek counselling.

The importance of social skills training

It has been well documented that one of the best predictors of recovery from psychological illness is the client's level of social skill prior to the onset of the disturbance, as noted in Table 1. Although the direction of causality has not been clearly established (i.e. whether lack of social skills causes psychological problems, or psychological problems cause a lack of social skills, or both), many therapists have held the working assumption that improving a client's social skills will improve his or her psychological functioning. With this in mind, Egan (1975) has suggested that 'It is utterly amazing that interpersonal skill building is left so much to chance in our society' (p. 21).

Although little research examining the efficacy of video-based social skills training programmes per se has been performed, several behavioural interventions have been shown to improve the social skills of trainees (Argyle, Bryant and Trower, 1974; Wolpe and Lazarus, 1966). Goldsmith and McFall (1973) found that a behavioural approach promoted better generalization of social skills to the outside world and resulted in greater pre–post test differences when compared to either a pseudotherapy control or an assessment-only control. Single case experiments utilizing behavioural approaches to social skills training have produced positive results with such disorders as depression (Lewinsohn and Atwood, 1969), sexual dysfunction (Edwards, 1972; Stevenson and Wolpe, 1960), homosexual anxiety (Duehn and Mayadas, 1976), occupational

Table 1 Studies relating psychological disorder and social skills deficits

---

Sexual dysfunction or deviation (Barlow, 1973; Barlow and coauthors, 1977; Feldman and MacCullock, 1965)

Depression (Lea and Paquin, 1981; Libet and Lewinsohn, 1973; Wells and coauthors, 1973)

Psychosomatic disorders (Barrios, 1980; Mitchell and Mitchell, 1971), schizophrenia (Bellack and Hersen, 1978; Bellack, Hersen and Turner, 1978; Hersen and Bellack, 1976)

Hysterical neurosis (Blanchard and Hersen, 1976)

Dating anxiety (Curran, 1978)

Psychological breakdown (Mednick and Shulsinger, 1968)

Urinary retention problems (Barnard, Flesher and Steinbook, 1966)

Obesity (McMillan, 1977)

Juvenile delinquency (Kornfield, 1974)

Marital problems (Eisler and coauthors, 1974)

Drug addition and/or alcoholism (Callner and Ross, 1976; O'Leary, O'Leary and Donovan, 1976; Van Hasselt, Hersen and Milliones, 1978)

---

satisfaction (Doran, 1976; Lange and Jakubowski, 1976), marital discord (Eisler and coauthors, 1974; Fensterheim, 1972) and passive/aggressive disorders (Eisler, Hersen, Miller and Blanchard, 1975).

During the past decade video has been increasingly utilized as a major component of behavioural social skills training programmes. Although much of the experimental research demonstrating the efficacy of video-based social skills training programmes have utilized college populations (see Thelen and coauthors, 1981), video-based social skills training programmes have much to offer other populations as well, including more disturbed types of clients (see Bellack and Hersen, 1977).

Characteristics of socially skilled persons

Before discussing specific video applications to social skills training, the characteristics of socially skilled persons need to be identified. In behaviour therapy, the terms assertion and social skill have often been used interchangeably (Bellack and Hersen, 1977). Assertion training has typically emphasized the outward expression of feelings in non-hostile ways (Lazarus, 1971). Recently the need for a more encompassing definition of social skill has been recognized. For example, Kelly, Keen, Kirkley and Patterson (1980) found that social popularity is not necessarily a function of assertive behaviours, particularly for females. Thus, identifying what socially skilled persons do and say necessitates the consideration of environmental, as well as personal, factors which affect behaviour. Moreover, the influence of the *person–situation interaction* is likely to be more important than either the environment or the individual alone (Endler and Magnusson, 1976). Because the specific components of effective social skills are somewhat variable and situation-dependent, the following descriptions may be helpful in characterizing socially skilled persons:

1. The socially skilled person knows which behaviours in his or her repertoire are likely to be rewarded and can perform such behaviours effectively

without experiencing anxiety (Libet and Lewinsohn, 1973). For example, some persons may utilize outstanding athletic, musical or conversational skills to obtain social reinforcement from others.

2. Conversely, the socially skilled person knows which behaviours in his or her repertoire are likely to be reinforcing to others. This category includes verbal and non-verbal aspects (e.g. using appropriate pitch and loudness of voice, establishing and maintaining eye-contact, smiling and selecting appropriate topics for conversation).

3. The socially skilled individual has the subtle ability to express both positive and negative feelings without the consequent loss of social reinforcement by infringing another's rights (Rimm and Masters, 1979).

4. The socially skilled individual attends to and accurately perceives the social context and the changing interpersonal demands of different situations and responds appropriately to them (Hersen and Bellack, 1976). As noted by Eisler and Frederiksen (1980): '. . . it may be permissible and functionally effective to ask a waitress to take your dinner back. The consequences of requesting the same from your mother-in-law might be quite dysfunctional and lead to the loss of your dinner' (p. 11). Similarly, the socially skilled individual is generally adept at perceiving the feelings and motivations of individuals and groups from other specific cultures or cultural stratifications. What is socially acceptable in one culture may be highly prohibited in others (see, in particular, Cheek, 1976; Jakubowski-Spector, 1973; Osborn and Harris, 1975; Wolfe and Fodor, 1975).

Assessment of social skills

Before beginning any video-based social skills training programme, the client's physiological, behavioural and cognitive response systems need to be assessed. If the therapist can gauge the relative involvement of each of these modalities in the overall problem, specific techniques may follow as the treatment method of choice (Lazarus, 1976, 1981). Of course, there presently exists no direct way to measure social skill physiologically; however, hand temperature, heart rate and other physiological measures can be used to assess the client's level of anxiety in different role-played or imagined social situations. Indeed, the socially unskilled person, in comparison with socially adept individuals, demonstrate higher physiological measures of anxiety in a variety of social situations (Borkovec and coauthors, 1974; Twentyman and McFall, 1975).

Not only can videotape be used to diagnose the client's overall social skills, it is particularly beneficial in pinpointing the specific skills in which the client is deficient. Clients can be videotaped in naturalistic situations, such as work or school (Hersen and coauthors, 1975), or, more conveniently, they may be videotaped while role-playing problematic social situations. Standardized tests can also be helpful in the assessment process. The Behavioural Assertiveness Test (BAT) developed by Eisler, Miller and Hersen (1973), for example, has the client role-playing 14 challenging social situations that require the expression of negative assertion; for instance: 'I ordered my steak well done, not rare. Please take this back.' A revised version of the BAT (BAT-R) has been developed to assess positive assertion (e.g. 'I would like to commend you on that project, well done') (Eisler and coauthors, 1975). Videotaping of these standardized scenes often speeds up the assessment process.

During the initial assessment, the therapist should determine whether the primary problem results from anxiety which is *inhibiting* effective interpersonal performance or whether a true behavioural *deficit* exists; i.e. the client has never acquired effective social skills. Lack of interpersonal skills may result from a historical background in which the client has simply not learned appropriate social behaviours or, as is perhaps more often the case, anxiety may be inhibiting or blocking the expression of these skills.

Developing a video-based social skills treatment programme

After assessment, development of a video-based social skills programme usually involves several specific intervention procedures. Basically, a video-based social skills training programme first will consist of procedures designed to reduce the social anxiety of the client; then video programmes of persons demonstrating effective social performance (models) are shown to the client; finally, the client is typically videotaped performing in simulated social situations both to evaluate the performance as well as to offer the client objective video feedback. However, within a general treatment framework, there is considerable opportunity for the therapist to implement specific, and sometimes quite innovative, techniques which would be beneficial to the client.

When anxiety interferes with performance of social skills

When anxiety is inhibiting or interfering with the expression of interpersonal skills, treatment should include a variant of systematic desensitization (Wolpe, 1973). If anxiety is particularly severe, Wolpe recommends that standard systematic desensitization be initiated before other treatments are attempted. With most clients, however, the therapist can immediately implement a video *rehearsal–desensitization* programme, an intervention developed by Piaget and Lazarus (1969) and later expanded by Hersen and Bellack (1976). Scenes involving either positive or negative interpersonal situations are typed on cards which then are sorted into a hierarchy from least threatening to most threatening for both the positive and negative scenes. These scenes can be specifically tailored to reflect the areas in which the client is experiencing difficulty. Beginning with the least threatening scenes, clients first observe video models behaving effectively in each of the social situations. Afterwards, they rehearse each of the scenes while being coached, videotaped and reinforced by the therapist. As they feel more relaxed and are responding effectively to some of the easier scenes, progressively more difficult interactions are attempted. Only after successful completion of a scene do clients move up the hierarchy of situations. Occasionally, it may be helpful to have them observe their performances on videotape with concomitant feedback from the therapist. Piaget and Lazarus (1969) provide a case description of the successful use of this procedure. In addition, Hosford and Brown (1975) have described the use of the *self-as-a-model* video technique which they used to help clients cope more effectively with anxiety-provoking situations.

Another means of reducing the social anxiety of clients is to present models on videotape which are shown to be reinforced after engaging in the anxiety-provoking behaviours. Such video demonstrations can produce a *disinhibitory effect* on the part of observers (Bandura, 1971; Rachman, 1972). Observing other people being rewarded for engaging in certain social behaviours often helps clients feel less anxious about performing the behaviours themselves. At the University of California, Santa Barbara, for example, clients have been taught to overcome various phobias using videotape self-desensitization programmes. One client, who was particularly fearful of spiders, was videotaped as she progressed through an *in vivo* systematic desensitization hierarchy. Her fear of spiders originated when one suddenly appeared hanging from her rear view mirror as she drove on the highway. Her fearful response almost resulted in an accident. The videotape of self-desensitization progressed systematically from looking at pictures of spiders, to touching a plastic spider, holding a jar of spiders in her lap, and finally (amazingly!) freeing a jar of non-dangerous spiders in the passenger compartment of her car as she relaxed comfortably in the driver's seat. The principal treatment merely involved having her observe herself on videotape successfully going through each step of the hierarchy.

When this videotape was shown to counselling psychology classes, students indicated that they also became somewhat desensitized to spiders simply by viewing the videotape. Similar programmes can be developed to desensitize anxieties related to various social situations, e.g. a hierarchy of scenes as one prepares to give a public speech. Video desensitization programmes have also been successfully used with snake phobias (Woody and Schauble, 1969) and fear of flying (Denholtz and Mann, 1975).

Observation of video models to promote social skills

When clients demonstrate a true deficit of social skills, simple treatment of anxiety is insufficient. Teaching new social skills may utilize one or a combination of strategies and techniques. Evidence from a variety of disciplines, including anthropological research (Bateson, 1936), experimental psychology (Dollard and Miller, 1941) and applied counselling settings (Thoresen and Hosford, 1973) suggests that probably the most pervasive form of human learning is *imitation*, or, more formally, *observational learning* or *modelling*. Simply stated, humans are predisposed to imitate the behaviours of other people. Individuals assess whether the models they observe are rewarded or punished for their behaviour as a guide for their own behaviour. Observation alone, however, without this added information, can produce quite long-lasting behavioural effects (Bandura, 1969, 1971, 1973, 1977b). Humans are not a *tabula rasa* for life—we have good memories—and it is probably not an overstatement to suggest that most of our complex behavioural and cognitive responses were initially learned vicariously, i.e. by observing others in real life settings or in media such as television. Thus, rather than attempting a tedious process of shaping specific behaviours using techniques of operant conditioning, therapists can help their clients acquire new complex behaviours relatively quickly and easily by having them observe models, either live or recorded on videotape, which demonstrate behaviours they need to learn. An equally important principle with implications for counselling is that behaviours can also be *reduced* and/or *extinguished* via these same learning procedures (Bandura, 1977b).

Presently few videotaped programmes exist that provide appropriate models of social behaviour. Television broadcasts are replete with either overly aggressive or passive social models. Social situations depicted on television are also often contrived, and are, of course, typically developed for their entertainment value rather than for educational purposes. Therapists may thus have to rely on their own resources to develop videotaped presentations of models behaving appropriately in particular social situations. In developing such programmes, a variety of variables can serve to enhance the effectiveness of the video modelling procedures.

First, only *appropriate* social behaviours should be presented. Since modelling has such a pervasive and powerful influence on human behaviour, people will often readily learn inappropriate social behaviours if they view such behaviour on the videotape. Also, the most relevant aspects of the modelled behaviour should be emphasized, e.g. by using freeze frame, close-ups, zoom shots, etc., so that the client will be sure to attend to the appropriate components of the model's behaviour.

In choosing types of models to present on videotape, research has shown that certain characteristics of actors will enhance the acquisition of new behaviours (Hosford, 1981). To maximize imitative learning, video models should be, in general:

1. Similar to the client in terms of age, cultural background, etc. (Baron, 1963; Hosford and de Visser, 1972; Kazdin, 1974)
2. Likeable (Sampson and Insko, 1966)
3. Physically attractive (Bandura and Huston, 1961)
4. Prestigeful (Bandura, 1977b; Duster and McAllister, 1973; Thoresen, Hosford and Krumboltz, 1970)
5. Powerful (Bandura, Ross and Ross, 1961; Grusec and Mischel, 1961; Mischel and Grusec, 1966)
6. Similar to the client in terms of personality and mood (Bandura, 1969; 1977b; Flanders, 1968; Thoresen and Hosford, 1973)

However, if clients are particularly anxious, then *coping models* (i.e. models who themselves appear to be anxious but are effectively learning to cope with the situation) are generally to be preferred over models that demonstrate mastery and ease in performing the task (Dillion, Graham and Aidells, 1972; Kazdin, 1974). As noted by Hosford (1981): 'Individuals who greatly desire to be highly successful along some dimension may, because they are already painfully aware of their inadequacies, resent models who exhibit these qualities at an exceptionally high degree' (p. 48). Table 2 provides a summary of desirable characteristics of video modelling presentations.

It is important to note that observational learning is a two-stage process (Bandura, 1977b). The first step of observational learning is the *acquisition* of new behaviours as the client observes the model. To acquire new behaviours

Table 2 Summary of characteristics of effective video modelling interventions
(Adapted from Perry and Furukawa, 1980)

Models should be:
  - similar to the client in terms of age, sex, race, attitudes and background
  - presented as having similar problems and concerns as the client
  - generally high in prestige
  - relatively (not greatly) higher in competence
  - observed to be rewarded for their appropriate behaviour
  - presented as warm and friendly persons
  - be physically attractive

Clients should:
  - be generally relaxed but alert
  - have a degree of uncertainty about the appropriateness of their behaviour
  - attend closely to the relevant aspects of the modelling presentation
  - view mostly exemplary aspects of their own behaviour, rather than their poorer
    performances, if video self-feedback is used (i.e. the self as a model)

Therapists should:
  - inform the client of the purpose and content of the videotape
  - minimize distractions
  - direct the client to focus on relevant aspects of the model's behaviour
  - present *coping models* (i.e. models which start out to be uncertain but progressively
    improve) to anxious clients
  - ask the client to summarize the main features of the presentation

To enhance performance and generalization:
  - present multiple models
  - reinforce the client for observing the model and summarizing main aspects of the
    presentation
  - reinforce the client for imitation of the model
  - provide incentives for performance in natural settings
  - follow up with client after intervention

through modelling, the observer must first pay particular attention to the important features of the modelled behaviour. Presumably, the observer is 'internalizing' the information presented by developing cognitive representations, both verbal and visual, which are stored in memory. To simply learn a new behaviour *cognitively* requires no actual practice. Clients who are uncertain about the appropriateness of their social behaviours will generally pay more attention to the modelled behaviours than those who erroneously believe they are socially skilled or simply do not realize that social skills can be learned.

The second stage of observational learning comes about when persons attempt to translate their cognitive representations of the modelled behaviours into actual behaviour. It has been suggested by several researchers (Bellack and Hersen, 1977; Gazzaniga, Steen and Volpe, 1979; Lazarus, 1981) that human cognitive, affective and behavioural systems are semi-independent. Observational learning first occurs in the cognitive system. Coded information must then be *translated* (by some as yet unknown neurological process) into the behavioural system before performance of the behaviour can occur. This *performance* stage of observational learning is generally more difficult than the first stage. It is often the case that while clients may *cognitively* know what to do, repeated behavioural practice is needed before they *behaviourally* know what to do. The more one practises, the more skill one is likely to have (Crossman, 1959). Although learning new behaviours via models is a two-step process in which both the cognitive and behavioural systems must be 'taught', it is often a more efficient route than operant conditioning in which the client may often attempt to guess the appropriate cognitive representations of the behaviour to be learned.

To ensure that clients can perform the social behaviours they have acquired (cognitively) by observing videotapes, rehearsal of appropriate social skills with the therapist is often necessary. Of particular utility are video vignettes which illustrate difficult social situations. Perlman, Koburn and Jakubowski-Spector (1973) have developed a series of video vignettes illustrating several difficult social situations requiring assertive behaviour. After watching the vignettes, clients are asked to respond as if they were actually in the situations. Combined with coaching, instructions and reinforcement, these vignettes amount to a very powerful behaviour change methodology, primarily because the level of *self-efficacy* belief (Bandura, 1977a) of clients increases as they realize that they are performing successfully in difficult (albeit simulated) social situations.

Videotapes of actual counselling sessions can also be used as an adjunct to counselling (or as counselling itself!) with clients who have similar problems. Hosford and Sorenson (1969) presented a videotape of a counselling session to socially anxious children who had difficulty speaking up in class. They note:

> We began with a student, Steve, who was identified by his teachers and parents as being unable to speak up in class and who had indicated that he would like help with his problem. The therapist made a videotape recording of the interview with Steve (who served as the model). . . . Basically the counseling session consisted of verbal interchanges between Steve and the therapist in which Steve responded to cues and questions as to what he might do to begin speaking up in class. Often the cues were such that Steve had little difficulty responding with a 'good' question. Whenever he suggested, for example, 'I would begin by asking a question,' he was reinforced with 'That's an excellent way in which to begin.' The interview was terminated after Steve had made several suggestions of things he might do (p. 203).

The dialogue below shows how the therapist on the videotape reinforced Steve's performance:

> *Counsellor*: . . . would you like to practise this now so that tomorrow you'll know what you are going to do?
> *Steve*: Uh huh. Okay.
> *Counsellor*: Now, why don't I pretend that I am your teacher? Now that's Mrs Jones, isn't it?
> *Steve*: Uh huh.
> *Counsellor*: Okay, class, it's time for science and we've been studying the stars. Is there anyone in here who has read anything about the stars?

Steve: I have.
Counsellor: Oh you have, Steve, good. What have you read about stars that you would like to tell us?
Steve: Well . . . the earth circles the sun every year.
Counsellor: Right! Now is the sun a star?
Steve: Uh huh.
Counsellor: Good. Now do you think maybe you could try that in Mrs Jones' class?
Steve: Uh huh. Okay. Suppose so (pp. 203–204).

After viewing the videotape students who had similar problems of speaking up in class indicated that they had learned several things to do to help them speak up in class.

With a little technical 'video magic' and imagination, variations in the presentation of video models can achieve additional therapeutic effects. Useful variations can include, at the discretion of the therapist, the use of printed graphic overlays, audio overdubbing, video vignettes and multiple models.

Printed video overlays and audio dubbing Printed video sub-titles and text and audio overdubbing (i.e. narration added to the audio track during post-production) can help to focus the client's attention on relevant aspects of the model's behaviour.

Although there have been some conflicting research results regarding any possible incremental effects of adding narration to video modelling present-ations (Hung and Rosenthal, 1981), if narration helps to focus the client's attention on the particulars of complex behaviour it may facilitate the acqui-sition of these new behaviours.

Graphic overlays are particularly appropriate to focus the client's attention to certain aspects of verbal behaviour occurring on the screen—particularly when audio dubbing may compete with the presentation of the model's verbal behaviour. Conversely, audio dubbing seems more appropriate when the thera-pist desires to focus the client's attention on visual rather than verbal aspects of the video presentation.

Video vignettes As noted earlier, video vignettes which portray various social situations can be used as stimuli to initiate role-play situations. Several such vignette presentations are currently available, including *Assertion Training for Women* (Perlman, Koburn and Jakubowski-Spector, 1973) and *Manage Your Stress* (CRM/McGraw Hill, 1980).

Even more realistic portrayal of social situations can be developed using large-screen video projection. In contrast to role-playing, large-screen video vignettes can present standardized situations to clients. Also, with good video production techniques and some imagination, very realistic video dramatiza-tions of problematic social situations may be developed which may have more impact than role-played situations with few props or effects.

Doyle, Smith, Bishop and Miller (1980) have developed a large-screen video vignette technique, which they have termed 'Social Interaction Training' (or SIT). The client stands three feet from the screen (the typical social interaction distance in American culture) and interacts with a life-size image as if he or she were actually in the social situation. The client responds directly on the image on the screen while the therapist observes. The vignette may be produced to provide a period of silence between stimulus presentations to allow for client responses or the machine may be placed in the 'pause' mode so that the image of the actor remains on the screen while the client responds.

To obtain a life-size image, the distance of the projector to the screen can be manipulated as well as the distance from the camera to the actor during recording. During taping of such vignettes, the actor is asked to look directly into the camera, as if the camera were a person. To avoid the problem of the client interfering with the projected light, translucent rear screen projection may be utilized, or, if such equipment is unavailable, the projector may be placed to one side of the client while he or she stands directly before the screen. To observe the client, the therapist should stand near the side of the screen in order to see more than a profile of the client interacting with the projected image. Given the availability of additional video equipment, a light and camera may be directed towards the client from a point near the screen to videotape his or her responses performed during the vignette. To provide continuity to the interaction during playback, the vignette and the videotape of the client may be edited together, or two playback machines may be utilized, altering the playback of the vignette with the performance of the client.

To date, large-screen video vignettes have been most extensively used by police departments to teach officers appropriate coping skills under stressful and/or potentially lethal situations. Doyle (1981) reports that officers exposed to such video vignettes were 'significantly more likely to react in a calming manner rather than belligerently, and similarly less likely to either over- or under-react to stressful situations' (p. 190). At an eight-month follow-up, the officers who participated in the interactive vignettes continued to maintain their gains over those in the control group.

Multiple models Learning is facilitated when appropriate responses to multiple social situations are illustrated on videotape by different types of models. For example, appropriate assertive responses can be demonstrated by different types of models (males, females, people of different ages and races, etc.) and for different environments (e.g. restaurants, supermarkets). The rationale for using multiple models is that the client is more likely to identify with one of the models, thus facilitating acquisition. Also, as the client is likely to encounter many different situations and persons in the environment, multiple models and multiple situations help to promote generalization (Bandura and Menlove, 1968).

Video self-observation to promote social skills

Another important technique to foster social skills is to have the client observe his or her own behaviour (as opposed to behaviour demonstrated by a model) on videotape. In fact, videotape is unsurpassed in ability to provide accurate, objective self-feedback. Video self-observation has been used in a variety of contexts, including teacher and therapist training programmes, sports, business and, of course, psychotherapy. Historically, Rogers (1942) used photographs in conjunction with phonograph recordings as a self-confrontation procedure. Cornelison and Arsenian (1960) also reported positive results using Polaroid pictures shown to patients of the their appropriate behaviours.

However, reactions to video self-confrontation may not always be positive. What happens to individuals when they view themselves on videotape? They see themselves, as the adage says, as others see them—but the experience is not always pleasant, is not always 'the giftie' that the poet Robert Burns imagined it would be. Rather, their self-concept is confronted with an image and sound which has the verdicality of stark reality; no longer can their defences easily hide their blemishes. The cognitive dissonance that can be generated from the discrepancies between the way persons think they come across and the way they see themselves come across can be quite emotionally arousing and, occasionally, quite aversive (Hosford, 1981; Schaefer, Sobell and Mills, 1971). Many studies have indicated that video self-confrontation increases effect levels (Bailey and Sowder, 1970; Boyd and Sisney, 1967; Danet, 1968; Geertsma and Reivich, 1969; Fuller and Manning, 1973; Jacobson, 1972; Kimball and Cundick, 1977; Kopel and Arkowitz, 1975; Nielsen, 1964). Perhaps one reason for emotional arousal may be that persons can see themselves communicate non-verbally, i.e. 'unconscious' communication is brought to awareness. Also, the degree of one's physical attractiveness (or lack thereof) likewise is brought in full view. It follows that there may be two quite distinct reactions to video self-confrontation, depending upon whether persons like or dislike the image they see.

Fuller and Manning (1973) found in their review of teacher training programmes that those who may benefit from video self-confrontation are generally young, attractive, verbal, intelligent and successful (or, to use their acronym, the YAVIS types). The 'victims' of video self-confrontation were, to use another acronym, the HOUND types: homely, old, unattractive, non-verbal, and dumb. Sanborn, Pyke and Sanborn's (1975) review suggesting that videotape self-confrontation used alone is an effective behaviour change technique was perhaps too enthusiastic, as has been pointed out by Gur and Sackeim (1978). Of particular importance in utilizing video self-confrontation is the assessment of the client's coping resources to deal with potentially aversive objective self-confrontation. Kimball and Cundick (1977) found that persons with 'low defensiveness' viewed themselves more negatively than persons with higher personal defences. Wicklund (1975) has suggested that the discomfort of self-confrontation may motivate behavioural changes, but Hung and Rosenthal (1981) point out that such self-confrontation, while providing the client with information about *what not to do*, does not, in itself, provide the client with information about *what to do*. Fuller and Manning (1973) concluded their review of video self-confrontation by stating: '. . . self-confrontation now seems to us more promising than we dared hope and more dangerous than we knew to fear' (p. 512).

For the YAVIS types, it has not been demonstrated that unedited video feedback *alone* generally facilitates social skills training. Treatment based on unedited video feedback has not been found to be superior to no-treatment control procedures in promoting social skills related to employment interviewing (Barbee and Keil, 1973), dating skills (Melnick, 1973) and marital social skills (Eisler, Hersen and Agras, 1973). Again, it appears that the effectiveness of video feedback in social skills training is a result of the combination of video feedback with other specific training methods. As Eisler and Frederiksen (1980) state: 'a review of the results obtained with the use of feedback in social-skills training would appear to indicate that it is of little use unless combined with other techniques which help the client acquire new social behaviours . . . (such as) coaching, modelling, and rehearsal . . .' (p. 38). Geertsma and Reivich (1969), as reported by Alger (1969), have commented that 'clinicians using videotape (feedback) for treatment purposes should be prepared to take an active role in relating to patients significant aspects of the play-back action' (p. 434). Indeed, Lambour (1975) found that the effectiveness of videotape feedback alone could be increased if clients (in this study, teachers) were 'cued' to look for specific behaviours or if they were praised for their performance.

However, when video self-observation techniques are used in a social skills training programme, there are various methods of video pre- and post-production and replay that can enhance the effectiveness of video self-feedback. Because many clients feel somewhat intimidated by the presence of video cameras, microphones, recording equipment and bright lights, such equipment should either be hidden from view or made as unobtrusive as possible. This is not to suggest that clients should be recorded surreptitiously, but rather, those who have agreed to be recorded should be helped to feel as relaxed and comfortable as possible. Cameras can be hidden behind one-way mirrors or by partitions with a small hole, or they can be placed several yards away if the camera has a zoom lens; microphones can easily be placed unobtrusively; video recording equipment can often be placed in another room. Typically, one can obviate the need for high intensity lights by using black and white video cameras which generally function quite well in normal light levels whereas colour cameras often require additional light sources.

Uses of video that often enhance the effectiveness of video feedback include such procedures as the self-as-a-model technique, interpersonal process recall, accelerated or decelerated playback, freeze frame, split screen, 'serial viewing' and instant replay. With the exceptions of the *self-as-a-model* and *interpersonal process recall* techniques, the clinical utility of these procedures has yet to be demonstrated empirically. Some of these methods which appear to be most clinically promising include:

The self as a model Video self-feedback is often more therapeutic if clients view only *exemplars* of their own behaviour. This method, termed *self-modelling*, or the *self-as-a-model* technique (see Dowrick in Chapter 9 of this volume; Hosford, 1981), can be seen as a variant of observational learning. However, in contrast to simple self-observation, after the client's behaviours are recorded all instances of the client's inappropriate behaviours are edited from the videotape. The client then observes only those portions of the videotape in which he or she is performing well (e.g. see Dowrick, 1978, 1979; Dowrick and Hood 1981). For a thorough discussion of this very promising technique (what we consider to be the video self-observation method of choice), see Chapter 9.

Accelerated or decelerated playback Another method of video self-feedback which may be useful with some clients is fast- or slow-motion video playback. By observing video playback in slow motion, clients can more readily see their subtle expressions and/or the reactions of others. Accelerated playback is particularly helpful in demonstrating fidgeting and nervous or repetitive body actions as well as the use (or disuse) of body gestures. Unfortunately, few video recorders on the market today offer accelerated or decelerated feedback.

Freeze frame By using the freeze frame (the 'pause' mode on most video recorders), a specific expression and/or feeling can be isolated and analysed. Clients sometimes are amazed at the hostile or very passive expressions on their faces captured on a video frame. Condon and Ogston (1966) reported successfully using still frames to isolate important non-verbal messages of clients which otherwise may have been missed during regular playback. When using video still-frames with clients with low self-esteem it is often advisable to keep the behavioural rule in mind: emphasize positive feedback; minimize negative feedback.

Split screen The split screen is sometimes useful to allow clients to observe others' reactions to their behaviour as they simultaneously view their own performance. This technique should perhaps be reserved for clients who are learning to master more social skills; otherwise the visual feedback may be largely negative. Professional looking productions typically require considerable equipment costs, including two cameras (one directed at the trainee, the other at the confederate participant) and two video recorders, as well as expensive post-production equipment. However, one can easily accomplish essentially the same effect with a strategically placed mirror, one camera and no post-production.

Serial viewing Some clients may report that they have not changed their behaviour much as a result of social skills training when, in fact, some rather impressive changes have occurred. That is, changes have occurred so gradually that clients hardly notice them. Such improvements can be dramatically demonstrated by editing together small segments of videotape of the client over a period of time. Fripp (1980) has reported that positive cognitive changes can often occur as a result of such 'before and after' viewing. This procedure can also help motivate clients to continue further with training.

Interpersonal process recall Yet another method to improve the effectiveness of video self-confrontation is a technique termed 'interpersonal process recall' (Kagan, Krathwohl and Miller, 1963; Kagan, Schauble and Resnikoff, 1969). In a manner similar to simultaneous feedback, clients can be videotaped interacting in a simulated social situation with another person. However, during playback of segments of the videotape, the therapist asks clients to verbalize what they were feeling, thinking, imagining, expecting or doing at different points during the videotaped interaction. The objective is to make clients conscious of their covert and overt behaviour during social interactions, and to analyse whether such covert and overt behaviours are functional or dysfunctional. This method of 'interpersonal process recall' has empirical support for its effectiveness (see, for example, Katz and Resnikoff, 1977).

Picture- or sound-only playback Sometimes videotape can present so much information so rapidly that it cannot be entirely assimilated by observers. However, by turning off either the picture or sound, clients can pick out information that they otherwise might have missed. With the sound turned off, individuals are more apt to direct their attention to their body posture and non-verbal communication without auditory distraction. With the picture turned off, they can focus more accurately on the tone and content of a discussion.

Recording when the client is alone By leaving the video recorder running while the therapist temporarily leaves the room, often clients will betray feelings they were hiding from the therapist or their feelings about therapy itself. Alger (1969) noted that after he suggested to a client that they view the portion of a videotape made after the therapist left the room, the client responded: 'Boy, wait till you see this.' The videotape showed the client pounding his fist on the arm of his chair after the therapist left, yet when the therapist returned the client greeted him with a very pleasant smile. Reviewing that portion of the videotape served as a significant starting point for a discussion regarding the inhibition of angry feelings in therapy.

Video as a component of a comprehensive social skills training programme

The effect of video observation of models or self is often insufficient in itself as a social skills training intervention. After reviewing over 52 studies on videotherapy, Hung and Rosenthal (1981) concluded that 'therapeutic gains only emerged if (video) was used as one facet of composite treatment programs' (p. 38). Although we can cite some exceptions overlooked in that review (see Dowrick in Chapter 9 of this volume), it is often true that video self-observation can be marred by defensiveness, denial and negative changes in self-concept. While observing models may promote cognitive representations of effective social performance, such knowledge must often be practised to be translated into effective actions. Thus, video social skills training techniques should be supplemented with other empirically based behaviour change methods that have been shown to be effective in producing desired outcomes. For example, *instruction* as an adjunct to video-based social skills training simply involves giving verbal instructions to the client such as 'speak louder' or 'look me in the eye'. To be maximally effective, instructions should be *specific and positive* (Azrin and Holtz, 1966; Cormier and Cormier, 1979). *Bibliotherapy* can also augment video social skills training. However, at the present time few popular books present comprehensive programmes based on empirical research, with the exceptions of *Your Perfect Right* (Alberti and Emmons, 1974) and *Responsible Assertive Behavior* (Lange and Jakubowski-Spector, 1976). When using *behaviour rehearsal* or *role-playing*, the client practises various interpersonal skills under the supervision of the therapist. Using shaping procedures, the therapist can carefully coach the client to 'try out' different behaviours which previously may have been alien to him or her (Hosford and de Visser, 1974). As noted earlier, video vignettes are particularly appropriate for initiating role-play situations. *Covert modelling* and *covert behavioural rehearsal* may be utilized to have the client mentally role-play difficult social situations for which video vignettes have not been developed or for which the therapist is unable to develop. Other situations may be difficult to deal with in the environment or in the training session (e.g. sexual or other intimate behaviours). What cannot occur in reality, however, can readily happen in the imagination. In such cases clients can simply visualize themselves, or others, dealing with the problematic situation effectively (Kazdin, 1974).

Just as the affective system (e.g. anxiety) can interfere with behavioural performance, so too can the cognitive system interfere with the performance of desired social behaviours (Jakubowski-Spector, 1973; Wolfe and Fodor, 1975). Thus, *cognitive restructuring* can also be used as an important adjunct to a video-based social skills training programme. An example of a social skills programme using video models designed to change observers' cognitions is discussed by Goodwin and Mahoney (1975). To decrease the disruptive behaviour of boys when taunted by their peers, a videotape was made of a boy being taunted but coping successfully with the verbal assault by using 'self-instructions'. Goodman and Mahoney relate:

> In addition to remaining ostensibly calm, looking at his taunters, and remaining in the center of the circle, the model was portrayed as coping with verbal assaults through a series of covert self-instructions. These thoughts, which were dubbed in on the tape, consisted of statements such as 'I'm not going to let them bug me' and 'I won't get mad' (p. 201).

Besides modelling, Goodman and Mahoney used cueing and behavioural rehearsal in the social skills training intervention. The percentage of time that these boys engaged in disruptive behaviour in the classroom decreased from approximately 60 to 10 per cent.

Another particularly important cognitive intervention for social skills training programmes is what might be called *rejection inoculation*. Similar to stress inoculation (Meichenbaum, 1975), the objective is to avoid mislabelling or overgeneralization of social rejections. Social rejections of various degrees and types occur frequently in everyday life; the person who makes his or her self-esteem too vulnerable to such inevitable situations is likely to withdraw and become depressed. Having the client interact with vignettes which portray various social rejections can help desensitize the person to such situations as well as help him or her learn appropriate responses to deal with them.

Finally, *in vivo practice and homework* is often helpful to evaluate the efficacy of the intervention as well as to provide additional generalization of newly acquired behaviours. If possible, this is best accomplished with the therapist present. For example, non-assertive clients may practise dealing with sales people in department stores while the therapist provides support and feedback. Clients can also practise social skills alone, such as telephoning a friend or acquaintance. Progressively more difficult assignments in the natural environment can be practised as the clients increase their repertoire of social skills. With portable video recording equipment, taping clients in the natural environment is becoming more convenient.

Evaluation of training

Evaluation of the efficacy of a video-based social skills intervention may be approached in much the same manner as the initial assessment. Clients may again be presented with video vignettes setting the stage for difficult social interactions and their videotaped responses to such vignettes may be evaluated. Gains in all three of the major regulatory systems (affective, behavioural and cognitive) often can be assessed. To avoid bias, final evaluation can be performed by therapists not involved in the training.

After approximately three to six months it is most advisable to contact the client to ensure that his or her interpersonal skills have not deteriorated. If so, further assessment and intervention should be considered.

McFall and Marston (1970) report a rather clever method (albeit involving deception) of assessing the effectiveness of assertion training. After involvement in the training, a confederate 'salesman' telephoned each person and used high pressure sales tactics to attempt to get the subject to subscribe to some magazines. Recordings of the telephone calls allowed the experimenters to assess the efficacy of the training programme by measuring the total time of the call before the subject terminated it, time to resistance, etc. Similar 'check-ups' can be performed without nefarious deception by having clients consent to such a future assessment; this in itself may help to motivate them to continue to monitor and correct their own behaviour.

Which treatment components and combinations are most effective?

Given the many techniques of video modelling, video self-confrontation and behavioural methods to supplement video presentations, which techniques have been demonstrated to be most effective in producing behaviour change in the desired direction? Several studies have examined the relative efficacy of various components of interpersonal skills training. In general, the research has indicated that behavioural rehearsal with feedback is superior to behavioural rehearsal without feedback (McFall and Marston, 1970). The most effective components in assertion training are behavioural rehearsal, coaching, modelling (covert and overt) and performance feedback (Friedman, 1971; Rathus, 1973). When used in conjunction with behavioural rehearsal and coaching, modelling, however, adds little to the effectiveness of the programme (Brown, 1977; McFall and Twentyman, 1973). Videotape feedback combined with verbal feedback is superior to verbal feedback alone (Edelson & Seidman, 1975). In their review of studies using videotherapy, Hung and Rosenthal (1981) noted that 'the worst results emerged if clients only viewed their own images or saw undesirable aspects of their own behaviour . . . replaying clients desirable role playing efforts brought the best results' (p. 26). They also suggested that better therapeutic results will be obtained if video self-confrontation presentations are at least 20 to 30 minutes in duration, and optimally about 40 minutes. Although observable behavioural improvements in social skills may be relatively rapid, changes in self-reports, self-statements and physiological measures of anxiety generally take longer to effect (McFall and Twentyman, 1973). Although there does seem to be evidence indicating some generalization between situations (Bellack and Hersen, 1977), the clinician would do well to attempt to 'programme' such generalization as well as *prime* the social environment such that the client receives adequate reinforcement contingent upon demonstration of his or her newly acquired socially skilled behaviours.

Custom tailoring a video social skills training programme

In summary, video applications in social skills training is a relatively young endeavour and experimentation with methods and procedures is still appropriate in clinical settings. Although we have presented a variety of techniques, exactly how and when these techniques and their various combinations should be used is best left to the discretion of the individual trainer or therapist. (For a detailed step-by-step approach for implementing a *general* social skills training programme see Fodor, 1980.) Table 3 lists some procedures which therapists may, at their option, use during each major step of the video-based social skills training programme. Within this general paradigm, therapists have much room to tailor 'custom' interventions to meet the specific needs of individual clients.

Table 3 Steps and optional procedures of a video-based social skills programme

Step 1. If anxiety is interfering with performance begin a desensitization procedure (Wolpe and Lazarus, 1966) and present appropriate coping models (Bellack and Hersen, 1977) on videotape which demonstrate in a graduated sequence the specific behaviours the client needs to perform. (*Optional techniques: present video-based systematic desensitization, live coping models, etc.*)

Step 2. Use available video programmes and/or develop custom ones in which models perform the behaviours the client needs to learn (see Table 2). Cue the client to attend to particularly relevant aspects of the modelled behaviours. Have the person imagine him or herself performing the demonstrated behaviours successfully. (*Optional techniques: present printed graphic overlays, audio dubbing, multiple models, etc.*)

Step 3. Break up components of complex behaviours demonstrated by the video models into more simple responses. Using role-playing methods (in conjunction with feedback, reinforcement and possibly live modelling), have the client practise first simple, then more complex, behaviours. Use video vignettes (see Perlman, Koburn and Jakubowski-Spector, 1973) wherein the client responds to video presentations of various social situations as if they were actually in the situation. Videotape the successful performance of the client and edit out instances of the client's inappropriate behaviours.

Step 4. Have the client observe him- or herself performing adequately on videotape. (*Optional techniques: self-as-a-model, accelerated or decelerated playback, freeze frame, split screen, serial viewing, video- or audio-only playback, interpersonal process recall, etc.*)

Step 5. Have the client practise, covertly and overtly, their behaviours observed on the videotape. Give feedback and assign homework in the natural environment. (*Optional techniques: videotape in vivo performances of client, interpersonal process recall, etc.*)

Step 6. After criterion is reached, follow up in three to six months. (*Optional techniques: confederate 'salesperson' calls—preferably with client's prior consent—and other real life checkup methods.*)

Future directions

Psychologists generally are not well educated in video technology, nor are professional video producers generally well educated in psychology. Thus, few quality video-based psychological interventions have been made available to the professional community. Hopefully the increasing use of video disk and home videotape will help make the productions of such video programmes economically attractive and thus encourage collaboration between the two professions. Therapists interested in video applications in therapy would also do well to keep abreast of developments in biopsychological research, particularly with regard to future discoveries related to the functioning and interrelationships among the sensory channels and information processing and storage systems of the human brain. More research is needed in this area in addition to research directed at specific video interventions in therapeutic/educational settings.

Perhaps by the turn of the century, advancing technology (including video in combination with computers, large-screen video projection, interactive home cable television and video disk) will have made video an integral component of most learning and therapeutic interventions. A videotape library of educational/therapeutic programmes ranging from systematic desensitization for a variety of phobias to specific social situations will, no doubt, become available. Such a video library of therapeutic interventions will allow more effective use of a therapist's time, as well as enhance the therapy process itself.

However, as history teaches, headlong leaps into a new technological era are likely to spawn problems, particularly ethical ones. Can therapists, for example, who are themselves products of a particular culture (and subculture), adequately assess which behaviours are considered to be socially skilled in their clients' culture or sub-culture? To help reduce the possibility of adverse personal effects resulting from video-based social skills training (also see Hargie, this volume), we suggest that an essential prerequisite for any behavioural, cognitive or physiological intervention is the *voluntary, informed consent* on the part of the client. The informed adult client should be the ultimate judge of what behaviours are in his or her best interests.

As a maturing and increasingly popular technology, video offers an exciting new area of exploration for therapists and researchers. Although we have presented a few promising video techniques which have the potential for improving social skills training, imaginative innovations with video (particularly in conjunction with other emerging technologies) are likely to produce still more effective therapeutic interventions to help alleviate human suffering.

References

Alberti, R. E., and Emmons, M. L. (1974). *Your Perfect Right*, Impact, San Luis Obispo, California.

Alger, I. (1969). Therapeutic use of videotape playback, *Journal of Nervous and Mental Disease*, **148**, 430–436.

Argyle, M., Bryant, B., and Trower, P. (1974). Social skills training and psychotherapy, *Psychological Medicine*, **4**, 435–443.

Azrin, N. H., and Holtz, W. C. (1966). Punishment, in *Operant Behavior* (Ed. W. K. Honig), Appleton-Century-Crofts, New York.

Bailey, K., and Sowder, A. (1970). Audiotape and videotape in self-confrontation in psychotherapy, *Psychological Bulletin*, **74**, 127–137.

Bandura, A. (1969). *Principles of Behavior Modification*, Holt, Rinehart and Winston, New York.

Bandura, A. (1971). Psychotherapy based upon modeling principles, in *Handbook of Psychotherapy and Behavior Change* (Eds. A. E. Bergin and S. L. Garfield), Wiley, New York.

Bandura, A. (1973). *Aggression: A Social Learning Theory Analysis*, Prentice Hall, Englewood Cliffs, New Jersey.

Bandura, A. (1977a). Self-efficacy: toward a unifying theory of behavioral change, *Psychological Review*, **84**, 191–215.

Bandura, A. (1977b). *Social Learning Theory*, Prentice-Hall, Englewood Cliffs, New Jersey.

Bandura, A., Blanchard, E. E., and Ritter, B. (1969). Relative efficacy of desensitization and modeling approaches for inducing behavioral, affective, and attitudinal changes, *Journal of Personality and Social Psychology*, **13**, 173–199.

Bandura, A., and Huston, A. (1961). Transmission of aggression through imitation of aggressive models, *Journal of Abnormal and Social Psychology*, **63**, 575–582.

Bandura, A., and Menlove, F. (1968). Factors determining vicarious extinction of avoidance behavior through symbolic modeling, *Journal of Personality and Social Psychology*, **8**, 99–108.

Bandura, A., Ross, D., and Ross, S. (1961). Transmission of aggression through imitation of aggressive models, *Journal of Abnormal and Social Psychology*, **63**, 575–582.

Barbee, J. R., and Keil, E. C. (1973). Experimental techniques of job interview training for the disadvantaged: videotape feedback behavior modification and microcounseling, *Journal of Applied Psychology*, **58**, 209–213.

Barlow, D. H. (1973). Increasing heterosexual responsiveness in the treatment of sexual deviation: a review of the clinical evidence, *Behavior Therapy*, **4**, 655–671.

Barlow, D. H., Abel, G. G., Blanchard, E. B., Bristow, A. R., and Young, L. D. (1977). A heterosocial skills behavior checklist for males, *Behavior Therapy*, **8**, 229–239.

Baron, R. (1963). Attraction toward the model and model's competence as determinants of adult imitative behavior, *Journal of Personality and Social Psychology*, **67**, 601–607.

Barnard, G., Flesher, C., and Steinbook, R. (1966). The treatment of urinary retention by aversive stimulus cessation and assertiveness training, *Behavior Research and Therapy*, **4**, 232–236.

Barrios, F. X. (1980). Social skills training and psychosomatic disorders, in *Social Competence* (Eds. D. P. Rathjen and J. P. Foryet), Pergamon, New York.

Bateson, G. (1936). *The Naven*, Stanford University Press, Stanford, California.

Bellack, A. S., and Hersen, M. (1977). *Behavior Modification*, Oxford, New York.

Bellack, A. S., and Hersen, M. (1978). Chronic psychiatric patients: social skills training, in *Behavior Therapy in the Psychiatric Setting* (Eds. M. Hersen and A. S. Bellack), Williams and Wilkins, Baltimore.

Bellack, A. S., and Hersen, M. (1980). *Research and Practice in Social Skills Training*, Plenum, New York.

Bellack, A. S., Hersen, M., and Turner, S. M. (1978). Role-play tests for assessing social skills: are they valid?, *Behavior Therapy*, **9**, 448–461.

Blanchard, E. B., and Hersen, M. (1976). Behavioral treatment of hysterical neurosis: symptom substitution and symptom return considered, *Psychiatry*, **39**, 118–129.

Borkovec, T. D., Stone, N. M., O'Brien, G. T., and Kaloupek, D. G. (1974). Evaluation of a clinically relevant target behavior for analog outcome research, *Behavior Therapy*, **5**, 503–513.

Boyd, H., and Sisney, V. (1967). Immediate self-image confrontation and changes in self-concept, *Journal of Consulting Psychology*, **31**, 291–294.

Brown, S. (1977). *An Experimental Investigation of Externally Mediated Self-feedback in Assertion Training*, Unpublished doctoral dissertation, University of California, Santa Barbara.

Callner, D. A., and Ross, S. M. (1976). The reliability and validity of three measures of assertion in a drug addicted population, *Behavior Therapy*, **7**, 659–667.

Cheek, D. K. (1976). *Assertive Black . . . Puzzled White*, Impact, San Luis Obispo, California.

Condon, W. S., and Ogston, W. D. (1966). Sound and film analysis of normal and pathological behavior patterns, *Journal of Nervous and Mental Disease*, **143**, 4.

Cormier, W. H., and Cormier, L. S. (1979). *Interviewing Strategies for Helpers*, Brooks-Cole, Monterey.

Cornelison, F. S., and Arsenian, J. A. (1960). A study of the response of psychotic patients to photographing self-image experience, *Psychiatry Quarterly*, **34**, 1–8.

CRM/McGraw–Hill (1980). *Manage Your Stress*, Del Mar, CA: CRM/McGraw-Hill Films, Del Mar, California (Film).

Crossman, E. R. F. (1959). A theory of acquisition of speed skills, *Ergonomics*, **2**, 153–166.

Curran, J. P. (1978). Skills training as an approach to the treatment of heterosexual-social anxiety: a review, *Psychological Bulletin*, **84**, 140–157.

Curran, J. P., and Monti, P. M. (Eds.) (1982). *Social Skills Training*, Wiley, New York.

Danet, B. (1968). Self-confrontation in psychotherapy reviewed, *American Journal of Psychotherapy*, **22**, 245–257.

Danish, S. J. (1971). Film-simulated counselor training, *Counselor Education and Supervision*, **September**, 29–35.

Del Vecchio, R., and Dundas, E. (1970). Tele-communications for mental health: prospects for the seventies and eighties, in *Videotape Techniques in Psychiatric Training and Treatment* (Ed. M. M. Berger), Brunner/Mazel, New York.

Denholtz, M. S., and Mann, E. T. (1975). An automated audiovisual treatment of phobias administered by non-professionals, *Journal of Behavioral Therapy and Experimental Psychiatry*, **6**, 111–115.

Dillion, P., Graham, W., and Aidells, A. (1972). Brainstorming on a 'hot' problem: effects of training and practice on individual and group performance, *Journal of Applied Psychology*, **54**, 487–490.

Doran, L. E. (1976). *The Effects of Assertion Training within a Career Awareness Course on the Sex-role Self-concepts and Career Choices of High School Women*, Unpublished Ph.D. dissertation, University of Illinois.

Dowrick, P. W. (1978). *How to Make a Self-model Film*, N.Z. Crippled Children Society, Auckland, New Zealand (Film).

Dowrick, P. W. (1979). Single dose medication to create a self model film, *Child Behavior Therapy*, **1**, 193–195.

Dowrick, P. W., and Hood, M. (1981). Comparison of self-modeling and small cash incentives in a sheltered workshop, *Journal of Applied Psychology*, **66**, 394–397.

Doyle, P. H. (1981). Behavior rehearsal to videotape simulations: applications, techniques, and outcomes, in *Videotherapy in Mental Health* (Eds. J. L. Fryrear and B. Fleshman), Charles C. Thomas, Springfield, Illinois.

Doyle, P. H., Smith, W. A., Bishop, P. C., and Miller, M. A. (1980). Simulated interaction training, in *Social Competence* (Eds. D. P. Rathjen and J. P. Foreyt), Pergamon, New York.

Duehn, W. D., and Mayadas, N. S. (1976). The use of stimulus/modeling videotapes in assertive training for homosexuals, *Journal of Homosexuality*, **1**, 373–381.

Duster, J., and McAllister, C. (1973). Effect of modeling and model status on verbal behavior in an interview, *Journal of Consulting and Clinical Psychology*, **40**, 240–243.

Edelson, R. I., and Seidman, E. (1975). Use of videotaped feedback in altering interpersonal perceptions of married couples: a therapy analogue, *Journal of Consulting and Clinical Psychology*, **43**, 244–250.

Edwards, N. B. (1972). Case conference: assertive training in a case of homosexual pedophilia, *Journal of Behavior Therapy and Experimental Psychiatry*, **3**, 55–63.

Egan, G. (1975). *The Skilled Helper*, Brooks Cole, Monterey.

Eisler, R. M., and Frederiksen, L. W. (1980). *Perfecting Social Skills*, Plenum Press, New York.

Eisler, R. M., Hersen, M., and Agras, W. S. (1973). Effects of videotape and instructional feedback on nonverbal marital interaction: an analogue study, *Behavior Therapy*, **4**, 551–558.

Eisler, R. M., Hersen, M., Miller, P. M., and Blanchard, E. B. (1975). Situational determinants of assertive behaviors, *Journal of Consulting and Clinical Psychology*, **43**, 330–340.

Eisler, R. M., Miller, P. M., and Hersen, M. (1973). Components of assertive behavior, *Journal of Clinical Psychology*, **29**, 295–299.

Eisler, R. M., Miller, P. M., Hersen, M., and Alford, H. (1974). Effects of assertive training on marital interaction, *Archives of General Psychiatry*, **30**, 643–649.

Endler, N. S., and Magnusson, D. (1976). Toward an interactional psychology of personality, *Psychological Bulletin*, **89**, 956–974.

Feldman, M. P., and MacCullock, M. J. (1965). The application of anticipatory avoidance learning to the treatment of homosexuality, *Behavior Research and Therapy*, **2**, 165–183.

Fensterheim, H. (1972). Assertive methods and marital problems, in *Advances in Behavior Therapy* (Eds. R. D. Rubin, H. Fensterheim, J. D. Henderson and L. P. Ullman), Academic Press, New York.

Flanders, J. (1968). A review of research on imitative behavior, *Psychological Bulletin*, **69**, 316–337.

Fodor, I. G. (1980). The treatment of communication problems with assertiveness training, in *Handbook of Behavioral Interventions* (Eds. A. Goldstein and E. B. Foa), Wiley, New York.

Friedman, P. H. (1971). The effects of modeling and role-playing on assertive behavior, in *Advances in Behavior Therapy* (Eds. R. D. Rubin, H. Fensterheim, A. A. Lazarus and C. M. Franks), Academic Press, New York.

Fripp, B. (1980). The breakthrough in videotherapy, *The Boston Globe*, October 5, 1980.

Fuller, F., and Manning, B. Self-confrontation reviewed: a conceptualization for video playback in teacher education, *Review of Educational Research*, **43**, 469–520.

Galassi, J. P. Galassi, M. D., and Litz, M. C. (1974). Assertive training in groups using video feedback, *Journal of Counseling Psychology*, **21**, 390–394.

Gazzaniga, M. S., Steen, P., and Volpe, B. T. (1979). *Functional Neuroscience*, Harper & Row, New York.

Geertsma, R., and Reivich, R. (1969). Auditory and visual dimensions of externally mediated self-observation, *Journal of Nervous and Mental Disease*, **148**, 210–223.

Goldsmith, J. B., and McFall, R. M. (1973). Development and evaluation of an interpersonal skill-training program for psychiatric inpatients, *Journal of Abnormal Psychology*, **84**, 51–58.

Goodwin, S. E., and Mahoney, M. J. (1975). Modification of aggression though modeling: an experimental probe, *Journal of Behavior Therapy and Experimental Psychiatry*, **6**, 200–202.

Gottheil, E., Backup, C., and Cornelison, F. (1969). Denial and self-image confrontation in a case of anorexia nervosa, *Journal of Nervous and Mental Disease*, **14**, 238–250.

Grusec, J., and Mischel, W. (1961). Model characteristics as determinants of social learning, *Journal of Personality and Social Learning*, **63**, 575–582.

Gur, R. C., and Sackeim, H. A. (1978). Self-confrontation and psychotherapy: a reply to Sanborn, Pyke and Sanborn, *Psychotherapy: Theory, Research and Practice*, **15**, 258–265.

Hersen, M., and Bellack, A. S. (1976). A multiple-baseline analysis of social-skills training for chronic psychiatric patients: rationale, research findings, and future directions, *Comprehensive Psychiatry*, **17**, 559–580.

Hersen, M., Turner, S. M., Edelstein, B. A., and Pinkston, S. G. (1975). Effects of phenothiazines and social skills training in a withdrawn schizophrenic, *Journal of Clinical Psychology*, **31**, 588–594.

Hosford, R. E. (1981). Self-as-a-model: a cognitive social learning technique, *The Counseling Psychologist*, **9**, 45–62.

Hosford, R., and Brown, S. (1975). Innovations in behavioral approaches to counseling, *Focus on Guidance*, **8**, 1–11.

Hosford, R. E., and Sorenson, D. L. (1969). Participating in classroom discussions, in *Behavioral Counseling: Cases and Techniques* (Eds. J. D. Krumboltz and C. E. Thoresen), Holt, Rinehart and Winston, New York.

Hosford, P., and de Visser, L. (1974). *Behavioral Approaches to Counseling*, APGA Press, Washington, D.C.

Hosford, R., and de Visser, I. (1972). *Ethnic Characteristics as Factors in Social Modeling*, Technical Report, U.S. Office of Education, Washington, D.C.

Hung, J. H., and Rosenthal, T. L. (1981). Therapeutic videotaped playback, in *Videotherapy in Mental Health* (Eds. J. L. Fryrear and B. Fleshman), Charles C. Thomas, Springfield, Illinois.

Jacobson, L. (1972). *The Effects of Brief Videotape Self-confrontation on Affect and Self-description*, Doctoral dissertation, University of Rochester.

Jakubowski-Spector, P. (1973). Facilitating the growth of women through assertive training, *The Counseling Psychologist*, **4**, 76–86.

Kagan, N., Krathwohl, D., and Miller, R. (1963). Simulated recall in therapy using videotape—a case study, *Journal of Counseling Psychology*, **10**, 237–243.

Kagan, N., Schauble, P., and Resnikoff, D. (1969). Interpersonal process recall, *Journal of Nervous and Mental Disease*, **148**, 365–374.

Katz, D., and Besnikoff, A. (1977). Televised self-confrontation and recalled affect: a new look at videotape recall, *Journal of Counseling Psychology*, **24**, 150–152.

Kazdin, A. (1974). Covert modeling, model similarity, and reduction of avoidance behavior, *Behavior Therapy*, **5**, 325–340.

Kelly, J. A., Keen, J. M., Kirkley, B. G., and Patterson, J. N. (1980). Reactions to assertive versus unassertive behavior: differential effects for males and females and implications for assertion training, *Behavior Therapy*, **11**, 670–682.

Kimball, H., and Cundick, B. (1977). Emotional impact of videotape and reenacted feedback on subjects with high and low defenses, *Journal of Counseling Psychology*, **24**, 377–382.

Kopel, S., and Arkowitz, H. (1975). The role of attribution and self-perception in behavior change: implications for behavior therapy, *Genetic Psychology Monographs*, **92**, 175–212.

Kornfield, J. L. (1974). Assertive training with juvenile delinquents, *Dissertation Abstracts International*, **35**, 1501–02 (University of Southern California No. 74–17, 354).

Lambour, G. P. (1975). *Variations of Videotape Feedback as a Mechanism of Behavior Change*, Unpublished doctoral dissertation, Ohio State University.

Lange, A. J., and Jakubowski-Spector, P. (1976). *Responsible Assertive Behavior*, Research Press, Champaign, Illinois.

Lazarus, A. A. (1971). *Behavior Therapy and Beyond*, Mcgraw-Hill, New York.

Lazarus, A. A. (Ed.) (1976). *Multi-modal Behavior Therapy*, Springer, New York.

Lazarus, A. A. (1981). *The Practice of Multimodal Therapy*, McGraw-Hill, New York.

Lea, G., and Paquin, M. (1981). Assertiveness and clinical depression, *The Behavior Therapist*, **4**, 9–10.

Lewinsohn, P. M., and Atwood, G. E. (1969). Depression: a clinical-research approach, *Psychotherapy: Theory, Research and Practice*, **6**, 166–171.

Libet, J. M., and Lewinsohn, P. M. (1973). Concept of social skill with special reference to the behavior of depressed persons, *Journal of Consulting and Clinical Psychology*, **40**, 304–312.

McFall, R. M., and Marston, A. R. (1970). An experimental investigation of behavior rehearsal in assertive training, *Journal of Abnormal Psychology*, **76**, 295–303.

McFall, R. M., and Twentyman, C. T. (1973). Four experiments on the relative contributions of rehearsal, modeling, and coaching to assertion training, *Journal of Abnormal and Social Psychology*, **81**, 199–218.

McMillan, M. (1977). Assertiveness as an aid in weight control, in *Assertiveness: Innovations, Applications, Issues* (Ed. R. Alberti), Impact, San Luis Obispo, California.

Mednick, S. R., and Schulsinger, F. (1968). Some premorbid characteristics related to breakdown in children with schizophrenic mothers, in *The Transmission of Schizophrenia* (Eds. D. Rosenthal and S. S. Kety), Pergamon, New York.

Meichenbaum, D. A. (1975). A self-instructional approach to stress management: a proposal for stress inoculation training, in *Stress and Anxiety* (Eds. I. Sarason and C. D. Spielberger), Vol 2, Wiley, New York.

Melamed, B. G., and Siegel, L. J. (1975). Reduction of anxiety in children facing hospitalization and surgery by use of filmed modeling, *Journal of Consulting and Clinical Psychology*, **43**, 511–521.

Melnick, J. (1973). A comparison of replication techniques in the modification of minimal dating behavior, *Journal of Abnormal Psychology*, **81**, 51–59.

Mills, M. E. (1980). *Decision and Motivation in the Selection Interview*, Paper presented at the meeting of the Western Psychological Association, Honolulu, May 1980.

Mischel, W., and Grusec, J. (1966). Determinants of the rehearsal and transmission of neutral and aversive behavior, *Journal of Personality and Social Psychology*, **3**, 197–205.

Mitchell, K. R., and Mitchell, D. K. (1971). Migrane: an exploratory treatment application of programmed behavior therapy techniques, *Journal of Psychosomatic Research*, **15**, 37–57.

Myrick, R. (1969). Effect of a model on verbal behavior in counseling, *Journal of Counseling Psychology*, **16**, 185–190.

Nauta, W. J. H., and Feirtag, M. (1979). The organization of the brain, *Scientific American*, **241**, 88–117.

Nielsen, G. (1964). *Studies in Self-confrontation*, Howard Allen, Cleveland, Ohio.

O'Leary, D. E., O'Leary, M. R., and Donovan, D. M. (1976). Social skill acquisition and psychosocial development of alcoholics: a review, *Addictive Behaviors*, **1**, 111–120.

Osborn, S. M., and Harris, G. G. (1975). *Assertive Training for Women*, Charles C. Thomas, Springfield, Illinois.

Perlman, J., Koburn, K., and Jakubowski-Spector, P. (1973). *Assertion Training for Women*, American Personnel and Guidance Association (Film).

Perry, M. A., and Furukawa, M. J. (1980). Modeling methods, in *Helping People Change* (Eds. F. H. Kanfer and A. P. Goldstein), Pergamon, New York.

Piaget, G. W., and Lazarus, A. A. (1969). The use of rehearsal desensitization, *Psychotherapy: Theory, Research and Practice*, **6**, 264–266.

Rachman, S. (1972). Clinical applications of observational learning, imitation, and modeling, *Behavior Therapy*, **3**, 379–397.

Rathus, S. A. (1973). Instigation of assertive behavior through videotape-mediated assertion models and directed practice, *Behavior Research and Therapy*, **11**, 57–65.

Reeder, C. W., and Kunce, J. T. (1976). Modeling techniques, drug-abstinence behavior, and heroin addicts: a pilot study, *Journal of Counseling Psychology*, **23**, 560–562.

Resnik, H. L. P., Davison, W. T., Schuyler, D., and Christopher, H. M. (1973). Videotape confrontation after attempted suicide, *American Journal of Psychiatry*, **130**, 460–463.

Rimm, D. C., and Masters, J. C. (1979). *Behavior Therapy—Techniques and Empirical Findings*, Academic Press, New York.

Rogers, C. R. (1942). The use of electrically-recorded interviews in improving psychotherapeutic techniques, *American Journal of Orthopsychiatry*, **12**, 429–434.

Saltmarsh, R. E., and Hubele, G. E. (1974). Basic interaction behaviors: a microcounseling approach for introductory courses, *Counselor Education and Supervision*, **13**, 246–249.

Sampson, E., and Insko, C. (1966). Cognitive consistency and performance in the autokinetic situation, *Journal of Abnormal and Social Psychology*, **68**, 184–192.

Sanborn, D. E., Pyke, H. F., and Sanborn, C. J. (1975). Videotape playback and psychotherapy: a review, *Psychotherapy: Theory, Research and Practice*, **12**, 179–186.

Sarason, I. G., and Ganzer, V. J. (1971). *Modeling: An Approach to the Rehabilitation of Juvenile Offenders*, Final report to the Social and Rehabilitation Service of the Department of Health, Education and Welfare, June 1971.

Schaefer, H. H., Sobell, M., and Mills, K. C. (1971). Some sobering data on the use of self-confrontation with alcoholics, *Behavior Therapy*, **2**, 28–39.

Serber, M. (1974). Videotape feedback in the treatment of couples with sexual dysfunction, *Archives of Sexual Behavior*, **3**, 377–380.

Stevenson, I., and Wolpe, J. (1960). Recovery from sexual deviations through overcoming non-sexual neurotic responses, *American Journal of Psychiatry*, **116**, 737–742.

Strupp, H. H., and Bloxom, A. (1973). Preparing lower-class patients for group psychotherapy: development and evaluation of a role induction film, *Journal of Consulting and Clinical Psychology*, **41**, 373–384.

Thelen, M. H., Fry, R. A., Fehrenback, P. A., and Frautschi, N. M. (1981). Developments in videotape and film modeling, in *Videotherapy in Mental Health* (Eds. J. L. Fryrear and B. Fleshman), Charles C. Thomas, Springfield, Illinois.

Thoresen, C., and Hosford, R. (1973). Behavioral approaches to counseling, in *Behavior Modification in Education*, Seventy-second Yearbook of the National Society for the Study of Education, Part 1, University of Chicago Press, Chicago, Illinois.

Thoresen, C., Hosford, R., and Krumboltz, J. (1970). Determining effective models for counseling clients of varying competencies, *Journal of Counseling Psychology*, **17**, 369–375.

Twentyman, C. T., and McFall, R. M. (1975). Behavioral training of social skills in shy males, *Journal of Consulting and Clinical Psychology*, **43**, 384–395.

Van Hasselt, V. B., Hersen, M., and Milliones, J. (1978). Social skills training in alcoholics and drug addicts: a review, *Addictive Behaviors*, **3**, 221–233.

Wells, K. C., Hersen, M., Bellack, A. S., and Himmelhock, J. M. (1973). *Social Skills Training for Unipolar Depressive Females*, Paper presented at the meeting of the American Association for the Advancement of Behavior Therapy, Atlanta, December 1973.

Wicklund, R. A. (1975). Objective self-awareness, in *Advances in Experimental Social Psychology* (Ed. L. Berkowitz), Vol. 8, Academic Press, New York.

Wine, J. D., and Smye, M. D. (1981). *Social Competence*, Wiley, New York.

Wolfe, J. L., and Fodor, I. G. (1975). A cognitive-behavioral approach to modifying assertive behavior in women, *Counseling Psychologist*, **5**, 45–52.

Wolpe, J. L. (1973). *The Practice of Behaviour Therapy*. Pergamon, Oxford.

Wolpe, J., and Lazarus, A. A. (1966). *Behavior Therapy Techniques*, Pergamon Press, New York.

Woody, R. H., and Schauble, M. S. (1969). Videotaped vicarious desensitization, *Journal of Nervous and Mental Disease*, **148**, 281–286.

Using Video
Edited by P. W. Dowrick and S. J. Biggs
© 1983 John Wiley & Sons Ltd

Chapter 11

Training Professional Skills

Owen D. W. Hargie

and

Christine Y. M. Saunders

Ulster Polytechnic, Northern Ireland

In this chapter we extend the analysis of the use of videotape in the training of social skills outlined in the previous chapter by focusing specifically on an area which has received increasing attention in recent years, namely the provision of specialized social skills training (SST) in order to improve the communicative ability of a range of professional groups. In particular, the emphasis will be on the provision of such training for what Ellis and Whittington (1981) have referred to as the 'interpersonal professions', including doctors, teachers, social workers, careers officers, youth leaders, nurses, health visitors, clergymen, sales personnel and managerial staff. In all of these areas, the ability to communicate effectively at an interpersonal level is a vital part of the job. It is hardly surprising, therefore, that in recent years increasing attention has been given to the development of systematic training programmes in the field of interpersonal relations for such professional groups.

While social skills training is a concept which has been attracting growing interest in recent years, it is not a unitary concept, in that more than one alternative paradigm is available for those who may wish to implement a programme of social skills instruction. Various attempts have been made to initiate such programmes in order to improve the social performance of trainees. These have ranged from the totally unstructured sensitivity training exemplified by, for example, T-groups at one end of the continuum to the very structured programmes of behaviour modification at the other. Between these two extreme types of training a number of other methods have been developed.

In this chapter we intend to describe one of these methods, namely the microtraining paradigm, which is now the most widely utilized form of SST for professionals. In particular, the role of closed circuit television (CCTV) and video replays will be featured, in terms of collecting ethnographic data in order to facilitate the pre-training phase of skill identification and also in terms of practical applications, alternative modes of usage and effects upon trainees during the training process. Specific examples of how these procedures have been applied across many discrete fields will be listed, and one of these applications will be considered in more depth, as a case study, to illustrate in practical terms the viability of this type of SST programme. Finally, important ethical considerations facing those responsible for designing and implementing such programmes will be raised, together with suggestions about how possible problems can be circumvented by careful planning and administration of programmes.

Training the professional

There are a number of approaches which can be adopted in relation to the training of professional social skills. The first, and perhaps most extreme form, is that of 'learning on the job'. The rationale behind this method is simply that if someone wants to learn how to be a social worker, teacher, or whatever, he or she should be given an opportunity to go ahead and practise while doing the job. The emphasis here is on learning by trial and error. There are, however, many dangers inherent in this approach. The learner may adopt behaviours which enable him or her to 'survive' but which are not the most appropriate for the job. On the other hand, the inexperienced learner may be unable to cope in certain situations, or may cope at the expense of the client. Argyle (1972), in reviewing research which has been conducted into learning on the job concludes that 'learning social skills simply by doing them can be remarkably unsuccessful' (p. 228).

Another method which often accompanies learning on the job is that of 'modelling the master'. This technique consists of the learner being assigned to an experienced professional and observing him or her at work for a period of time, prior to performing the same kind of tasks. The rationale here is obviously akin to the notion of apprentices learning from being with a master craftsman. While this approach has advantages over the more extreme on the job method in isolation, it is not without its difficulties. Master professionals will have their own attitudes, personality, age, sex and behavioural style, all of which may be different from those of the trainee. These differences will cause problems for the trainee when attempting to model the master. Furthermore, the trainee will learn only those skills portrayed by the professionals observed, and these are unlikely to be exhaustive of the total possible range of skilled behaviour available. Stones and Morris (1972) point out that in terms of professional interaction this form of training 'stands for imitation rather than analysis' (p. 10).

Given the problems inherent in both of these methods, it is obvious that training is desirable prior to job experience. Indeed, this principle is now widely accepted in the training of most professionals, with training programmes being organized in colleges, polytechnics and universities for a wide range of professional groups. Until fairly recently, however, the practical elements of such courses have tended to concentrate upon the lecture or seminar mode of teaching as a means of imparting information about professional practice. This approach, consisting of much talk and little action, tended to displease both trainer and trainee alike, since there was an obvious gap between the theoretical college input on the one hand and practical fieldwork on the other.

It was as a result of trying to bridge this gap in the training of teachers that microteaching was first introduced at Stanford University in 1963. Microteaching was basically a scaled-down teaching encounter where trainees could put into practice, in the safe college environment, techniques which would be useful to them later in the classroom. In this respect, microteaching represented a systematic attempt to bridge the gap between education theory lectures and classroom practice. Attempts to devise this systematic approach resulted in the notion of simplifying the teaching situation. This was achieved by reducing the number of pupils in a class to between five and ten; by reducing the length of lessons to between five and ten minutes; by focusing upon one teaching skill at a time; and by organizing microteaching in college (Brown, 1975).

By coincidence, in 1963 Keith Acheson, a researcher at Stanford, was experimenting with the use of the, then new, video-recording system in relation to the preparation of trainee teachers for classroom experience. The resulting chance marriage of the videotape recorder and a programme of microteaching at Stanford was a union which resulted in fruitful offspring. The combination of these two aspects generated a great deal of enthusiasm among teacher trainers in a large number of countries. Surveys of microteaching in the United States (Ward, 1970), West Germany (Brunner, 1973), Australia (Turney and coauthors, 1973) and the United Kingdom (Hargie and Maidment, 1979) have indicated widespread dissemination of this training method in institutions throughout the world.

As microteaching usually takes place in a carefully monitored college environment, researchers in education have also been attracted to this training method. Much of the early research in microteaching was concerned with ascertaining just how successful this technique really was. Research reviews by Turney and coauthors (1973), Brown (1975), Hargie and Maidment (1979) and Malley and Clift (1980) have illustrated that the methods and procedures employed in microteaching have proved to be invaluable in the preparation of student teachers for classroom experience. Furthermore, this technique has been shown to be consistently well received by trainers and trainees alike—a fact which has undoubtedly contributed to the rapid spreading of microteaching into teacher education. As Allen (1980) points out this popularity is based 'not so much on research evidence as upon the satisfaction of the teacher education staff, the teaching candidates and the school personnel involved in its use' (p. 148).

Following the success of microteaching, Allen Ivey developed the micro-counselling technique at Colorado State University (and later at the University of Massachusetts) as a method of teaching, interviewing or counselling behaviour (Ivey and coauthors, 1968). This was the first adaptation of the micro-teaching method to another profession and it heralded the beginning of a large number of parallel developments in other fields. All of these methods now fall under the umbrella term of microtraining, and the central procedures used constitute what is known as the microtraining paradigm.

Microtraining paradigm

The training procedures which follow have evolved at Ulster Polytechnic over approximately the last ten years as a result of a critical appraisal of current research, together with an evaluation and refinement, where necessary, of existing microtraining courses designed to meet the needs of a wide range of professional trainees. The microtraining paradigm described here is comparable with the training processes employed in many other institutions, not withstanding idiosyncratic differences arising from this model as the direct product of negotiation between, and collaboration with, college tutors, professional practitioners, microtraining staff and trainee students in one institution. We would argue that, since the training procedures draw extensively upon research into the elements and processes of interpersonal interaction and extensive practical experience, it would be unfitting to alter radically or even omit certain phases of this microtraining paradigm without adequate evidence at either a theoretical or empirical level to justify such changes.

The microtraining model comprises three distinct but mutually interdependent phases: (1) preparation, (2) training and (3) evaluation (see Figure 1).

Phase I—preparation

This is perhaps the most important phase of the entire programme since it is dependent upon the ability of tutors to identify relevant skills for practice. Although most skills are generic to a wide variety of both dyadic and group interactions, there are some which are more appropriate to specific professional areas than others. For instance, although the use of reinforcement skills may be encouraged in student teachers to motivate their pupils to learn (Rosenshine, 1971), in the counselling context a minimum of reinforcement would be more relevant, since it would be maleficent to reinforce positively a very depressed client (Ivey and Authier, 1978). In addition, we cannot assume that all skills selected for training be given equal weighting in terms of their efficacy in one professional area. For example, the skill of oral higher order cognitive questioning would appear to be a crucial skill for a teacher in secondary education since it is related to pupils' achievement (Turney and coauthors, 1975). On the other hand, an understanding of non-verbal behaviour plays a much larger role in the skill repertoire of infants' teachers, since the language, vocabulary and syntactical patterns of five-year-old children are still fairly limited (De Landsheere, 1973).

Clearly, then, there is a need to identify and label discrete behaviours in a number of professional situations where communication is at a premium. This can be done by direct observation of practising professionals, by extensive discussions with professionals and college tutors to generate skills used by competent practitioners and by literature research, both empirical and theoretical, to ascertain what preceding work has been carried out.

Phase II—Training

There are four parts to the training phase, namely: skill analysis, skill discrimination, skill practice and focused feedback.

Skill analysis This takes the form of a lecture input in which trainees are provided with a theoretical rationale for each skill, relevant research findings

Figure 11.1 Microtraining paradigm

Phases	Procedures	Techniques	Resources
Preparation	Identification of Skills	Direct Observation Consultation with Professionals Empirical Literature Search Theoretical Literature Search	Access to Placement Facilities Books, Journals Research Studies
	Skill Analysis	Linked Theory Lecture	Hand-outs Illustrative Examples
	Skill Discrimination	Workshop Session	Live or Video-taped models Schedules Cueing Written Exemplars
Training	Skill Practice	Small Scale Practice with Role Play Sequences	Video-recording Equipment
	Focused Feedback	Video Play Back Tutor Feedback Peer Feedback Client Feedback	Video Recordings Observation Schedules Rating Schedule
Evaluation	Real Practice	Actual practice on Block Placement with Pupils or Clients. Supervision by Professionals Tutors and Teachers/Field Workers	All School or Field Work Placement Facilities
		Feedback To Course Planners	

pertaining to the use of each skill and, finally, descriptions of the behavioural elements included in each skill. This is followed by a critical examination of the advantages and disadvantages of utilizing the skill in specific professional contexts.

Skill discrimination Such workshops enable trainees to identify the skill in action, critically analyse its behavioural components and evaluate its effectiveness in a particular professional situation. In order to facilitate this procedure, 'model' videotapes are constructed and presented to exemplify each skill. There is a great deal of research evidence to show that the acquisition of social behaviour is facilitated by imitating or 'modelling' the behaviour of significant others (Bandura, 1969, 1977). However, the preparation of models for use in micro-training programmes is a demanding task, since a number of factors must be considered in the construction of such modelling materials and procedures. These will be discussed later in the chapter when the role of CCTV and video is considered.

Skill practice These sessions are designed and organized to resemble as closely as possible the kind of situation a professional is faced with daily in the normal course of his or her work. Therefore, commonly recurring situations in a variety of professional areas need to be identified and defined, and role-plays written to encapsulate precisely the 'real' situation. However, not all practice sessions are simulated. In courses such as teaching and careers guidance, for instance, it is advisable to involve school pupils in order to authenticate the training process. In other courses, such as counselling, health visiting and social work, simulations are essential, given problems such as client confidentiality. In addition, research by Goldthwaite (1969) has indicated that trainees who role-play clients actually demonstrate higher levels of skill acquisition than those who role-play the professional. In operational terms, each skill is practised in a scaled-down encounter for a short period of time, approximately seven to ten minutes, and is video recorded by a remote controlled camera which is operated by a tutor in a connecting tutorial playback room. (For a more complete description of this phase of training see Tittmar, Hargie and Dickson, 1977). Although each skill is practised individually there is opportunity towards the end of the course for the trainee to integrate the skills in a final practice session.

Focused feedback Such sessions consist of verbal comments by both tutor and other trainees in the group, in addition to the playback of the trainee's performance on videotape. This form of focused group tutorial feedback is an essential element in trainees' skill acquisition. A fuller description of the processes involved will be provided in the following section relating to the role of CCTV and video.

Phase III—evaluation

Following a programme of microtraining, each trainee is required to complete a period of fieldwork placement in which he or she will hopefully be given the opportunity to display some of the skills acquired during training. Trainees, assisted by college tutors and fieldwork supervisors, should be encouraged to make a critical evaluation of the skills in the light of practical placement experience. Any additional skills identified or refinements made to existing skills which become apparent during placement can be fed back into the training programme itself in order to strengthen its validity.

The role of CCTV and video

Although a great deal of research has been undertaken to ascertain the effectiveness of microtraining procedures using closed circuit television (CCTV) and video replay (Borg, 1969; Fortune, Cooper and Allen, 1967; Ivey, 1971) relatively few studies have focused specifically on the effects which CCTV recording and video feedback have on improving trainees' skill performance (exceptions are Bierschenk, 1972, 1974; MacLeod, 1977a). Yet despite Allen and Ryan's (1969) claim that video replay is not an essential element of microteaching, Griffiths (1972), in a scrutiny of present day practice, notes that 'it has been unusual to hear of the implemention of a microteaching programme without television involvement' (p. 16).

Much of the rationale for the inclusion of a video recording system in these training programmes is based on the assumption that feedback, i.e. the information provided to trainees immediately following their performance, is a powerful influence in helping trainees acquire new skills and strategies. However, surprisingly little is known about the processes involved in self-viewing in microtraining, and what evidence there is suggests that mechanical feedback procedures are more complex than might initially be realized (Griffiths, 1974). Feedback, though, is only one of the four uses which video systems have in a course of microtraining. The other three areas in which video recorders can assist trainees to identify, analyse, acquire and evaluate a range of social skills in any one of the professional areas previously mentioned, are skill identification, model tape construction and discrimination training.

Skill identification

How do course planners arrive at a valid checklist of skills with which to equip trainees so that their first interactional encounters in their chosen profession will be neither internally stressful nor disastrous in their consequences? One basic way is to observe directly the behaviour of professionals in action. Mattarazo, Phillips, Wiens and Saslow (1965) identified a number of counselling skills using this method, and Flanders (1968) developed a compendium of teaching skills by systematically recording the frequency of pre-specified teaching behaviours. An alternative procedure is to have extensive discussions with professional practitioners and college-based tutors to facilitate the identification and analysis of the skills used by competent interactors.

Saunders and Saunders (1980) used this technique, aided by videotapes of classroom lessons, to identify the kind of skills student teachers should possess at the end of a four-year B.Ed. programme. More specifically, video recordings of students teaching different areas of their main subject were made so that specimen lessons of a range of activities were available for analysis of teaching behaviour. Clearly, the success of deriving teaching skills from videotape observation depended upon the ability of the observers to perceive patterns of behaviour accurately, which in turn assumed a common understanding and operational agreement about the features of the teaching behaviour under observation. In all, the observers in this study, who were made up of practising teachers and college tutors, identified 14 basic teaching skills. However, there is no reason why the techniques developed in this research could not be applied to other professionals bent on identifying key communication skills.

Model tape construction

While modelling procedures used in microtraining courses have their genesis in Bandura's (1969, 1977) research, which shows that complex human behaviour can be learned by viewing and imitating or 'modelling' from others, there remain unresolved important issues regarding the type and use of such models. Thus the preparation of model tapes is a demanding task since, as yet, our knowledge of a number of factors concerning the construction and use of videotaped material remains relatively incomplete. Yet it is fair to say that some tentative generalizations have emerged which are useful to consider when preparing model tapes.

Firstly, for models to be effective, the key skill elements must be specifically defined in behavioural terms and clearly exemplified in the model's performance on tape. Secondly, there must be a high degree of association in the trainees' mind between them and the model, if some change in trainee performance is to be effected. For instance, observing an outstandingly proficient performance by a competent professional might overwhelm rather than encourage the trainee since the gap between his or her own experience and that of the model's is too great to bridge. On balance, it would appear that a variety of models—competent, coping, real life and role-played—should be deliberately selected to cater for a diverse range of trainee ability (Gillmore, 1975; Young, 1969). Thirdly, although symbolic modelling procedures can be utilized effectively (e.g. analysing written transcripts of questioning skills) trainees appear to derive more benefit from the experience of viewing the skill rather than merely reading about it (Koran, 1969). Fourthly, when constructing a model tape to exemplify specific use of a particular skill it is important to record the response that action has on the behaviour of the respondents. For example, for a teaching skill to be judged appropriate, consideration should be given to the effects of that skill upon the responses of pupils. Thus, it is important when constructing 'simulated' model tapes to record the interaction between respondents since this helps to clarify the objectives of the skill in terms of consequent respondent behaviour. A fifth aspect to consider is whether or not the personal characteristics of the model (e.g. age, sex, perceived status) affect trainees' perceptions of the behaviours being modelled. Although the research literature is sparse there is evidence to suggest that trainees identify more closely with models who approximate their own characteristics (Resnick and Kiss, 1970). Finally, the inclusion of some form of cueing, i.e. directing the observers' attention to significant aspects of the model's behaviour, tends to increase the model's effectiveness (Turney and coauthors, 1973).

Although these are only some of the main factors to consider when devising model videotapes, it is important to note them if models are to be effective in sensitizing trainees to appropriate professional behaviour patterns.

Discrimination training

A number of researchers (Kissock, 1971; Griffiths, 1977; Wagner, 1973) have provided evidence to show that while the practice element of microtraining is a means whereby trainees can demonstrate what they have learned, it is not the learning vehicle itself. Instead, learning appears to take place at a cognitive level when trainees are encouraged to discriminate in lecture and seminars, by means of modelled exemplars, effective and ineffective use of the skill in action. Learning will be enhanced if observation schedules, ratings of effectiveness and questions requiring covert answers are given to trainees. Thus it would seem that some form of linkage of verbal meaning to perceived behavioural indices is essential to the acquisition of appropriate skill behaviour.

Practice and feedback

Whereas the skill discrimination aspect of the training programme can be shown to be effective in shaping social skills, without supplementary skills practice, the microtraining course would remain less than attractive to many students. Practice sessions are extremely motivating to trainees since they provide them with the opportunity to try out (in practice) what they have previously learned (Hargie, 1980).

In operational terms, trainees are ideally organized into small groups of five or six each with a supervizing tutor. Each trainee practice session should, if possible, be video recorded. At the beginning of each training programme and before the skills practice sessions commence, each trainee should be given the opportunity to self-view on videotape for the first time in order to overcome the 'cosmetic effect' of first-time self-viewing (Allen and Ryan, 1969). Evidence from a number of researchers suggests that individuals viewing themselves for the first time are often preoccupied with the size, shape and general characteristics of their face and body and ignore their actual behaviour (Travers, 1975). However, with increasing exposure to the videotape MacLeod (1977b) demonstrated that student teachers typically 'became preoccupied with the behaviour they see and the consequences of that behaviour and fail to take note of the appearance of their body' (p. 203).

The advantages of self-viewing cannot be overstated since it encourages trainees to develop both a critical self-awareness and an awareness of others which would be difficult to achieve otherwise (Fuller and Manning, 1973). However, self-analysis is improved if trainees, while viewing the playback of their performance, are required to focus on specific aspects of their behaviour. Morrison and MacIntyre (1973) found, for instance, that the value of video feedback on its own is valueless unless students are trained to observe and evaluate specific aspects of their performance. Thus some form of observation schedule, which contains a checklist of behavioural indicators together with a predetermined rating scale, should be used when viewing the playback of a trainee practising an individual skill. In addition, tutor feedback comments are important since some trainees devalue their performance as portrayed on video and require their tutors to provide effective reinforcement in order to correct the imbalance (Watts, 1973). In fact, variety may be the order of the day for most trainees if we consider Griffiths' (1977) research, in which groups of students each received one particular type of tutorial feedback during video replay sessions in microteaching. In a follow-up questionnaire designed to assess student attitudes to each of these tutorial styles, Griffiths found that 'all groups want more of what they did not receive and less of what they did receive' (p. 141).

Applications to professional practice

The microtraining approach has been applied to a large number of different professional groups, including careers advisers (Dickson, Hargie and Tittmar, 1977), clergymen (Kriesel, 1975), college lecturers (Cannon, 1979), counsellors (Miller, Morrill and Uhlmann, 1970), doctors (Authier and Gustafson, 1974), health visitors (Tittmar, Hargie and Dickson, 1978), industrial supervisors (Bradley, 1975), librarians (Jennerich, 1974), managers (Smallwood, 1977), nurses (Authier and Gustafson, 1976), occupational therapists (Furnham, King and Pendleton, 1980), police officers (Danish and Brodsky, 1970), psychologists (Goodwin, Garvey and Barclay, 1971), selection interviewers (Lewis, Edgerton and Parkinson, 1976), speech therapists (Boone and Prescott, 1971) and teachers (Hargie, Tittmar and Dickson, 1978a), among others.

To illustrate how the microtraining paradigm can be applied in practice, it is useful to look closely at one particular professional group. To this end we will describe the programme used with students on a four-year full-time B.A. honours degree in social work at Ulster Polytechnic. We believe that readers will be able to apply aspects of this example to their own professional situations. The first 18 months of the course is devoted to grounding in discipline studies (psychology, sociology, social policy) with accompanying social work orientation seminars. After 18 months, students are selected for the mainstream B.A. social work degree. Shortly after this selection, students are provided with their microtraining programme, as a preparation for their first experience of fieldwork placement, which occurs at the beginning of their third year of study.

Microtraining with social work students was first introduced at Ulster Polytechnic in 1972, and the programme described here is the result of a continual process of development and refinement which has occurred during the intervening years. This programme consists of lectures, seminars, analysis of videotapes of social work interaction and role-plays where students act out various types of situations pertinent to social work.

The first step, then, is to provide students with a lecture/seminar input on the social skill under consideration. This consists of an analysis of the theoretical rationale for the skill, an outline of relevant research findings relating to the use of the skill and a description of the behaviour associated with the skill. This is followed immediately by an analysis of videotapes (either 'real' or role-play exemplars) to highlight how the skill may be used in various social work situations; at this time students are required to discuss the strengths and weaknesses of the interaction presented in order to encourage the development of a sense of critical awareness. Later in the week students are given an opportunity to put the skill into practice in a simulated social work case. We have found it useful to allow at least one day between the lecture/seminar stage and the practical stage of training since it gives students time to assimilate the information given and to read further about the skill under review.

The practical sessions take place in the Social Skills Training Centre at Ulster Polytechnic (for a full description of this Centre see Hargie, 1980). Practicals take the form of role-plays of various types of situations likely to be encountered by social workers. These roles are written by the social work tutors at the Polytechnic, based upon real situations with which they have had experience. The roles involve a range of contexts including dyadic interviewing and counselling encounters, and various types of small group interactions (such as family scenes or case conferences).

The roles are acted out in the SST Centre, with each student in turn being given the chance to play the role of the social worker. These simulations are recorded on video by the tutor, and then played back on a television monitor with accompanying discussion and evaluation. Over the duration of the microtraining programme, students will have had experience of some 40 to 50 social work role-plays. This provides them with an invaluable insight into many of the problems with which they will later be faced in the field, and it also prepares them with a repertoire of useful strategies for dealing with a variety of social situations which they may encounter during social work placement. Assessment of the microtraining programme takes the form of a workbook in which students are required to evaluate their practical performance in terms of their use of the social skills under review. Students are not assessed directly in terms of their practical performance at this time, since this would be both anxiety-provoking for the student and would reduce the learning potential to be derived from the exercise.

A number of social skills are studied during the course of the programme. These include non-verbal communication, questioning, reflection of feeling, paraphrasing, rewarding, active listening, sustaining, explaining, self-disclosure, set induction (opening an interaction) and closure (closing an interaction). As Hargie, Saunders and Dickson (1981) in their review of skills point out, these 'are generally regarded as being the central skills of interpersonal communication' (p. 17). However, other skills currently being investigated at Ulster Polytechnic include presenting (specifically related to the presentation of a particular case in a case conference) and confronting (drawing attention to incompatible pieces of information which relate to a person's situation). It is anticipated that other skills will also be identified to add to our ever-increasing knowledge of social work practice.

Microtraining, therefore, represents the first preparatory phase in the training of social work students for practical experience, which leads to the next step in their practical training, namely, the first period of fieldwork practice. Programmes similar to the one briefly described here have been reported by Howard and Gooderman (1975), Hargie, Tittmar and Dickson (1978b), Lewis and Gibson (1977) and Ivey and Authier (1978), who all illustrate how such an approach can be applied to the training of social workers.

We have attempted to illustrate briefly how video facilities can be incorporated into a practical programme of microtraining, both to facilitate the discrimination of skills during lectures and to provide a frame of reference and accurate feedback during practicals. This facilitates the analysis, evaluation, reflection and consolidation of professional social skills. Obviously the microtraining methods and procedures described here in relation to social workers could easily be applied to a large number of other professional groups.

Ethical considerations

In any programme of training in interpersonal relations, there are a number of ethical issues which must be examined (Ivey and Authier, 1978). When training professionals there are at least five such issues which need further consideration. These are:

1. *Have trainers the right to intervene in the behaviour of trainees?* This question is fundamental to the whole concept of providing some form of training in communication for professionals. It has already been answered in the affirmative earlier in this chapter, when we considered the alternatives to such training—none of which was really satisfactory. Provided that trainees fully recognize their rights to withdraw, trainers in fact have a responsibility to help trainees by offering such training.
2. *Do such training programmes produce uniformity and reduce the freedom of expression of the individual?* On the contrary, the programme goals should clearly set out to enlarge the repertoire of possible behaviour open to the individual, thereby providing a greater freedom of choice than might otherwise have prevailed. Trainers should be aware of individual differences among trainees and encourage them to develop patterns of behaviour to suit their personality. In this way, no attempt is made to mechanize social interaction or produce robot-like professionals. Here, the emphasis should always be on the individual as decision maker, in terms of which behaviour he or she chooses to employ in any situation.
3. *Is it wrong to subject trainees to criticism during video feedback tutorials?* The tutorial aspect of microtraining is an area where no firm conclusions have been reached regarding the value of tutors and peers during feedback sessions. Research tends to suggest that, whether or not tutors may be instrumental in effecting changes in trainee behaviour, trainees nevertheless desire the presence of a tutor during video replays (Hargie and Maidment, 1979). The role of peers during this stage is an aspect which has been largely ignored by researchers. It would appear, however, that tutor sensitivity is important in terms of picking up a trainee who may be suffering unduly, either from observing an unsuccessful performance or from scathing criticisms made by peers. The video feedback tutorials are important and potent aspects of training and, given appropriate management by a tutor, should not cause unnecessary stress to trainees.
4. *Do SST programmes train people how to manipulate others?* In one sense this is

true, in that trainees, following training, should be aware of a number of techniques which can be used to influence others. The trainee, however, must decide how to use these techniques. If a trainee does decide to use this knowledge malevolently, this still does not negate the validity of the training. Just because some individuals write poison pen letters or obscene slogans on walls does not mean that it is unethical to teach people how to write! The vast majority of professionals will use the new skills learned in SST in a constructive and meaningful fashion.

5. *Are there not dangers in recording an individual's behaviour on videotape during training?* The answer here is that there are dangers, and steps must be taken by trainers to circumvent these. Strict control of all videotapes used during training is essential. Tapes should be wiped clean as soon as possible after practicals. If a tape is to be kept and used again for any purpose (such as for research or as a model tape for future teaching) the permission of all participants on the tape must be obtained in writing. By adopting procedures such as these, it should be possible to guarantee complete confidentiality to all trainees in terms of access to any videotape on which they are to be recorded.

Conclusion

In this chapter we have attempted to outline the central theoretical and practical considerations involved in the training of professional skills. In particular, the microtraining paradigm has been highlighted as the most widespread and systematic form of training in this field. As we have illustrated, the microtraining paradigm had its origins in the microteaching technique developed at Stanford University, and is a method of preparing trainee teachers for classroom experience. The success of microteaching, in which the use of CCTV and videotaping played a crucial role, soon led trainers in other fields to adapt this technique to meet their own requirements.

In most of these cases trainers have modified the original microtraining format to suit their own particular requirements, and, indeed, there is no one 'fixed' or 'set' microtraining format. Rather, one of the advantages of this approach is the flexibility inherent in the method. The crucial aspects, however, are the emphases on the identification of the core social skills involved in professional interaction and on providing trainees with an opportunity to acquire these skills in a safe environment as a preparation for fieldwork practice.

Thus, the microtraining technique has been operative for quite some time. During this time, a great deal of research has been conducted in the field. The general outcome from this research has been to demonstrate that microtraining is an effective method for improving the communicative competence of trainees; that it is often more effective than alternative training approaches; and that it is well received by both trainers and trainees alike. Ivey and Authier (1978), in reviewing research and practice in microtraining, conclude that: 'Experience and research has led to the conclusion that specific commitments to single skills and general adherence to the microtraining framework leads to the greatest benefit for the largest number of trainees and clients' (p. 392).

For training professional skills, therefore, it would seem that the benefits to be gained from the use of videotaping can be increased by incorporating this resource within a coherent and organized microtraining framework. Otherwise, as emphasized earlier, it is probable that the use of CCTV and video if used in an unsystematic fashion may have little value other than that of gimmickry.

References

Allen. D. (1980). Microteaching: a personal review, *British Journal of Teacher Education*, **6**, 147–151.

Allen, D. W., and Ryan, K. A. (1969). *Microteaching*, Addison-Wesley.

Argyle, M. (1972). *The Psychology of Interpersonal Behaviour*, Penguin, Harmondsworth.

Authier, J., and Gustafson, K. (1974). Using video to develop communication skills, *Biomedical Communications*, **2**, 38–42.

Authier, J. and Gustafson, K. (1976). Application of supervised and nonsupervised microcounselling paradigms in the training of registered and licensed practical nurses, *Journal of Consulting and Clinical Psychology*, **44**, 707–709.

Bandura, A. (1969). *Principles of Behavior Modification*, Holt, Rinehart and Winston, New York.

Bandura, A. (1977). *Social Learning Theory*, Prentice-Hall, Englewood Cliffs, New Jersey.

Bierschenk, B. (1972). Self-confrontation via closed-circuit television in teacher training: results, implications and recommendations, in *Didakometry*, Vol. 37, University of Malmö, Sweden.

Bierschenk, B. (1974). Perceptual, evaluative and behavioural changes through externally mediated self-confrontation, in *Didakometry*, Vol. 41, University of Malmö, Sweden.

Boone, D., and Prescott, T. (1971). *Application of Videotape and Audiotape Self-Confrontation Procedures to Training Clinicians in Speech and Hearing Therapy*, Mimeo, Speech and Hearing Centre, Denver University, Colorado.

Borg, W. R. (1969). *The Minicourse as a Vehicle for Changing Teacher Behavior, The Research Evidence*, Far West Laboratory for Educational Research and Development, Berkeley, California, Paper presented at AERA Annual Meeting, Los Angeles, California.

Bradley, C. (1975). Microcounselling: a tool for the preparation of supervisors, *Journal of Industrial Teacher Education*, **13**, 24–31.

Brown, G. (1975). *Microteaching a Programme of Teaching Skills*, Methuen, London.

Brunner, R. (1973). Microteaching an den Hechschuler der Bundesrepublik Deutschland, *Psychology in Erzieh U Unterr*, **20**, 269–279.

Cannon, R. (1979). The Design, Conduct and Evaluation of a Course in Lecturing, *PLET*, **16**, 16–22.

Danish, S., and Brodsky, S. (1970). Training of policemen in emotional control and awareness, *Psychology in Action*, **25**, 368–369.

De Landsheere, G. (1973). Analysis of verbal interaction in the classroom, in *Towards a Science of Teaching* (Ed. G. Channon), pp. 110–122, NFER, Buckinghamshire.

Dickson, D., Hargie, O., and Tittmar, H. (1977). The use of microcounselling in the training of employment advisory officers, *The Vocational Aspect of Education*, **29**, 45–47.

Ellis, R., and Whittington, D. (1981). *A Guide to Social Skills Training*, Croom Helm, London.

Flanders, N. A. (1968). Interaction analysis and inservice training, *Journal of Experimental Education*, **37**, 126–132.

Fortune, J. C., Cooper, J. M., and Allen, D. W. (1967). The Stanford summer microteaching clinic, *Journal of Teacher Education*, **18**, 384–393.

Fuller, F. F., and Manning B. A. (1973). Self-confrontation reviewed: a conceptualization for video playback in teacher education, *Review of Educational Research*, **43**, 469–528.

Furnham, A., King, J., and Pendleton, D. (1980). Establishing rapport: interactional skills and occupational therapy, *Occupational Therapy*, **October**, 322–325.

Gillmore, S. (1975). The effects of modelling on student teachers' questioning behaviours: a study in the micro-teaching context, Unpublished M.Ed. thesis, University of Glasgow.

Goldthwaite, D. T. (1969). A study of M.T. in the pre-service education of science teachers, *Dissertation Abstracts International*, **29**, 3021A.

Goodwin, D., Garvey, W., and Barclay, J. (1971). Microconsultation and behavioural analysis: a method of training psychologists as behavioural consultants, *Journal of Consulting and Clinical Psychology*, **37**, 355–363.

Griffiths, R. (1972). *Some Troublesome Aspects of Microteaching*, Paper presented to the Annual Conference of the National Closed Circuit Television Association, University of Stirling, 1972.

Griffiths, R. (1974). The contribution of feedback to microteaching technique, in *Microteaching Occasional Papers* (Ed. A. J. Trott), pp. 17–24, No. 3, APLET.

Griffiths, R. (1977). The preparation of models for use in microteaching programmes, in *Microteaching Occasional Papers*, (Ed. A. J. Trott), pp. 47–55, No. 3, APLET.

Hargie, O. D. W. (1980). *An evaluation of a microteaching programme*, Unpublished Ph.D. Thesis, Ulster Polytechnic, Northern Ireland.

Hargie, O., and Maidment, P. (1979). *Microteaching in Perspective*, Blackstaff Press, Belfast.

Hargie, O., Saunders, C., and Dickson, D. (1981). *Social Skills in Interpersonal Communication*, Croom Helm, London.

Hargie, O., Tittmar, H., and Dickson, D. (1978a). Miniteaching: an extension of the microteaching format, *British Journal of Teacher Education*, **4**, 113–118.

Hargie, O., Tittmar, H., and Dickson, D. (1978b). Microtraining: a systematic approach to social work practice, *Social Work Today*, **9**, 14–16.

Howard, J., and Gooderman, P. (1975). Closed Circuit TV in social work training, *Social Work Today*, **6**, 194–197.

Ivey, A. E. (1971). *Microcounselling: Innovation in Interviewing Training*, Charles C. Thomas, Springfield, Illinois.

Ivey, A. E., and Authier, R. J. (1978). *Microcounselling: Innovations in Interviewing, Counselling, Psychotherapy and Psychoeducation*, Charles C. Thomas, Springfield, Illinois.

Ivey, A., Normington, C., Miller, C., Morrill, W., and Haase, R. (1968). Microcounselling and attending behaviour: an approach to prepracticum counsellor training, *Journal of Counseling Psychology*, **15**, 1–12.

Jennerich, E. (1974). *Microcounselling in Library Education*, Unpublished doctoral dissertation, University of Pittsburgh.

Kissock, C. (1971). *A Study to Test the Value of MT in a Programme of Video Modelling Instruction* . . . , Ph.D. thesis, University of Minnesota.

Koran, J. J. (1969). The relative effects of classroom research and subsequent observational learning on the acquisition of questioning behaviour by pre-service elementary science teachers, *Journal of Research in Science Teaching*, **6** (3), 217–223.

Kriesel, H. (1975). *The Teaching of Basic Counselling Skills to Theology Students: A Comparison, within a Values Context, of the Microcounselling Paradigm with the Skills Practice Approach*, Unpublished dissertation, Claremont, School of Theology.

Lewis, C., Edgerton, N., and Parkinson, B. (1976). Interview training—finding the facts and minding the feelings, *Personnel Management*, **8**, 29–33.

Lewis, J., and Gibson, F. (1977). The teaching of some social work skills: towards a skills laboratory, *British Journal of Social Work*, **7**, 189–211.

MacLeod, G. (1977a). The effects of videotape and skill-related feedback on students' perceptions of their microteaching performance, in *Investigations of Microteaching* (Eds. D. MacIntyre, G. MacLeod and R. Griffiths), pp. 205–213, Croom Helm, London.

MacLeod, G. (1977b). A descriptive study of students' perceptions of their microteaching performance, in *Investigations of Microteaching* (Eds. D. MacIntyre, G. MacLeod and R. Griffiths), pp. 194–205, Croom Helm, London.

Malley, J., and Clift, J. (1980). *A Review and Annotated Bibliography of the Microteaching Technique*, Royal Melbourne Institute of Technology, Melbourne, Australia.

Mattarazo, R., Phillips, J., Wiens, A., and Saslow, G. (1965). Learning the art of interviewing: a study of what beginning students do and their patterns of change, *Psychotherapy: Theory, Research and Practice*, **2**, 49–60.

Miller, C., Morrill, W., and Uhlmann, M. (1970). Microcounselling: an experimental study of pre-practicum training in communicating test results, *Counsellor Education and Supervision*, **9**, 171–177.

Morrison, A., and MacIntyre, D. (1973). *Teachers and Teaching*, 2nd ed., Penguin Education, Harmondsworth.

Resnick, L. B., and Kiss, L. E. (1970). Discrimination training and feedback in shaping teacher behaviour, Paper presented at the Annual Meeting of AERA (ED 039 175).

Rosenshine, B. (1971). *Teaching Behaviours and Student Achievement*, IEA Studies, No. 1, NFER.

Saunders, E., and Saunders, C. (1980). *The Assessment of Teaching Practice*, Monograph, Ulster Polytechnic.

Smallwood, R. (1977). Using CCTV in management training: means of using recorded material to provide effective feedback in interpersonal skill training, *Journal of European Industrial Training*, **1**, 23–24.

Stones, E., and Morris, S. (1972). *Teaching Practice: Problems and Perspectives*, Methuen, London.

Tittmar, H. G., Hargie, O. D. W., and Dickson, D. A. (1977). Social skills training at Ulster College, *PLET*, **14**, 300–305.

Tittmar, H. G., Hargie, O. D. W., and Dickson, D. A. (1978). The moulding of health visitors: the evolved role played by minitraining, *Health Visitors Journal*, **51**, 130–136.

Travers, R. M. W. (1975). Empirically based teacher education, *The Educational Forum*, **39**, 417–433.

Turney, C., Cairns, L. G., Williams, G., Hatton, N., and Owens, L. C. (1975). *Sydney Micro Skills*, Series 2 handbook, Sydney University Press, Australia.

Turney, C., Clift, J., Dunkin, M., and Traill, R. (1973). *Microteaching Research, Theory and Practice*, Sydney University Press, Australia.

Wagner, A. (1973). Changing teacher behaviour: a comparison of MT and cognitive discrimination training, *Journal of Educational Psychology*, **64**, 299–305.

Ward, B. (1970). *A Survey of Microteaching in NCATE Accredited Secondary Education Programmes*, Stanford University, California.

Watts, M. W. (1973). Behaviour modelling and self-devaluation with video self-confrontation, *Journal of Educational Psychology*, **64**, 212–215.

Young, D. B. (1969). Modification of teacher behaviour using audio, video-taped models in a microteaching sequence, *Educational Leadership*, **26**, 394–403.

Using Video
Edited by P. W. Dowrick and S. J. Biggs
© 1983 John Wiley & Sons Ltd

Chapter 12

Video and the Community

Leonard Henny

Sociology Institute, Utrecht

The most attractive feature of the use of video in community processes is its possibility to provide feedback in a relatively spontaneous manner. This holds for larger communities, like a neighbourhood or an 'action group'. It becomes ever more applicable the smaller the size of the group which is involved.

Historical development

There is nothing new in using moving images in social processes. Shortly after the Russian revolution, in the early twenties, two pioneer Soviet film-makers, Alexander Medvedkin and Dziga Vertov, organized a tour with a filmtrain which was equipped with cameras and projection facilities. At each station along the railroad the two filmmakers showed films about the new ways of life in post-revolutionary Russia, calling upon the population to combat alcoholism and teaching the people to prevent tuberculosis. Medvedkin and Vertov, however, did not limit themselves to only showing films; they also made films on the spot, which they developed in a laboratory on the train, and showed to the stunned crowds gathered at the railway station the next day. Thus they made short documentaries about the working conditions in local factories, inviting the people to discuss these conditions and to think of improvements which could be proposed to the local managers before the train would move on to the next station (Henny, 1976).

Theory

The theoretical foundation for Medvedkin and Vertov's filmwork can be found in the treatises by Sergei Tretjakov (1972), who argued that a new society needs a new relation between the author/artist and the public. Tretjakov was the first to propagate 'deprofessionalization' in the arts and in community leadership. Art, including cinematography, would transcend through all aspects of daily life:

> The public should make its own art, and the artist should no longer be the idolized hero of the stage. The artist (or filmmaker) should be an 'operator', who fulfils the

function of a middleman between the people that make up the audience about its own messages. . . . There are uncounted numbers of unwritten books in the minds of the people. These books got stuck inside the people by default of their capacity to bring them out.

The artists' job, according to Tretjakov, is to make people write their own history, to stage their own drama.

The coming of Stalinism brought an early end to the transformation of Tretjakov's ideas into reality. But it is certainly not a historic accident that the near-revolutionary events of 1968 in Europe, in the United States and in Prague brought new life to the dreams of Tretjakov. The examples set by Medvedkin and Vertov became an inspiration to the media collectives which were founded in many countries both in Europe as well as in Japan in the later part of the sixties. Jean-Luc Godard, for instance, called his collective 'Groupe Dziga Vertov'. Another media collective in Bordeaux was named after Medvedkin. A Dutch media collective is called 'Kinoglas'. The 'post-1968' period coincided with the appearance of video equipment on the consumer market. Godard is credited for having been the first to propagate the use of video as a tool in political mediawork. In 1968 in Montreal, Canada, and in 1969 at the newly established university of Vincennes he introduced video in his media teaching. Soon the new medium became called 'guerilla video' or 'operative video'; the period of the great expectations concerning the 'liberating capabilities' of video had begun (Gauthier, 1979). Hans Magnus Enzensberger, at that time one of the leading theoreticians in the use of video, predicted in 1969 that video would become a major instrument in converting the one-way communication prevalent in the mass media (the 'Master's Voice' speaking to the millions) to a two-way communication between citizen groups within and among communities. In Enzensberger's view, video could make Bertold Brechts' hope come true that the mass media would one day no longer be merely a *distribution system*, serving the needs of a power élite, but would become a *communication system* which would contribute to the redistribution and equalization of information and thereby of power and even wealth in society.

Although the social movements supporting basic social change, as formulated by the leaders of the student and workers' revolt of 1968, did not obtain hegemony, their ideals and principles did not die out, but continued to operate in a legitimatized underground. In many parts of Europe, Japan and the United States the year 1968 was followed by a development of radical media groups. Some of the most well known of these are Newsreel in various cities in the United States, Crepac/Scopcolor in France, Liberation Films in England, Cineclub in Holland, the Filmcentrum in Stockholm, for instance. For the first years of their existence these groups worked primarily with film (16 mm or Super 8). A common factor was that they produced their films in close cooperation with the emerging protest movements: the anti-Vietnam war movement, the ecology movement and the civil rights movement (in the United States). Their ideal was to have citizen groups make their own productions, which become more of a possibility as video equipment became more available. One of the most successful efforts in this respect were the video programmes made in support of the strike at the Lip watch company in France in 1972, where for the first time workers occupied the factory and kept it going in spite of the decision by its owner to stop production and lay off the workers. The video programmes, partly made by the workers themselves, have contributed to the mobilization of national support which led to the victory of the Lip workers at the time.

The expectations by the early advocates that video could somehow become a revolutionary force that would lead to Marshall McLuhan's (1964) 'global village' did not, however, come true. Video continued to be used among local citizen action groups, but in comparison to the total use of video in society (in corporations, in government agencies, by the military and the police), the use of video for conscientization purposes (i.e. as a tool for generating discussions in an emancipatory manner among citizen groups) has remained relatively marginal (see *Videomagazin*, 1980).

Yet there are many ways in which video can be used and in which video is used in support of community-oriented activities. These uses vary along a broad range of applications inside and towards various communities. In this article we will give some attention to two examples: one is on a global level to help increase international understanding among various population groups in the global community; the other is the use of video by women as a means to strengthen the women's movement.

Video and the global community

Here we see a wide range of applications such as the use of video to help bridge the information gap concerning population groups at the other end of the globe or, for instance, the use to help improve the relationship among separately living population groups within a community, such as the relationships between migrants and the people of the 'host' community.

In most countries of the former colonial powers (Western Europe, the United States, Japan) there are citizen groups which take it as their major concern to inform their fellow countrymen about unacceptable social conditions in specific Third World countries. Such solidarity committees often make use of video as a means of informing people in the 'Welfare State' about the view of various liberation movements in the Third World. The film and videotape *Nicaragua, September 1978* by Frank Diamant, for instance, has fulfilled an important function in mobilizing moral support and financial funds for the reconstruction and for literacy campaigns in Nicaragua after the revolution in that Middle American country.

A more immediate connection with the situation in the Third World can be obtained through the making of video productions with refugees from the Third World. One example is the programme which the Manchester Film and Video Workshop made with refugees from Chile. The making of the videotape became a learning experience, both for the Chileans as well as for the British who helped them make the tape (Wade, 1980). The Chileans learned to break through their sectarian divisions. In the beginning only Chileans belonging to the MIR party were involved. As the project progressed they became aware that, in order to convince a British audience, it would be necessary to produce a tape that represented the broader Chilean community and not just one tiny segment thereof. It so happened that in the final version of the tape only non-MIR members appeared on the screen! For the British participants in the programme it was revealing to learn about the differences among the Chilean refugees and to realize that these differences could be overcome in the interest of the common objective: to reach a larger audience.

Refugees are not the only representatives of the Third World in Western Europe. Migrant workers coming from a wide range of Third World countries experience hardships in their new environments. Video groups have been instrumental in helping migrants to improve communication among themselves, as well as with the large population in the host country (see Pavelka, 1980).

Some theoretical notions concerning the applicability of video for migrants have been brought forward by Stig Svärd (1978), who comes to the conclusion that video is of special importance to migrants because they are 'at the bottom of the communication system in the new country', while most of their social problems are one way or another related to communication deficiencies. Svärd points out that migrants belong to at least three communication systems: that of their home country, that of the new community in which they are living and that of the migrants in the new country (see Figure 12.1). Within the migrant community there are again information sub-systems in accordance with the various nationalities and ethno-religions as well as political subdivisions that tend to exist among migrants from a particular country. Svärd sees four major communication tasks for the organizations that are the information channels for the various segments among the migrants:

1. Informing the authorities of the majority society of the conditions and the aspirations of the various migrant communities

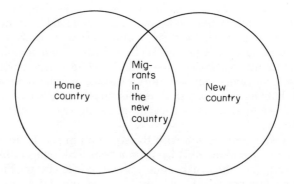

Figure 12.1 Migrants belong to at least three communication systems: that of their home country, that of the new country in which they are living and that of migrants in the new country

2. Channelling information from the majority society to the members of the minority organizations
3. Providing a link between migrants in the new society
4. Providing information and cultural productions, e.g. films, videotapes, from the home countries

Thus Yugoslav immigrants in Sweden are given access to videotapes made in Yugoslavia to inform them about developments in their home country and to keep them in contact with Yugoslav culture. These tapes are shown on a regular basis at community centres in Sweden where Yugoslavs meet each other. A good number of video groups have produced video programmes in close cooperation with immigrants, for instance to inform them about their rights in the host country. In Holland the Studio for Information of Minorities, which is fully sponsored by the Dutch government, produces video productions of this type in nine languages.

At a grass-roots level there are a number of examples where video has been used to bridge the gap between foreign migrants and the population of the host country. In Western Europe it is becoming more and more clear that many of the migrants who moved as temporary workers during the economic boom in the sixties from the Mediterranean countries to the North will not return to their home country, either for political reasons or because there is no employment for them in the countries from where they came. Now that there is an economic downturn in most of the northern West European countries, tensions are beginning to grow up, particularly in the larger cities, where there are considerable concentrations of workers of Moroccan, Turkish, Yugoslav or Iberian origin.

In Germany a number of community projects have been executed or started to improve the level of understanding of the Germans for the foreign immigrants. The Medien Operative in Berlin, for instance, is presently (1981) making a series of videotapes about Turkish workers in Berlin which draws special attention to the situation of the so-called second generation. One such example takes the case of the children of Turkish guestworkers, who are already acculturated to German society and are most probably never going to return to their home country, but at the same time experience considerable hostility when looking for jobs and for rooms in Germany. The same subject is being dealt with by media collectives in other European cities like Bremen (Weber, 1978), the Hague and Utrecht, Holland (Henny, 1980), Manchester, England (Wade, 1980), and Belleville, France (*Mon Oeil*, Collectif de Distribution, 1980).

The uses of video so far described all relate to intercultural and interethnic communication. Problems that keep presenting themselves in this area of video application are typically related to language differences. These difficulties are not limited to the differences in language as such, but to the 'ways of seeing' as they tend to be culturally defined in each ethnocultural community. Video, though itself also subject to being beset by the problem of understandability, has shown to be able to perform a bridging function between otherwise separately living communities, as it may concretize discussions that otherwise remain abstract and vague by lack of imagery about those living 'on the other side'.

Video and the women's movement

Another example of an area of social concern in which video has been widely used is the women's movement.

As Monika Hielscher (1979) points out, women have been victimized by the commercial mass media in (s)exploitation films and other media since the invention of photography. The emergence of the women's movement has in part been a reaction against the production of an image of women as submissive servile creatures. From 1970 on this image became redressed in the media. There was even a wave of commercial films on themes on women's issues. However, up to 1980 most of these films were made by male directors and all-male filmcrews, 'who seldom or never were able to communicate the authentic experiences and feelings of women. In many cases these "woman films" were mere expressions of male anxieties vis à vis the changing role of women in society'.

Given this development it is not surprising that at least some women were fascinated by the possibilities offered by video to effect the false portrayal of women by making their own films. According to Yvonne Mignot-Lefebvre (1979) video programmes made by women for women have the largest circulation in France, and most newly established video groups are women's video collectives, such as Videa, M'SAM and Insoumuses in Paris, Videoteuses in Montpellier and some others outside Paris. Women video collectives also exist in Italy, West Germany and Holland.

Some of the most effective videograms, in terms of distribution, are the video programmes made on the role of women in the occupation of the Lip factory in France: *La Lutte des Femmes à Lip et Ailleurs* (the women's struggle at Lip and elsewhere) and *Une Autre Façon de Militer: Le Groupe Femmes de Lip* (another way of militant action: the women's group at Lip). These videograms have been effective in rallying nationwide support for the workers at Lip and contributed to the conscientization about leadership and women's participation in the strike. Another videogram that has obtained national exposure in France is *Les Prostituées de Lyon Parlent*, about the occupation of the church of Saint-Nizier by a large group of prostitutes in 1975 to protest about the exploitation by their bullies and the battering by their clients. During the occupation, video monitors were placed on the sidewalks outside the church to inform the passers by of the reasons for the occupation. In the Year of the Woman, 1976, the women collective Insoumuses made a video programme *Maso et Miso Vont en Bateau* (Maso and Miso go in a boat), which protests in a humorous way the pretentions of the French officials who claim to speak for all women while actually reinforcing existing stereotypes and prejudices. In this case the video-tape gives a point-by-point correction from a feminist point of view on a speech by Françoise Giroud, the French Secretary of State in charge of women's affairs.

I have dealt relatively extensively with the French productions, primarily because the situation in France seems to be the most advanced as far as the activities of women in video-making is concerned. However, similar groups and productions have come to the fore in other countries, notably in West Germany where the first woman video collective called Bildwechsel (change of images) was established in Hamburg in 1980. In Germany, like in France, videograms produced by women protest against sexual exploitation, as for instance in the videogram *Gehst du zum Weihnachtsmarkt, vergiss die Peitsche nicht* (in case you go to the Christmas fair don't forget the whip). The tape documents a feminist action to stop the sale of whips, which are advertised by sexshops meant to be used by men for sadistic use on women. Other German tapes are concerned with the desired rupture of daily chores and routines for women (e.g. tapes by Rosemary Blank), the efforts to get men involved in sharing tasks normally done by women: *Frauen aktivieren Männer* (women activate men) and the role of women in the production process in unionization and in dealing with the issues of abortion (Videomagazin, 1977).

The use of video by women has as one of its primary objectives to promote 'another view on women by women'. The primarily male-oriented and male-determined image of women as portrayed in the mass media is now more and more offset by images generated by women—sometimes exclusively made by women and sometimes even destined 'for women's eyes only'. Some of the productions are explicitly feminist in language—verbally as well as visually. A first international feminist film and video festival, held in Amsterdam in 1981, has shown the breadth in scope of productions and purposes within the women's image-making movement.

Methods in community video

In the field of methodology we can see again a great variety in methods in the applications of video equipment. It ranges from individualized video, used for helping people to learn from seeing themselves, to the use of video as a tool in community organizing. Here we will limit ourselves again by presenting a few examples, focusing primarily on the organizing function of video in social processes.

Most uses of video in community work have been rather spontaneous and therefore not very methodological. There are, however, a few examples where the use of video has been made an integral part of a strategy in community action and development.

One of the most interesting ways in which video is used as a social feedback apparatus in community organizing is exemplified by the work of Workgroup 2000, an advocacy planning group in Amersfoort, Holland. This video unit makes up part of an Advocacy Planning Agency and has developed a systematic method of stimulating citizen participation in neighbourhood rehabilitation planning. The method is called 'community self-research through video'. The method consists of three basic stages, each of two months. The *first phase* is the making of a visual inventory of problems and wishes among residents. The video film which is the end result of this phase is shown to as many residents as possible, either in their own home or in community centres.

Thus in the *second phase* the residents react to the statements made by the fellow residents in the first tape. A second video programme summarizes what issues residents or resident groups have found concensus on and where there were 'hot issues' that led to controversies within the community. It contains a number of proposed improvements often supported with visual examples of solutions to urban problems in other cities. This second video programme is then shown, mainly in people's homes. It works as follows: one person invites in a number of neighbours and after showing the programme (on the family television set) an intense discussion automatically tends to develop which often goes on until late into the night. These discussions are always attended by members of the staff of Workgroup 2000 who take notes and try to encourage people to state their preferences and objections vis-à-vis the given proposals, as clearly as possible. The combined discussions normally lead to a list of priorities regarding a set of solutions, which in a *third phase* are tested at a community-wide meeting. Here again a third video programme is shown, which summarizes a set of concrete solutions. This videotape at a later stage is also shown to the municipal planning board which is to ratify any plans that are executed at the neighbourhood level.

The use of video provides a number of advantages in the citizen participation process. From the start, when the first scenes of the video programmes are shot, there is a direct interest on the part of the residents. The video programmes generate spontaneous reactions and make the problems more understandable and eventually the solutions more imaginable. The residents often complain that the first programme (phase 1) presents too negative a picture of the neighbourhood showing it as if it only had problems and as if there were nothing good in the neighbourhood. Consequently, the positive aspects of the neighbourhood tend to come spontaneously to the fore, and these are to be stressed and strengthened in the planning process.

One aspect that is very important in the production of the videotapes is the identifiability of what is shown on the television screen. On the one hand, this has the function that people get emotionally involved in the problems of and the possible solutions for their neighbourhood. On the other hand, there is also the danger that people get too distracted by looking at their neighbours, recognizing certain idiosyncracies and forgetting that the purpose of the showing is to produce concrete proposals instead of simply providing entertainment for the spectators! For that reason it often proves to be necessary to show a tape twice in order to help the spectators to overcome this handicap of 'seeing and being seen on television', which for most people is quite an experience, particularly when it happens for the first time.

There is another potential danger in using video in this manner—it may be used in a manipulative way. Using close-ups of cracks in deteriorated housing may create the idea that all housing in the neighbourhood are as delapidated as the house that is being filmed. The use of music or the application of special lenses or optical effects may create wrong impressions. Sometimes municipal officials want to censor certain parts of the films. But Workgroup 2000 has so far been able to retain the confidence of both residents and municipal authorities, which certainly is an accomplishment, considering the problems that generally beset citizen participation procedures in residential rehabilitation (Rutten and Snel, 1978).

Another example is the research by the European Centre for Social Welfare Training and Research in Vienna (Gauthier, 1979; Pavelka and Salaun, 1978). This Centre took the initiative to make an inventory of poverty in a peripheral region near the Czech border. In addition to compiling statistical data, the researchers also made video interviews with the indigent families as well as with local 'opinion leaders'. Midway in the research, the team members organized hearings in local bars in which the video interviews were shown. The villagers then discussed the opinions expressed by the persons interviewed and the living conditions as they appeared from the tape. These discussions were also filmed with video, which made it possible to add the people's reactions to the original material. Subsequently the original interviews and the reactions were edited onto one videotape.

This compilation tape was then presented in Vienna to representatives of organizations concerned with the alleviation of poverty in Austria. Representatives from the poverty stricken region were also present at this screening. The showing of the tape and subsequent explanation impressed the administration in Vienna (the press was also present) in such a manner that it resulted in a breakthrough of the long-standing apathy of the government. Video had accomplished something that the lengthy reporting about social abuses in Austria had not been able to achieve.

Thus video as an organizing tool has proven to be useful, provided that it plays only a part in a well thought-through strategy of community work. 'Instant video', as had happened in the sixties, has less and less chance of succeeding since people have become used to sophisticated video programmes on television. Very few people will nowadays watch a programme just because it is on video (as a novelty). They tend to only really watch it as long as it is watchable and/or relevant to their concerns.

Future developments

In the early eighties we see on the distribution side a vast network of tape-renting organizations spreading out, as well as the existence of local cable television stations which may to a certain degree broadcast video programmes with an orientation to community problems made at local video centres. The experience up to now has been that it requires special pressure to have cable television open its facilities to such use of their channel. There are some moderately successful experiments, notably in England and the Netherlands (Henny, 1980). However, much has still to be done to require real public access from the perspective of basic democratic action in the immediate future. On the production side we see a broadening scope of issues being dealt with through video in interactive processes. Many cities have public video centres where local groups or institutions like schools and libraries have access to equipment and know-how which enables them to make their own programmes.

Among the 'spontaneously' set up video collectives we see a great instability in their continuity. As some of the oldest groups disappear we also see the coming of many new ones. An important factor leading to instability is the continuous lack of funds to pay full-time staff members. It has been proven to be impossible to run a self-sufficient non-commercial video centre to deal with community needs. Most video groups are dependent upon subsidies from governmental and private agencies. In the Anglo-Saxon countries (the United Kingdom and United States in particular) funds for video work tend to be given exclusively by local arts councils or art foundations, which tend to have a set of criteria for the allocation of funds that does not correspond with the (social) aims of the videomakers. Many videomakers do consider themselves as artists, but generally their social engagement is for them more important than mere artistic production for the sake of artistic production. Many video-makers have become real 'artists' in the metaphorical sense in producing grant proposals!

On the European continent money for video work is partly provided by social welfare agencies. In France many video activities are financed under the heading of 'animation socio-culturelle'. The purpose of the agencies providing these funds tends to be 'integrative', i.e. to bring minority populations in line with social welfare policies, most often designed at the national level, which leaves relatively little room for helping people to find and maintain their own cultural identity.

In Holland and Scandinavia video centres have been able to obtain funds from a great variety of sources. This explains in part the relative variety in the ideological lines among the video centres in these countries. West Germany is a separate case as very little financial support can be obtained from the State. Worse, even, some video centres have been searched and harassed by the police, in the wake of the police search for the kidnappers of Schleyer whose kidnapping had once been 'demonstrated' on an amateur videotape (evidence enough for the Ministry of Justice to suspect video centres in West Germany of complicity with the Baader-Meinhoff group).

Let us conclude with a few speculations concerning the immediate future. In all it can be predicted that the 'video explosion' (i.e. the above proportional growth in the market of video equipment) will primarily take place in the commercial use of video, i.e. in commercial establishments, in education and government, and particularly in the home-video area (the recording and play-back of television programmes). In the mid eighties video is likely to become a home-movie substitute, thus replacing or adding to the Super 8 film cameras, now in use for filming the family.

Future support for community video will remain largely dependent upon the availability of government funds. In a later phase it is foreseeable, however, that video equipment will be so widely available in homes that some of this equipment will also be used for community relationships, as is now (though incidentally) the case with Super 8 film equipment.

In all countries almost all funding is agreed upon on a project-by-project basis. This hampers the continuity of the video centres. In some countries (notably Holland and France) some video centres are fully organized and financed by the government. This brings the advantage that more people can gain access to the use of video equipment on a continuous basis. The Studio for the Information on Minorities in Utrecht, Holland, is a good example. Here minority groups and organizations can, for a nominal fee produce video programmes with professional equipment and with the aid of professionals. A video library makes these tapes available to other groups who show an interest in seeing these video programmes (including schools and community centres). The disadvantage of full government sponsorship is, however, that the centre is apt to become an instrument of government policy and that the existence of such a centre is used as an alibi for not funding private initiatives that for one reason or another cannot be executed by the centralized studio. There is enough evidence to support the view that full government sponsorship tends to limit the possibilities for airing fundamental criticism on social issues, particularly whenever they are controversial, such as the energy debate and the issue of inter-racial relations in ethnically mixed population areas. Nevertheless, the social controversies of the eighties will certainly be portrayed and discussed with the help of video programmes, whether they are made with public or private funds. In addition there will be extra controversy on who controls the access to video facilities and what will be the boundaries set by those controlling these to the freedom of speech and image-making on video.

References

Enzensberger, Hans Magnus (1969). *Baukasten für die Theorie der Massenmedien*, Kursbuch 20, Suhrkamp Verlag, Frankfurt a/Main.

Gauthier, Guy (1979). Libres antennes, ecrans sauvages, in *Autrement*, nr. 17, Paris, February 1979.

Henny, Leonard (1976). Filmmakers as part of a revolutionary intelligentsia, in *The Intelligentsia and the Intellectuals* (Ed. Aleksander Gella), pp. 175–178, Sage, Beverley Hills, California.

Henny, Leonard (1980). *Community Video in Holland*, Sociological Institute, Utrecht, Holland.

Hielscher, Monika (1979). Frauen sehen Frauen, Frauen filmen Frauen (Women see women, women film women), *Videomagazin*, Hamburg, May 1979, pp. 49–52.

McLuhan, Marshall (1964). *Understanding Media*, McGraw-Hill, New York.

Mignot-Lefebvre, Yvonne. Quand les femmes ont pris les machines: l'appropriation de la technique vidéo par les femmes (When the women took charge of videotechnology), *Cinemaction*, No. 9, Paris, Autumn 1979, pp. 89–95.

Mon Oeil, Collectif de Distribution (1980). *Dix Années de Vidéo 1970–1980* (Annotated catalogue of videograms), distributed by *Mon Oeil*, 20 Rue d'Alembert, 75014 Paris, Tel. 327.6900.

Pavelka, Franz (1980). Migrants and video, report on an international workshop, *Eurosocial*, Newsletter No. 18 of the European Center for Social Welfare Training and Research, Vienna, Austria.

Pavelka, Franz, and Salaun, Herbert (1978). *Political Mediation through Video*, European Center for Social Welfare Training and Research, Vienna, Austria (Videotape).

Rutten, Jan, and Snel, Maarten (1978). 'Bewoners Zelfonderzoek, een vorm van action research', (Residents self research, a form of action research), in PLAN, Amsterdam, 1978, p. 30–35.

Svärd, Stig (1978). 'Migrants and Video, a working paper', in: ibid pp. 3–9.

Tretjakov, Sergei (1972). *Lyrik, Dramatik, Prosa*, published in Germany by Reclam Verlag, Leipzig (1972), originally published in Russian.

Videomagazin (1977). Videofilme zu Problemen und dem Kampf von Frauen (Videotapes on the problems on the struggle of Women). *Videomagazin*, Hamburg, West Germany, January 1977, pp. 57–58.

Videomagazin (1980). Bürgermedium Video? (Video a bourgeois medium?), *Videomagazin*, Special Issue, nr. 18/19, Hamburg, January 1980.

Wade, Graham (1980). *Street Video, An Account of Five Video Groups*, pp. 58–72, Blackthorn Press, Leicester.

PART III

INTRODUCTION (THEORY)

Simon J. Biggs

Theoretical perspectives on the process taking place when one sees oneself on tape have been few and far between. They might almost be thought of as ranging across a spectrum. One end consists of attempts to use video along lines dictated by an existing school of thought, while the other consists of attempts to write about video as a unique experience. This section begins with a brief survey of such attempts.

Perhaps the clearest examples of one end have arisen from workers using theories of interpersonal perception, most predominantly attribution theory and objective self-awareness theory. Attribution theorists point to the fact that people attend to cues in their environment while actively involved in achieving their ends. The observer who is watching this event would, on the other hand, focus upon these actors, and would attribute more responsibility to them than they would themselves. Video can be used to turn an actor into an observer, and thus change their attributions (see Storms, 1973; Wright and Fichten, 1976). An attempt to compare the viewer's perspective with that of an actor or an observer (Biggs, 1980) has recently concluded somewhat differently. Viewing may be similar to observing in terms of direct access to behaviour and similar to acting in terms of access to personal memories, but should not be equated with either. It is suggested that each of these perspectives involves a combination of factors emerging from differences between the self and others and between taking part in an event and looking on.

Adherents to objective self-awareness theory have concerned themselves with events which turn the person's attention inwards and those which focus attention onto tasks in the outside world. Video would be seen as an event which increases introspection and has been used as such by Duval (1976). In both cases a particular quality of video, changing perspective or increasing self-awareness, has been used to bring about a predetermined effect. The danger here is that this process could be used to explain the *total* value of video by using it in conformity with the theory rather than exploring the wide range of effects that it might evoke. The part may, in theoretical terms, be speaking for the whole.

Perhaps the closest case of a theory 'tailor-made' to video comes from Willener, Milliard and Ganty (1976). They claim that by a successive process of 'standing outside' and 'looking back in' viewers migrate away from the 'givens' of a role or situation. By so doing viewers become aware of latent possibilities for action. A dialectical perspective emerges from this whereby viewers become able to step into, out of and against existing states of affairs. The experience of video is seen by these workers as the psychic equivalent of the moebius strip and as being of great complexity.

In the present section each contributor has started by examining an existing perspective which has been used as a springboard to understanding video itself. Each has explored the particular value of the medium and attempted to suggest how the emerging theoretical insights might influence practice and the rights and obligations of both the viewer and the video user.

Trower and Kieley have begun by noting the negative effects that video feedback can have on self-esteem. These results would be predicted by objective self-awareness theory and the analysis which follows hinges upon a distinction between public and private perspectives in self- and interpersonal perception. Concrete suggestions have been made for interventions which incorporate aspects of rational–emotive therapy in order to balance biases in perception created by the medium itself.

Shotter has used existing concepts from hermeneutics to throw light on the special case of seeing oneself. He has emphasized that behaviour is both directed and intentional, in the case of both viewers and observers. He has opposed this view to that held by the attribution theorists. Shotter has been particularly concerned by the lack of spontenaity that such representations of the self can produce, and emphasizes the reciprocal duties that the parties involved must respect.

Finally, Biggs has explored the relationship between the video user, the actor who has become a viewer and the context in which they find themselves. He has attempted to unmask some of the implicit power relationships in situations where people are being taped or are watching tapes of themselves and of other people. There follows an analysis of the ways in which video can enhance or inhibit change, and suggestions have been made which may make the former most likely.

References

Biggs, S. J. (1980). The me I see; acting, participating, observing and viewing and their implications for video feedback, *Human Relations*, **33**, 575–588.

Duval, S. (1976). Conformity as a function of personal novelty and being reminded of the object status of the self, *Journal of Experimental Social Psychology*, **12**, 87–98.

Storms, M. (1973). Videotape and the attribution process: reversing actors and observers points of view, *Journal of Personality and Social Psychology*, **16**, 319–328.

Willener, A., Milliard, G., and Gantry, A. (1976). *Videology and Utopia*, Routledge and Kegan Paul, London.

Wright, J., and Fichten, C. (1976). Denial of responsibility, videotape-feedback and attribution theory: relevance to behavioural marital therapy, *Canadian Psychological Review*, **17**, 219–230.

Using Video
Edited by P. W. Dowrick and S. J. Biggs
© 1983 John Wiley & Sons Ltd

Chapter 13

Video Feedback: Help or Hindrance? A Review and Analysis

Peter Trower

and

Brian Kiely

Hollymoor Hospital, Birmingham

In this chapter we shall be concerned with the use of video feedback (VF) as a therapy technique with mental health clients, either in its own right or as an adjunct to other techniques, such as social skills training. The main question—as with all therapy techniques—concerns the efficacy of VF. Does it produce positive, negative or neutral effects? The main question spawns a number of corollary ones. What type of client does it affect and in what way? Which aspects of its use produce positive versus negative results? We shall propose that there are some empirical grounds, and substantial theoretical grounds, for believing that VF can have beneficial effects but may also be harmful if used in certain ways. It seems to us vitally important to try to explain and predict such effects, and the main purpose of this chapter will be to develop some principles.

The chapter will be structured in the following way: firstly, the known therapeutic consequences of VF will be briefly reviewed; secondly, we shall selectively review some cognitive social-psychological theories and attendant research which help to explain the cognitive and perceptual processes believed to underlie the occurrence of beneficial or harmful outcomes. Finally, we shall pull together the various strands in a comprehensive account that attempts to predict the conditions and circumstances in which VF may have negative effects. We shall also suggest therapy procedures for overcoming some of the traps inherent in the use of VF.

The arguments—for and against

The practical usefulness of video lies in the hardware—an exact and immediately available film record of the person in interaction and thus a unique source of information about performance. Many behaviour change therapies rely upon objective and measurable feedback which the patient can monitor precisely, reliably and immediately (Kanfer, 1970). The potential benefit of VF is that it brings an apparently objective feedback technology to the complex area of social behaviour. In other words, VF presents an apparent source of unbiased, raw data feedback, which gives the actor/viewer the opportunity to identify previously unknown or unconscious elements of behaviour. Since so much social behaviour is automated and 'mindless' (Langer, 1978) such identification is a necessary step before self-initiated behaviour change can take place. There seems to be a strong, and widely believed, *prima facie* case for the effectiveness of VF as a therapy technique for helping to produce positive change.

However, we question this apparent face validity of VF, which may deceive therapists and others into making the common assumption that VF enables the self-viewer to perceive his behaviour 'objectively'.

We put forward a null hypothesis—that VF can be consistently ineffective in bringing about therapeutic change and may even be harmful. A summary of our argument is as follows: VF is not perceived as unbiased, raw data information but is *interpreted* both by the self-viewer and observers. Many psychiatric patients, such as depressives (Beck, 1976), characteristically have cognitive sets within which they *negatively distort* self-related information and apply the same interpretive bias to VF. Such patients draw *evaluative inferences* of personal failure, helplessness, etc., from negative information, experience lowered self-esteem and either increased depression or anxiety and worsening of performance. Finally, the deteriorated performance provides further confirmatory evidence of the negative self-evaluation, thus completing a loop which is best described as a self-fulfilling prophecy (Trower, 1981).

The evidence

We turn firstly to the empirical evidence regarding the efficacy of VF. Recent reviews of the literature relating to the clinical uses of VF have struck a very cautious tone regarding its therapeutic efficacy (e.g. Bailey and Sowder, 1970; Hung and Rosenthal, 1978). In part this caution is a consequence of the poor methodology of the clinical studies to date, a situation which we feel largely precludes meaningful interpretation of the literature taken as a whole. However, the present brief and selective account of VF in therapy will introduce the reader to a few of the possible consequences of VF. The above reviews are recommended for more detailed accounts of the literature.

There appears to be increasing awareness that VF is not inevitably therapeutic. One of the commonest reported consequences of VF is that a wide range of clients find it aversive and anxiety-provoking (e.g. Carrere, 1954; Cornelison and Arsenian, 1960; Geertsma and Reivich, 1965; Moore, Charnell and West, 1965). Danet (1968) makes the point that some patients may not be strong enough to 'deal with the strong emotional impact and anxiety arousal inherent in any self-image experience' (p. 256). Evidence in support of this contention is not hard to find. Reivich and Geertsma (1968) found that many patients' symptoms worsened in reaction to VF, the behaviour of schizophrenics becoming more bizarre, depressives more self-deprecating and neurotics responding with their own 'characteristic defensive styles'.

A second study, this time involving couples engaged in marital therapy, reported that the use of VF produced significantly worse results than were obtained with couples who did not receive VF—of nine couples shown VF, two men committed suicide and four couples separated (Alkire and Brunse, 1974). While the results of both these studies were relatively severe in certain cases, some clients did show improvement in the VF condition of each. Indeed, some authors have viewed the shock properties of VF as beneficial in that it seemingly aroused and motivated clients to change and improve, e.g. Cornelison and Arsenian (1960) and Moore, Charnell and West (1965) with a wide range of in-patients, and Sobell, Sobell and Mills (1973) with alcoholics.

Other consequences of VF relate more directly to the self-perception process. In marital therapy, for example, VF increased the willingness of one or both partners to blame themselves for their marital problems (Alger and Hogan, 1966; Kagan, Krathwohl and Miller, 1963). With a variety of in-patients VF improved the accuracy of their self-description, a goal viewed by some clinicians as an important component of successful psychotherapy (Braucht, 1970; Geertsma and Reivich, 1965). Very probably related to such changes in self-descriptive accuracy is the effect VF has been discovered to have on an individual's self-esteem. In one study, the self-esteem of alcoholics fell as a consequence of VF, although no changes in drinking behaviour were subsequently found (Paredes and coauthors, 1969). In similar vein, VF was again found ineffectual in changing clients' behaviour, this time in assertive training (Brown, 1980). Additionally, and according to Bandura (1977) just as important for subsequent therapeutic outcome, VF lowered clients' self-efficacy expectations.

In reviewing the various studies we find a confusing diversity of effects of VF. Generally acknowledged as aversive and anxiety-arousing, VF can prove beneficial, anti-therapeutic or ineffectual, to some extent irrespective of the nature of the client group. As indicated by the studies of Alkire and Brunse (1974) and Reivich and Geertsma (1968), among others, individual differences exist which can influence quite markedly the subsequent effect of VF. Such differences include severity of disorder and length of hospitalization (Braucht, 1970), and the individual's characteristic defence mechanisms (Kipper and Ginot, 1979). Finally, one other source of variation in the effectiveness of VF is the use of therapist focusing by which the self-viewer's attention is guided to the relevant aspects of the VF. In many instances such focusing has proven beneficial and on occasion crucial to the therapeutic efficacy of VF (e.g. Cavior and Marabotto, 1976; Edelson and Seidman, 1975; Geertsma and Reivich, 1965).

Cognitive processes in perception and performance

The body of research on the effects of video in no way straightforwardly supports the 'face validity' hypothesis of VF as an effective therapy instrument per se, and to understand better the fact that VF can under varying circumstances produce a range of effects—positive, neutral *and* negative—we need to explore some of the complex perceptual and cognitive processes involved in video viewing, which after all is a special case of *person perception*. Our argument is that a viewer/actor does not perceive VF—the stimulus—as objective data to which he directly and predictably responds, as in an S-R model, but interprets the information in certain ways, in accordance with known principles of cognitive processing, with predictable behavioural and emotional effects.

Psychologists broadly encompassed in the 'cognitive social' domain have for many years theorized and demonstrated that individuals perceive stimuli in terms of cognitive categories which served to select and group information according to rules. Bruner (1957) suggests perception is best conceived as an act of categorization. Since these categories imply rules for classifying information, the perceiver is seen as actively deciding whether new information would allow her to place the stimulus person into a particular personality category. This is the view of the person as a perceptual problem-solver—she approaches each situation with an expectation or hypothesis and tests this against 'reality'. In Asch's (1946) classic study, students organized standard stimulus materials in ways which were internally consistent but quite different between individuals, and often including qualities not in the original. Bruner and Tagiuri (1954) suggest that perceivers employ implicit personality theories to guide their inferences, while Kelly (1955) calls these hypotheses *personal constructs*, which together form a consistent construct system or system of beliefs about the world. In similar vein, Mischel (1973) develops the notion of encoding strategies and personal constructs, by means of which people make personality judgements about self and others on the basis of behavioural, physical and other cues, i.e. people make inferences from events and actions to 'underlying' traits or dispositions (e.g. from talking a lot to extraversion, or from smoking to oral fixation). Since personal constructs greatly mediate the impact raw 'stimuli' have on an individual, they are clearly important in social learning and social behaviour.

The classic attribution theories

Categorization of stimuli is, however, only one of the ways that individuals try to explain and understand their social worlds, and the study of these processes has given rise to a number of influential and sophisticated models grouped under 'attribution theory'. To understand the significance of VF we must further consider these processes.

One of the tasks confronting the social observer is to identify the cause to which some action can best be *attributed*—a causal judgement. A second related task is to make inferences about the *attributes* of a person or situation—a social inference. A third task is to make prediction about future actions and outcomes—a social prediction (Ross, 1978). Heider (1958) is widely credited with first clearly formulating the causal judgement problem. He asserted that the amount of personal causality attributed to an actor would depend upon the observer's estimate of the balance between personal compared with environmental forces. An event would be attributed to an 'internal' disposition on the basis of judged ability, traits and motives, etc., and to an 'external' situation on the basis of task difficulty, luck, incentive, peer pressure, etc.

Looking at the problem in this way, how do people make inferences about the *attributes* of persons or situations *from* an action (or effect)? Jones and Davis

(1965) put forward a theory of correspondent inferences in which high correspondence means that an action, say of dominance, is believed to infer (correspond to) an internal disposition of dominance. The factors which lead a perceiver to such an inference include not only the actor's intention, ability and knowledge, but also non-common effects (effects which could not equally be attributed to a number of other causes) and low social desirability of effects. One may conceptualize this as out-of-role behaviour, since in-role behaviour (conforming to social norms, etc.) is uninformative about the individual. Two further factors claimed to increase dispositional inference are increased 'hedonic relevance' of the action to the perceiver, i.e. one that tends to promote or thwart the perceiver's purposes, and 'personalistic' in that it was judged to be uniquely conditioned by the perceiver's presence if the perceiver believes himself to be the recipient of the actor's intentions.

A further major development of attribution theory is made by Kelley (1967). He argues that people make causal attributions by means of an intuitive version of the analysis of variance, i.e. effects are attributed to those causal factors—self/other persons, situations and entities—with which they covary. Thus an action will be attributed to a person if uniquely and consistently associated with him, but to a situation if people in general consistently and concensually have the same reaction. In addition, people develop causal schemata (Kelley, 1972), i.e. assumed patterns based on learned assumptions about the world, with which they deal rapidly with new situations in which they have limited information.

Recent emphasis in attribution research has, however, tended to move away from logical schemata towards a more thorough understanding of the sources of systematic bias or distortion in judgements that lead people to 'misinterpret events and hence to behave in ways that are personally maladaptive, socially pernicious . . .' (Ross, 1978, p. 345).

The first identified (Heider, 1958) and most often cited bias is the tendency for attributers to underestimate the impact of situational factors and overestimate dispositional factors in controlling behaviour.

Another general area of bias is noted by Bem (1972) and Kelley (1967) in their comparisons of interpersonal and self-perception. They argue that the process of drawing inferences about the self is similar, if not identical, to that used in arriving at inferences about others, but for the products of these separate processes to be comparable, the same information would need to be available for the self as for another. That this is not necessarily the case has been recognized by both Kelley and Bem as a potential and consistent source of attributional bias which results in an attributional differential being created between actors and observers.

Jones and Nisbett (1972) have extended this latter point to include the possibility that not only is the information available to actors and observers differentially distributed between them, it is also differentially processed by them. The evidence of the available information varies, dependent on their differing perspectives, such that they selectively attend to that which is most prominent in the visual field. Elaborating what was to be called 'the fundamental attribution error' (Ross, 1978), Jones and Nisbett propose, on the basis of these divergent perspectives, that there is an enduring tendency for observers to attribute the behavioural choices of actors to internal dispositions whereas the actors attribute the same choices to situational forces.

The self-awareness theories

This said, it is to objective self-awareness theory, as originally stated by Duval and Wicklund (1972) and revised by Wicklund (1975) that we turn for a framework in which to explain not only these actor–observer differences but also for a possible description and explanation of the self-viewer's perspective. Objective self-awareness theorists (e.g. Duval and Wicklund, 1973; Duval and Hensley, 1976) agree with Jones and Nisbett that attentional focus is a crucial determinant of subsequent attributions, as shown in a study by Duval, Hensley and Cook (in Duval and Hensley, 1976, pp. 184–186). However, they view the differences between actors and observers as less static. The usual attentional focus of individuals is seen much as that described by Jones and Nisbett—i.e. actors typically focus attention on their environment whereas observers concentrate on the actor. Extending this, Duval and Wicklund believe that the respective attentional focus can be manipulated within the total situation (i.e. without altering the individual's access to any aspect of the situation) with corresponding changes in each individual's attentional perspective. Self-focusing of the actor's usual external focus produces a state characterized by an awareness of the self's object status in the world. The term 'objective self-awareness' is used to draw a contrast with the usual state of 'subjective self-awareness' in which the self is only the subject, not the focus, of conscious attention. Situational factors bringing about an increase in the proportion of total attention spent self-focused include the presence of mirrors (Carver and Scheier, 1978) and cameras (Davis and Brock, 1975). It follows from the attention–attribution idea that such increased self-focused attention results in increased self-attribution, and this is shown in experiments with mirrors (Duval, 1972; Duval and Wicklund, 1973), and video images (Arkin and Duval, 1975; Duval, Hensley and Neely, 1975; Storms, 1973). In contrast, it is also possible to increase the proportion of total attention focused on the environment, with a corresponding increase in attributions to the environment by both actors and/or observers (Arkin and Duval, 1975; Duval and Wicklund, 1973). By combining increased attention to self by actors and decreased attention to actors by observers, three studies have reversed the usual actor–observer difference (Arkin and Duval, 1975; Biggs, 1979; Storms, 1973). Actors shown video images of themselves were significantly more dispositional in their attributions than observers whose attention had been directed away from the actors. Indeed, in two studies there was a non-significant tendency for self-viewing actors to overdispositionalize relative to 'normal' observers. These findings serve to underline the flexibility of the attributional process, regardless of perspectives.

While VF has been shown to alter the actor's attributional perspectives such that it resembles that of the observer, this resemblance may be superficial. Firstly, the self-viewer may exhibit self-serving biases in his perceptual processing, much as does the actor and the observer. By way of an example, Biggs (1979) found that not only did self-viewers' attributions to self increase, they were more likely to do so when their behaviour was favourable. This is a point we will return to later when we discuss disproportional influences on attribution. Secondly, a change in the attributional perspectives is far from being the only consequence of objective self-awareness. Another important result of self-focusing is the onset of evaluation. As Sartre (1956) points out in his distinction between the planes of action and reflection, self-evaluative thought is considered to be possible only when the self is viewed as an object, for only then can it stand as one of the terms in an evaluative relation. When objectively self-aware, the individual is thought to be more aware of both his actual performance and his standards. To the extent that a self-ideal discrepancy exists, self-focusing will enhance the effect usually felt as a consequence, be it positive or negative (Scheier, 1976; Scheier and Carver, 1977). A further consequence of self-focused self-evaluation is a change in self-esteem in the direction of the discrepancy (Ickes, Wicklund and Ferris, 1973). One important qualification to both these latter points is the existence of a negativity bias such that self-awareness exacerbates the changes in affect (Kanouse and Hanson, 1972) and self-esteem (Ickes, Wicklund and Ferris, 1973) which are consequent on discrepancies. In addition to the initial reaction of self-evaluation, self-focusing on negative discrepancies produces behaviour directed at avoiding the self-focusing stimuli (Duval, Wicklund and Fine, in Duval and Wicklund, 1972, pp. 16–21), the degree of avoidance engaged being proportional to the size of the discrepancy and the time spent self-focused (Gibbons and Wicklund, 1976). Finally, in the case of negative discrepancies, an inescapable objective self-awareness will result in attempted discrepancy reduction such that behaviour will change in the direction of the salient standards (e.g. Carver, 1974; Duval, Hensley and Neely, 1975; Scheier, Fenigstein and Buss, 1974). However, in certain cases discrepancy reduction fails to take place because of an overconcern with self-evaluation due to objective self-awareness, producing disruptions in the smooth flow of behaviour (Liebling and Shaver, 1973).

While Duval and Wicklund view the determinants of attentional focus to be entirely situational, Buss (1980) has proposed the existence of a dispositional influence, namely the trait of self-consciousness as measured as a scale developed by Fenigstein, Scheier and Buss (1975). This is seen as the enduring tendency of persons to direct attention to either the private, unshared aspects of the self such as emotions and bodily processes (private self-consciousness) or to their public, observable aspects such as appearance or behaviour (public self-consciousness). Given circumstances which increase attention to the private self (e.g. introspection, which the authors suggest may be brought about by the client role in therapy) or the public self (e.g. VF as suggested by Buss), the theory predicts that the effects of such increased attention will be most marked in individuals high in the corresponding trait. High private self-consciousness has been found to result in the intensification of affective states following mood induction (Scheier and Carver, 1977) and increased self-attribution in imagined situations (Buss and Scheier, 1976), these effects being independent of the individuals' level of public self-consciousness. In its turn, high public self-consciousness is held to increase awareness of discrepancies in the public aspects of the self, decrease self-esteem and increase attributions to the self. For example, Fenigstein (1979) found that when public self-conscious individuals were rejected by a peer group—a public event—they were much more likely to accept responsibility for the rejection than low self-conscious individuals. More relevant to the therapeutic setting, specifically the use of VF, Kiely (1980) reported that high public self-conscious males attributed more to themselves in a social interaction when a camera was present than did low self-conscious males, as predicted by Buss (1980). These results were qualified, however, by an unpredicted trend in the opposite direction by female subjects. While such sex differences are not predicted by self-consciousness theory, Kiely suggested that the results obtained were confounded by the sex difference in attributional style noted by Ickes and Layden (1978). Put crudely, women were found to attribute success to luck or others and failure to themselves, in contrast to men who attributed success to themselves and blamed fate or others for failure. The influence of a subject's sex paralleled findings relating to the subject's level of self-esteem—the attributions of high self-esteem subjects, regardless of sex, resembled those of males, whereas those of low self-esteem subjects resembled those of females.

The existence of such enduring influences on attributions fits well with our earlier discussion of biases and errors in the attribution process and also with the findings of individual differences in relation to VF in therapy. The importance of such attributional styles for our discussion of VF in therapy is highlighted by the growing literature which views attributional styles as central to mental health. For example, Beck (1967) talks of depressives as exhibiting an attributional style which is consistently distorting, leading to 'a bias against themselves' (p. 234); as such, their style is very similar to that displayed by the low self-esteem subjects in Ickes and Layden's study (1978). Relatedly, Kiely (1980) carried out a study which sought to explore the attributional style, should it exist, of individuals characterized by a high level of neuroticism (as measured by Eysenck and Eysenck's EPI, 1964) and to gauge the effect of VF on this style. High neuroticism (N) subjects were found to have a very markedly more external focus of attribution than low N subjects in the absence of VF. This finding fits well both the psychoanalytic literature relating to the neurotic's external focus of blame, identified as a defence mechanism to protect the idealized self-image (e.g. Yachnes, 1975), and also Heider's (1958) acceptance of psychodynamic influences on the attribution process. The effect of VF, however, was to cause high N subjects to become significantly more internal in their attribution than in the no VF condition, a complete reversal of the previous high N to low N difference being noted. That such a sharp shift in attributional focus should occur in high N subjects was explained tentatively by Kiely in terms of a collapse of their defensive style in the face of the awareness inducing properties of VF. In the case of neurotics, as opposed to those showing a high measure of neuroticism, it would be expected that the effect of VF was less marked due to the relatively stronger defensive style.

In summary, we have briefly reviewed attributional theories and other models of cognitive processing to help understand how social information in the form of VF is interpreted. We have argued that VF is not perceived by the self-viewer objectively as raw data, but like any other social information is cognitively processed and interpreted. Included in the factors which influence this processing is the individual's attributional style.

Public versus private perspectives

The first assumption we questioned was that VF is received 'objectively' as raw data. We now turn to question a second assumption (see also Biggs, 1980), also intuitively 'obvious' and probably widely believed, that the self-viewer will have the same perspective as others and therefore form the same impression of himself that others form of him. We need firstly to identify and define this 'public perspective' and then consider whether it is shared by the self-viewer, since if it is not, this will have important consequences for the use of video.

Firstly, the *public perspective* (how we view others) probably contains the 'fundamental attribution error' (Ross, 1978), namely the tendency to overestimate the importance of personal or dispositional factors and neglect situational forces. It would seem that VF brings the self-viewer to make the same error—perhaps even more so on occasion (Arkin and Duval, 1975; Biggs, 1979; Storms, 1973). Secondly, the public perspective entails the role of observer (Argyle and Williams, 1969) and therefore does not involve objective self-awareness (Duval and Wicklund, 1972) or public or private self-consciousness (Buss, 1980). Thirdly, the observer only has 'public' behavioural information available, and by virtue of motivational and other complex attributional biases (Ross, 1978) will tend to identify 'attributes' quite different in kind from the self-viewer. Nonetheless, the observer will probably assume, under certain conditions, that the self-viewer will share the public perspective, discounting or forgetting the role of self-consciousness, etc.

Let us consider in more detail the self-viewer's, or *private, perspective*. Firstly, he will probably reverse his usual, situational attributional tendencies and, like the observer, become dispositional. The difference is that seeing himself as the responsible 'personality' will come by way of a surprising or even 'shocking' discovery. Secondly, he will immediately be in a state of self-awareness. Thirdly, he will be in possession of both internal and external information with which to form self-dispositional judgements (Biggs, 1980).

Buss (1980) would argue that the self-viewer becomes aware at this point of his public image or self as a social object and would make comparisons between what he sees and his personal (internal) standards; where he found a discrepancy, he may experience social anxiety, embarrassment, shyness and related feelings, and a loss of self-esteem.

Goffman (1969) has also developed the notion of self as a social object in his book *The Presentation of Self in Everyday Life*. He argues in his dramaturgical model that a person is on stage for others and 'presents' himself by various public manipulations, has front regions where the presentation goes on and back regions which he tries to keep hidden from public view by various deceits and concealments. At certain points the individual becomes afraid that back regions are being exposed, which cause the individual embarrassment or extreme anxiety. It may be the fear of failure or collapse in self-presentation that is the basis of social phobia. It may be that VF presents to the individual precisely the kind of information about his behaviour which he construes as exposure.

Drawing on Goffman's presentation of self, and also on objective self-awareness theory, the following account might be argued. The individual constantly works to present himself when with others, but does not normally reflect upon this, or indeed any other aspect of self as object, unless something happens to remind him of his status as a social object. Video feedback not only does this but provides him with precisely the information he needs (and normally does not have in polite society) to inspect the contents, as it were, of his self-presentation. Motivated to manage his impressions competently, he will focus upon possible shortcomings in behaviour, discrepancies between his internal standards and actual achievements. Such perceived imperfections or faults in presentation might be speech errors, accent, autistic gestures, a whole range of 'unskilled' or inappropriate behaviour like gaze aversion, blank or hostile expression, gaffes, and so on. One obvious group for inspection, which Biggs (1979) has researched, would be 'leakage' cues to anxiety, which Ekman and Friesen (1969) show are mainly displayed in leg and foot movements, i.e. less controlled areas, but in social phobics might be blushing and shaking, where control breaks down partially or completely in a panic attack.

The 'shock' of first having VF, noted in the clinical literature, illustrates that self-monitoring is the immediate reaction—the primary response—to such feedback. The imperfections seem to leap out and are the salient features for selective attention and memory.

Not only does the individual perceive faulty presentation cues in himself, but believes others perceive them too, since he assumes their salience will be obvious in the public arena. He also assumes others will invest such failure with the same degree and kind of negative evaluation that he does. In time these cues recede, either by habituation (Wicklund, 1975) or self-modification, and the public perspective may take over. This change in perspectives may be the secondary response. However, neither habituation nor modification may take place in some clients, e.g. social phobics.

We suggest that the individual views himself from the private perspective and is not aware, at least initially, of the public perspective, but indeed assumes that others will share his private view and therefore perceive the same failings in his self-presentation, rendering him transparent. In contrast, others view the individual from the public perspective and are not aware of the individual's private perspective (unless certain conditions hold, certain thresholds crossed), but indeed assume that the individual shares the public perspective and therefore forms the same dispositional impression that they do.

If there are divergent perspectives, the self-viewer will be attending to different aspects of his behaviour or, if the same, interpreting (reacting to) them differently. Biggs (1979) has indeed found differences of this kind. One implication here is that the self-viewer will fail to attend to the relevant interpersonal (i.e. public perspective) cues, but will vigilantly attend to presentation cues which are not even perceived by the other, and the value of video feedback will be undermined. Others (particularly therapists) will assume he *is* attending to relevant cues and may fail to provide corrective guidance, the value of which was illustrated in the clinical literature mentioned earlier.

The individual's belief that others will adopt his private perspective and 'see through him' is understandable but unlikely, in most circumstances, to be true. Firstly, he knows the impression he is trying to manage and how far he falls short, but this is information to which he has priviliged access and others will have no such evidence (with certain notable exceptions, e.g. within families and friendship groups). Secondly, the other will be occupied primarily in processing the individual's speech and the mainly non-verbal cues to personality, attitudes and other dispositions. Given that consciousness has a limited information processing capacity, faulty elements will be the least likely to be processed, unless severe enough or in other ways forced into prominence. As Dittman (1978) says, 'nonfluencies are far more frequent than we realise, since the listener very kindly edits them out as he tries to follow what the speaker is saying'.

Goffman (1969) says that people go to some length, probably unconsciously, to help any accepted member of the community to maintain face by ignoring faulty performances or giving justificatory accounts. Finally, the other person does not have the same emotional investment in another individual's disfluencies and will be less likely to attend to them, remember them or evaluate them. However, against the evidence, the self-viewer will persist in believing that they are transparent to others in all their imperfections.

We argue then that the self-viewer perceives himself on video quite differently from others. This brings us to our third point: because of this private, self-aware perspective, VF may, in certain individuals, confirm negative self-beliefs, lower self-esteem, increase levels of anxiety and consequently may damage 'mental health'.

Referring back to our earlier discussion of objective self-awareness theory, a major consequence of such self-awareness is an increased recognition of any personal shortcomings which may exist, self-focused attention being found aversive as a result. Wicklund (1975) describes how a young man, following some severe criticism of his timidity, which provoked self-awareness, withdrew into solitude to escape this self-focused attention. Whenever circumstances arose to remind him of his self-status, e.g. being with other people or on seeing a reflection of himself, say via VF, his attention would turn towards that salient trait on which he was originally berated, i.e. his timidity. In other words, salient traits such as timidity will receive more attention as a consequence of VF than they would in its absence. Another of the reactions to self-focused attention mentioned earlier is the attempt to escape from it, since it is aversive and anxiety-provoking. In cases of the chronically shy, for example, this could lead to social withdrawal, while for alcoholics it might serve to increase their drinking, their habitual response to anxiety. A third reaction is motivation to reduce the discrepancy—except in depressives, say, who may have no hope of doing so.

Our contention is that so-called normals will cope with, and benefit from, VF but that certain vulnerable individuals, including many patients, may not—hence the wide range of results noted in the clinical literature. One distinguishing characteristic of such vulnerability is the disposition to be high in self-consciousness. This would include those with a 'shyness' trait (Crozier, 1979), who, among other things, express fears of looking foolish in front of others, and certain patient groups, particularly social phobics. As follows from self-consciousness theory (Buss, 1980), these dispositionally self-conscious individuals (both private and public) will be most affected by situations and roles which cause self-reflection, e.g. patient status in skills training and other

psychiatric settings, including the use of VF. As already noted, the consequences of such high self-consciousness include an increased tendency to see
themselves as causal agents of an event (e.g. Buss and Scheier, 1976; Fenigstein,
1979) and exacerbation of an effect such as depression (Scheier and Carver,
1977).

Another characteristic of the vulnerable is low self-esteem which Ickes and
Layden (1978) have associated with a distinct self-blaming attributional style.
The low self-esteem subject is typical of a broad range of psychiatric patients,
particularly depressives and anxiety states. It is such a person who present
most worry with VF. Videotaping and VF may simply produce worse performance than normal in such individuals. Brockner and Hulton (1978) found low
self-esteem subjects performed worse than high self-esteem subjects in front of
an audience, no differently in a control condition and *better* when instructed to
concentrate on a task (which reduced self-consciousness). Add this to the
well-substantiated finding that low self-esteem subjects, e.g. depressed clients,
selectively attend to self-defaming information, and we have the possibility that
video simply exacerbates a particular vicious circle: patients made self-aware
on camera focus on negative attributes, suffer a loss of motivation, which causes
a reduction in effort and give less attention to tasks, producing worse results,
confirming initial negative beliefs.

This is one example of an 'exacerbation cycle'—an explanatory model ex-
pounded by Storms and McCaul (1976). They say that any distinctive dysfunctional behaviour such as insomnia, stuttering or sexual impotence (their
examples) produce objective self-awareness, which as we have seen usually
leads to increased negative affect about the self as well as dispositional attributions to the self. The outcome is a negative self-labelling or self-diagnosis of
inadequacy, or 'mental illness', or worse. It may be that video provides just
the self-focusing effect together with just the type of information (perceived
from the private perspective) needed to fuel such self-labelling in vulnerable
individuals. If our patient is actually exposed to a sample of his social deficiencies—which is undoubtedly practised in skills training—the scene is well
set for establishing or confirming such negative self-beliefs: the evidence is
there before his eyes, a situation exacerbated by his belief that his faults are
transparent to everyone. After all, the therapist may be pointing them out,
perhaps in front of a group of others. It is little wonder that the patient may
drop out of treatment—escaping the aversive experience. It is possible he may
recall the image whenever his attention is self-focused and help to constantly
remind him of his status.

Recommendations

An examination of research findings in the cognitive therapy literature suggests a common theme in the main emotional/behavioural disorders. This
common theme is to be found in the cognitive processes of such disturbed
patients. Of a number of processes identified (Rehm, 1977), we shall focus on
two. The first concerns the *direction* of attributions, namely for any given
behaviour the direction of attribution can be persons or situations; and the
second concerns the evaluation of the attributed behaviour, namely whether it
is good or bad. Affectively disordered patients evaluate negatively and are

attributively self-directed (Abramson, Seligman and Teasdale, 1978) they see their actions as bad or poor and see themselves as responsible (not others or the situation). Following from this they view their 'poor' performances as evidence of their poor self-worth ('I behaved foolishly, therefore I am a fool').

According to rational emotive therapy theory (Wessler and Wessler, 1980), this form of inferring, and the evaluative conclusions they lead to, generate emotional disturbance such as anxiety, depression and avoidance behaviours. Since neurotic patients commonly have such a pattern of thinking, video feedback in our view carries a high risk factor of exacerbating the process. In particular, it strongly influences the direction of attribution (i.e. to self). How then can these damaging effects be dealt with so that clients can benefit from video information? Cognitive therapy and RET tackle and try to change both the inferences and evaluations of the patient. At the level of attributional inferences the therapist tries to train the patient to examine objectively the various possible situational causes, e.g. attribute failure to the difficulty of the exam rather than lack of ability. Some social situations are inherently more 'difficult' than others and more likely to produce failed skills and anxiety (Trower, in press). The client assumes uniqueness and therefore dispositional responsibility for his behaviour ('I'm the only one'), a tendency exacerbated by the perceptual saliency and self-focusing effects of VF. He probably also generalizes from his own biased perspective to that of others ('Others will attribute my behaviour to my "inadequacy" '). Video feedback may give him a biased picture of the general view, with himself at the centre and therefore the causal focus. Cognitive therapy can help the patient modify his attributions and related, often contradictory, inferences by logical and empirical challenges and proofs.

While VF may actually *alter* the direction of attribution (from situation to person) it cannot alter the evaluation, which the self-viewer himself carries with him. However, given a strong evaluatively negative tendency, VF will undoubtedly help the client magnify it and generalize from it, and will help him bring previously unknown self-related information under the same biasing stereotypic belief. By means of his transparency assumption, it may lead him to assume that his newly perceived, VF mediated performances, privately defined as social failures, are also publicly viewed and defined as social failures. This 'mortifying' discovery had best be dealt with at the time of VF also by means of cognitive therapy. The disputing and disproving method will in this case be directed at the client's catastrophizing, irrational self-worth constructs and 'demanding philosophy' (Ellis, 1977). One method of using RET is to get the client to carry out an ABC analysis on segments of the video during playback (Wessler and Wessler, 1980). ABC analysis consists of identifying first an emotional reaction—anger, anxiety or depression. This is termed the emotional *consequence* (the C in the ABC sequence). The next step is to identify the *activating* event (the A in the sequence) which triggered the emotional consequence. Lastly, the therapist helps the client identify the irrational evaluation or *beliefs* (B) that led to C and finally helps the client *dispute* (D) and disprove them by means of a socratic 'questioning' dialogue or logical and empirical disputation and behavioural assignments designed to disprove the beliefs.

Video feedback can be utilized as an activating event, triggering in the client emotional consequences and their mediating beliefs. Suppose the client notices on video his nervous foot and hand movements, speech errors and long pauses, and so on (A), and immediately feels depressed (C). The tape is stopped and RET commenced. The therapist probes the client's inferences and evaluations until the central irrational beliefs (catastrophizing, generalizing, self-downing, demanding, thinking, etc.) are revealed so that disputing can commence. The earliest VF sequences will, of course, take some time to work through, but as the patient gains more insight, develops expertise in challenging his cognitions and works out appropriate self-statements, the process will be speeded up, especially as the ABC patterns tend to repeat themselves time and again in the same client. The fact that video can be repeatedly played back means that the patient can rehearse the ABCD procedure as often as required and without the therapist necessarily being present. Intending practitioners will find that any of the RET or cognitive therapy manuals (e.g. Wessler and Wessler, 1980) give practical guidance on procedure.

References

Abramson, L. Y., Seligman, M. E. P. and Teasdale, J. D. (1978). Learned helplessness in humans: Critique and reformulation. *Journal of Abnormal Psychology*, **87**, 47–74.

Alger, I., and Hogan, P. (1969). Enduring effects of videotaped playback experience on family and marital relationships, *American Journal of Orthopsychiatry*, **39**, 86–94.

Alkire, A., and Brunse, A. J. (1974). Impact and possible casualty from videotape feedback in marital therapy, *Journal of Consulting and Clinical Psychology*, **42**, 203–210.

Argyle, M., and Williams, M. (1969). Observer observed? A reversible perspective in person perception, *Sociometry*, **32**, 396–412.

Arkin, R., and Duval, S. (1975). Focus of attention and causal attributions of actors and observers, *Journal of Experimental Social Psychology*, **11**, 427–438.

Asch, S. E. (1946). Forming impressions of personality, *Journal of Abnormal and Social Psychology*, **41**, 258–290.

Bailey, K. G., and Sowder, W. T. (1970). Audiotape and videotape self-confrontation in psychotherapy, *Psychological Bulletin*, **74**, 127–137.

Bandura, A. (1977). Self-efficacy: towards a unifying theory of behavioral change, *Psychological Review*, **84**, 191–215.

Beck, A. T. (1967). *Depression: Clinical, Experimental and Theoretical Aspects*, Hoeber, New York.

Beck, A. T. (1976). *Cognitive Therapy and the Emotional Disorders*, International Universities Press, New York.

Bem, D. J. (1972). Self-perception theory, in *Advances in Experimental Social Psychology* (Ed. L. Berkowitz), Vol. 6, Academic Press, New York.

Biggs, S. (1979). *Videotape Feedback and Self Awareness*, Unpublished doctoral thesis, Senate Library, University of London (British Library Ref. D.29862/80).

Biggs, S. (1980). The me I see: acting, participating, observing and viewing and their implications for videofeedback, *Human Relations*, **33**, 575–588.

Braucht, G. N. (1970). Immediate effects of self-confrontation of the self-concept, *Journal of Consulting and Clinical Psychology*, **35**, 95–101.

Brockner, J., and Hulton, A. J. B. (1978). How to reverse the vicious cycle of low self-esteem: the importance of attentional focus, *Journal of Experimental Social Psychology*, **14**, 564–578.

Brown, S. D. (1980). Videotape Feedback: effects on assertive performance and subjects' perceived competence and satisfaction, *Psychological Reports*, **47**, 455–461.

Bruner, J. S. (1957). Going beyond the information given, in *Contemporary Approaches to Cognition* (Eds. J. S. Bruner, E. Brunswik, L. Festinger, F. Heider, K. F. Muenzinger, C. E. Osgood and D. Rapaport), Harvard Universities Press, Cambridge, Massachusetts.

Bruner, J. S., and Tagiuri, R. (1954). The perception of people, in *Handbook of Social Psychology* (Ed. G. Lindzey), Vol. 1, Addison Wesley Publishing Company Inc., Cambridge, Massachusetts.

Buss, A. H. (1980). *Self-Consciousness and Social Anxiety*, W. H. Freeman & Co., San Francisco, California.

Buss, D. M., and Scheier, M. F. (1976). Self-consciousness, self-awareness and self attribution, *Journal of Research in Personality*, **10**, 463–468.

Carrere, M. J. (1954). Le psychoc cinematographique, *Annales Medico-Psychologiques*, **112**, 240–245.

Carver, C. S. (1974). The facilitation of aggression as a function of cognitive self-awareness and attitude towards punishment, *Journal of Experimental Social Psychology*, **10**, 365–370.

Carver, C. S., and Scheier, M. F. (1978). Self-focussing effects of dispositional self-consciousness, mirror presence and audience presence, *Journal of Personality and Social Psychology*, **36**, 324–332.

Cavior, N., and Marabotto, C. M. (1976). Monitoring verbal behaviours in a dyadic interaction, *Journal of Consulting and Clinical Psychology*, **44**, 68–76.

Cornelison, F. S., and Arsenian, J. (1960). A study of the response of psychotic patients to photographic self-image experience, *Psychiatric Quarterly*, **34**, 1–8.

Crozier, W. R. (1979). Shyness as a dimension of personality, *British Journal of Social and Clinical Psychology*, **18**, 121–128.

Danet, B. N. (1968). Self-confrontation in psychotherapy reviewed, *American Journal of Psychotherapy*, **22**, 245–258.

Davis, D., and Brock, T. C. (1975). Use of first person pronouns as a function of increased objective self-assurance and prior feedback, *Journal of Experimental Social Psychology*, **11**, 381–388.

Dittman, A. T. (1978). The role of body movements in communications, in *Nonverbal Behaviour and Communication* (Eds. A. W. Siegman and S. Feldstein), Erlbaum, Hillsdale, New Jersey.

Duval, S. (1972). Causal attribution as a focus of attention, in *A Theory of Objective Self-awareness* (S. Duval and R. A. Wicklund), Academic Press, New York.

Duval, S., and Hensley. (1976). Extensions of objective self awareness theory, in *New Directions in Attribution Research* (Eds. J. Harvey, W. Ickes and R. Kidd), Earlbaum, Hillsdale, New Jersey.

Duval, S., Hensley, V., and Neely, R. (1975). *Attribution of an Event to Self and Helping Behaviour as a Function of Contingous verses Noncontingous Presentation of Self and Event*, Unpublished manuscript, University of Southern California.

Duval, S., and Wicklund, R. A. (1972). *A Theory of Objective Self-awareness*, Academic Press, New York.

Duval, S., and Wicklund, R. A. (1973). Effects of objective self-awareness on attribution of causality, *Journal of Experimental Social Psychology*, **9**, 17–31.

Edelson, R. I., and Seidman, E. (1975). Use of videotape feedback in altering inter-personal perceptions of married couples: a therapy analogue, *Journal of Consulting and Clinical Psychology*, **43**, 244–250.

Ekman, P., and Freisen, W. (1969). Nonverbal leakage and cues to deception, *Psychiatry*, **32**, 88–105.

Ellis, A. (1977). *Reason and Emotion in Psychotherapy*, Citadel, Secanous, New Jersey.

Eysenck, H. J., and Eysenck, S. B. G. (1964). *Manual of the Eysenck Personality Inventory*, University of London Press.

Fenigstein, A. (1979). Self-consciousness, self-attention and social interaction, *Journal of Personality and Social Psychology*, **37**, 75–86.

Fenigstein, A., Scheier, M. F., and Buss, A. H. (1975). Public and private self-consciousness: assessment and theory, *Journal of Consulting and Clinical Psychology*, **43**, 522–527.

Geertsma, R. H., and Reivich, R. S. (1965). Repetitive self-observation by video tape feedback, *Journal of Nervous Mental Disorders*, **41**, 29–41.

Gibbons, F. X., and Wicklund, R. A. (1976). Selective exposure to the self, *Journal of Research in Personality*, **10**, 98–106.

Goffman, E. (1969). *The Presentation of Self in Everyday Life*, Penguin, Harmondsworth, Middlesex.

Heider, F. (1958). *The Psychology of Interpersonal Relations*, Wiley, New York.

Hung, J. H. F., and Rosenthal, T. L. (1978). Therapeutic videotaped playback: a critical review, *Advances in Behaviour Research and Therapy*, **1**, 103–135.

Ickes, W. J., and Layden, M. A. (1978). Attributional styles, in *New Directions in Attribution Research* (Eds. J. Harvey, W. Ickes and R. Kidd), Vol. 2, Lawrence Erlbaum Associates, Hillsdale, New Jersey.

Ickes, W. J., Wicklund, R. A., and Ferris, C. B. (1973). Objective self-awareness and self-esteem, *Journal of Experimental Social Psychology*, **9**, 203–219.

Jones, E. E., and Davis, K. E. (1965). From acts to dispositions: the attribution process in person perception, in *Advances in Experimental Social Psychology* (Ed. L. Berkowitz), Vol. 2, Academic Press, New York.

Jones, E. E., and Nisbett, R. E. (1971). *The Actor and the Observer: Divergent Perceptions of the Causes of Behavior*, General Learning Press, Morristown, New Jersey.

Kagan, N., Krathwohl, D. R., and Miller, R. (1963). Stimulated recall in therapy using videotape: a case study, *Journal of Counselling Psychology*, **10**, 237–243.

Kanfer, F. H. (1970). Self-monitoring: methodological limitations and clinical applications, *Journal of Consulting and Clinical Psychology*, **35**, 148–152.

Kanouse, D. E., and Hanson, L. R. (1972). Negativity in evaluations, in *Attribution: Perceiving the Causes of Behavior* (Eds. E. E. Jones *et al.*), General Learning Press, Morristown, New Jersey.

Kelley, H. H. (1967). Attribution theory in social psychology, in *Nebraska Symposium on Motivation* (Ed. D. Levine), University of Nebraska Press, Lincoln, Nebraska.

Kelley, H. H. (1972). *Causal Schemata and the Attribution Process*, General Learning Press, Morristown, New Jersey.

Kelly, G. A. (1955). *The Psychology of Personal Constructs*, Vols. 1 and 2, Norton, New York.

Kiely, B. (1980). *Therapeutic Use of Videotape Feedback*, M.Sc. dissertation, University of Aston in Birmingham.

Kipper, D. A., and Ginot, E. (1979). Accuracy of evaluating videotape feedback and defense mechanisms, *Journal of Consulting and Clinical Psychology*, **47**, 493–499.

Langer, E. (1978). Rethinking the role of thought in social interaction, in *New Directions in Attribution Research* (Eds. J. Harvey, W. Ickes and R. Kidd), Vol. 2, Lawrence Erlbaum, Hillsdale, New Jersey.

Liebling, B. A., and Shaver, P. (1973). Evaluation, self awareness and task performance, *Journal of Experimental Social Psychology*, **9**, 297–306.

Mischel, W. (1973). Towards a cognitive social learning reconceptualization of personality, *Psychological Review*, **80**, 252–283.

Moore, F. J., Charnell, E., and West, M. J. (1965). Television as a therapeutic tool, *Archives of General Psychiatry*, **12**, 218–220.

Paredes, A., Ludwig, K. D., Hassenfeld, I. N., and Cornelison, F. S. (1969). A clinical study of alcoholics under audiovisual self-image feedback, *Journal of Nervous and Mental Disease*, **148** 449–456.

Rehm, L. P. (1977). A self-control model of depression, *Behaviour Therapy*, **8**, 787–804.

Reivich, R. S., and Geertsma, R. H. (1968). Experience with videotape self-observation by psychiatric inpatients, *Journal of Konsal Medical Society*, **69**, 39–44.

Ross, L. (1978). The intuitive psychologist, in *Cognitive Theories in Social Psychology* (Ed. L. Berkowitz), Academic Press, New York.

Sartre, J.-P. (1956). *Being and Nothingness*, Philosophical Library, New York.

Scheier, M. F. (1976). Self-awareness, self-consciousness and angry aggression, *Journal of Personality*, **44**, 627–644.

Scheier, M. F., and Carver, C. S. (1977). Self-focussed attention and the experience of emotion: attraction, repulsion, elation and depression, *Journal of Personality and Social Psychology*, **35**, 625–636.

Scheier, M. F., Fenigstein, A., and Buss, A. H. (1974). Self-awareness and physical aggression, *Journal of Experimental Social Psychology*, **10**, 264–273.

Sobell, M. B., Sobell, L. C., and Mills, F. C. (1973). Alcoholics treated by individualized behavior therapy: one year treatment outcome, *Behaviour Research and Therapy*, **11**, 599–618.

Storms, M. D. (1973). Videotape and the attribution process: reversing actors' and observers' points of view, *Journal of Personality and Social Psychology*, **27**, 165–175.

Storms, M. D., and McCaul, K. D. (1976). Attribution processes and the emotional exacerbation of dysfunctional behavior, in *New Directions in Attribution Research* (Eds. J. H. Harvey, W. J. Ickes and R. F. Kidd), Vol. 1, Earlbaum, Hillsdale, New Jersey.

Trower, P. (1981). Social skills disorder, in *Personal Relationships in Disorder* (Eds. R. Gilmour and S. Duck), Academic Press, London.

Trower, P. (in press). Social fit and misfit, in *Social Behaviour and Context* (Eds. A. Furnham and M. Argyle), Allyn and Bacon, New York.

Wessler, R. A., and Wessler, R. L. (1980). *The Principles and Practice of Rational-Emotive Therapy*, Jossey-Bass, San Francisco.

Wicklund, R. A. (1975). Objective self-awareness, in *Advances in Experimental Social Psychology* (Ed. L. Berkowitz), Vol. 8, Academic Press, New York.

Yachnes, E. (1975). Neurotic pride, *American Journal of Psychoanalysis*, **35**, 27–32.

Using Video
Edited by P. W. Dowrick and S. J. Biggs
© 1983 John Wiley & Sons Ltd

Chapter 14

On Viewing Videotape Records of Oneself and Others: A Hermeneutical Analysis

John Shotter

Department of Psychology, University of Nottingham

Of course in this you fellows see more than I could see. You see me.
Joseph Conrad, *Heart of Darkness*

Introduction

What does it mean to see oneself on a television screen? Rather than directly exploring the experience of viewing records of ourselves and others on videotape, I shall approach the matter indirectly by first providing an account of how ordinary people both experience themselves and others in their daily encounters, and I shall contrast the experience of viewing videotape records with this. There is first the fundamental problem of how one grasps one's own and other people's existence as distinct, individual persons at all, before one can turn to the problem of what determines the kind of person they are—whether they are or not, say, self-conscious, or concerned with self-display, or whatever.

I want to begin in this manner as what I have to say is heavily dependent upon a particular account of social being and social perception, one which recognizes its inherent *intentionality* or its *directedness*—the fact that all mental activity is directed by an agent in some way. This account is opposed in almost every detail to theories currently held in social psychology (e.g. Eiser, 1980), and especially in attribution theory (e.g. Jones and Nisbett, 1971), that perception is simply a matter of mechanical 'informational processing'. I do not want to argue that that theory is wrong in its entirety—for we clearly can and sometimes do logically *infer* people's mental states from our objective observations of them—and we do occasionally understand them in analogy with ourselves—but such a theory cannot be the whole story. Firstly, if it really were the case that we *only* ever interpreted patterns of movement in the world on analogy with our own, then, logically, on encountering movements similar to our own, how could we ever conclude that they were in fact the movements of another, alien self, and not simply our own movements there too? It is only because we can sense that the activity, although like ours, is not actually *directed* by us that we can sense that another personality is at work in it.

Secondly, it lacks a 'developmental' aspect, and consequently cannot account for the acquisition of the particular cultural categories and 'mechanisms' (the mechanical procedures) in terms of which the actual information processing involved might take place. Unless people also have a direct, non-inferential, non-mechanical access to one another's psychic states, the source of such categories and routines remains a mystery. There must be another more immediate, extralinguistic mode of communication (or communion) prior to the establishment of the categories used in our more explicit, linguistic communications—a basic mode of communication within which the transmission of the more specialized, cultural forms of communication may take place.

Thirdly, such a theory suggests that people are left untouched in their *being* by such experiences and that it is just a matter of people—who are already clear as to who and what they are—gathering information relevant to decisions about how they should act. However, encountering other people, as well as viewing oneself on videotape, is not just an epistemological matter; it is an ontological one too. *People are changed* by their encounters. They are changed, as we shall see, not just in their knowledge, but in the whole mode of their relationship to both themselves and to others—in their very being in fact. Thus there is a 'developmental' aspect to be considered here too.

The intentionality of action and the mediatory function of joint action

Intentionality

It is the problem of how personality characteristics are perceived at all—for clearly they are not apparent as objects in immediate perception—which arouses our concern with intentionality. As I have already mentioned, human action—whether the *deliberate* action of individuals acting alone or the *spontaneous* (joint) action of people simply reacting to one another in a social context—always has an intentional quality to it: it is not only always *directed* in some way, but it is also *intrinsically interconnected with the world* in which it has its being. It always 'points beyond itself', so to speak, to a 'something' which no matter how vague is always something other than itself.

It was Brentano (1973, from an original publication of 1874) who was essentially responsible for introducing this conception of intentionality (as he called it) into *descriptive psychology* in an attempt to clarify the distinction between mental and physical phenomena. All our psychological activities—thinking, believing, desiring, loving, hating, and the like—are, he claimed, 'directed upon' objects, whether such objects actually exist or not. In other words, human beings 'in' their actions exhibit a tendency towards *either* fitting themselves appropriately to their circumstances *or* their circumstances appropriately to themselves—towards, as Searle (1979) calls it, the achievement of a *mind-to-world* or a *world-to-mind* fit. Thus an action in its very occurrence indicates (or implies), in the way in which it is being directed by the agent, both a structured context into which it fits (within which its sense, function or use can be understood) *and* a whole realm of other possible next actions also appropriate to that context—actions which, if performed, will of course modify that context.

It is as if—and this is another way of visualizing the nature of intentional processes—agents can progressively determine or *specify* regions of the world beyond themselves by their actions. Thus an action in progress, while having so far produced a degree of specification into its content, still leaves that content open to further specification, but only *specification of an already specified kind* (Shotter, 1980). An action now, a smile say, determines in some sense what counts as an appropriate response to it in the future—not the precise form of response but at least the style. Not all responses (a slap in the face, for instance) would be appropriate, although, even here, it is a matter of the context in which the slap is delivered which determines its appropriateness.

Meeting: handshaking and mutual gazing

We can now turn to the problem of the perception of personality. Let us consider the paradigm case of people meeting one another: i.e. of two people shaking each other's hands and simultaneously looking each other in the eye. There is an almost magical or clairvoyant aspect to such an encounter which is taken so much for granted ordinarily that its theoretical importance is obscured. What is amazing in such an encounter is that we come to appreciate *through* it (and I want to pick up on its *mediatory* properties in a moment) another person—a self different from our own. Its special nature may be appreciated empirically simply by grasping another person's hand and shaking it out of the context of a meeting, and/or by not meeting a person's gaze as such, but by simply looking (as an opthalmologist might) at the surface of their eyes. Fingarette (1967) has discussed the first of these two situations and pointed out:

> We shake hands—not by my pulling your hand up and down or your pulling mine, but by spontaneous and perfect cooperative action. Normally we do not notice the subtlety and amazing complexity of this coordinated 'ritual' act. This subtlety and complexity become evident, however, if one has had to learn the ceremony from a book of instructions, or one is a foreigner from a non-handshaking culture (p. 148).

It is not, as when I just grasp someone else's hand, a matter of me just touching them, in a proper meeting it is a matter of me, in touching them, *also being touched by them*. This is a part of what it is for people to properly meet one another. It is not just a unidirectional relationship of perceiver to perceived; the relationship is bidirectional or reciprocal. The reciprocity has to be there for the experience to be accounted a meeting. I experience a 'directing' at work in the activity (joint) which I know to be not my own. In such circumstances, I do not simply constitute another person as an object of my own perception, but a *social institution* is established between us in which we both share, and in which self and other are operative as mutually constitutive polarities and experienced by one another as such.

With looking, too, one may carry out such 'experiments'. Heron (1970) discusses the distinctions in our experience noticeable when one's gaze is ignored and the other person looks instead at one's eyes as objects. One's sense of being in a world in which one is recognized as a person disappears and one begins to feel that one cannot continue to *be* a person. Intellectually, one is unchanged, of course; it is not that one does not still have the knowledge of how to be a person. The phenomenon is *motivational*. Mental activities are 'released' by their context; not by that context actually causing them directly, but by its meaning or significance—by the projects it holds out to or affords the person as an agent. An environment in which one is not recognized as a person does not afford one a personal mode of being. The experience of encountering such a world is objectively frightening; one feels, as Laing (1960) puts it, 'ontologically insecure'.

The directedness of action and the use of mediatory processes

It is through the directedness of our mental activities that we can control their content—whether, for instance, as agents we hide ourselves from or reveal ourselves to others in our actions, or whether as observers we direct our attention to people as objects or as persons. Heron (1970) describes in his paper some of the various modes of looking at other people available to us.

Essentially he notes in them a threefold directedness:

1. One can direct one's awareness away from one whole area of experience towards another, as when one turns from perception, say, to memory, or from phantasy to reflective thought, or from withdrawn observation to active participation in the world.
2. One can then direct one's attention, of course, to specific objects or contents within the area of experience selected.
3. One can then direct one's awareness within a particular moment of experience, in a particular mode or manner: e.g. reverentially or skeptically, descriptively or evaluatively, and so on. It is, of course, the way in which we direct our gaze (or our handshaking) which determines our experience, and it is up to us whether we direct ourselves to see persons as objects or whether to discriminate a personal content in their activity. Normally, we do see through people's activities to their mental contents; only unusually do we not do so.

We have now reached a convenient point at which to break off to discuss the *mediatory* function of human action—the way in which the activity going on between people can both serve as a *means* as well as presenting a *meaning* (and have, as some writers have put it, *duality of structure*—e.g. Giddens, 1979). Most of the time in social interaction, in what elsewhere I have called *joint action* (Shotter, 1980), in a conversation say, we are unaware of the actual mediating process itself; we grasp something *through* it. Heider's (1958) view can be cited as typical here:

> One might say psychological processes such as motives, intentions, sentiments, etc., are the core processes which manifest themselves in overt behaviour and

expression in many ways. The manifestations are then directly grasped by p, the observer, in terms of these core processes; they would otherwise remain undecipherable. By looking through the mediation, p perceives the distal object, the psychological entities that bring consistency and meaning to the behaviour; p's reaction is then to this meaning, not to the overt behaviour directly, and this reaction is then carried back by the mediation to o, etc. (p. 34).

It is through the mediatory process of the activity between myself and another that I can grasp a mental content, a content given to it by the way in which that activity is directed by myself or by the other. In its *duality of structure*, a mediatory act, an utterance say, functions both as an outgoing *means* through which actors may express themselves and as an incoming process through which recipients may look back to see a *meaning*, to see the performer's motive, intention, or sentiment, etc. Thus, when I perceive the activity of another, I may direct my gaze in such a way as to perceive in it either a physical realm of events or a psychological realm of contents; I may pick up in the pattern of interwoven activity between us shapes or forms, *or* meanings—thus to achieve, in an extended Searlean terminology, a *mind-to-mind* direction of fit, a knowledge of other minds. Furthermore, I may direct my gaze towards another with the intention not just of perceiving their state of mind but also of expressing my own regarding them—whether of hostility or affection, of censure or affirmation, etc.—and hence to express a meaning in *my* look in response to theirs, and so on.

The intrinsic vagueness of meanings

Such meanings, however—in a look of boredom, say, or of surprise—are both vague and specific at the same time; they presage the *style* of the activity to come rather than any particular response. In other words, an expression can be seen as specifying a set of possibilities, any and only one of which can be actualized and made determinate by the particular expression coming to play its part in a specific context. Much of our puzzlement about the nature of meaning arises, as Merleau-Ponty would put it, not from any 'testimony of consciousness' but from a widely held 'prejudice in favour of an already determined, objective world': the belief that the nature of everything in existence is already in some sense, somewhere, fully specified. If we refer back here to the intentional nature of human action—that it may not yet, if still in progress, have a fully specified content—it is such that its contents may still be open to further specification; its meaning may only partially be specified.

We must bear these comments in mind when attempting to understand the meaning of being videotaped, or of being confronted with a videotape recording of oneself, for there is clearly no one single meaning to be discovered, only an enormous range of possibilities, each one specific only in its context. At best we may be able to outline their general *style or styles*.

The moral ecology of everyday social life; rights and duties

Social situations not only afford us different opportunities for action but they also make different demands upon us. In fact, our social world is also a *moral* world, a world in which our *selves*—which as a socially conferred status is held by us only with other people's 'permission', so to speak—are at risk. We may find ourselves degraded from our full status at socially autonomous individuals at any time (Garfinkel, 1956; Goffman, 1968). We have to be careful to appreciate the *duties* such moral situations demand of us as well as the *rights* they afford us, for what we have a right to do in one situation we have no right to do in another. In fact, our moral world can be seen as an ever-changing sea of opportunities and limitations, of enablements and constraints, with its character transformed by each action which takes place within it. What is at stake in all of this is the reproduction of the social order: people must do only what it is legitimate to do; they must be responsible for their actions *and know how to account for them or justify them to others if called upon to do so*. Associated with each role in the ecology of daily social life at large is a set of rights and duties, and people in such roles must appreciate their nature. Clearly, the nature of these roles is changed if people's conception of their relations to themselves and to others is changed—either by the videotape experience or in some other way.

In particular, I want to discuss what seem to be the rights and duties associated with the three major roles in life: as first person performers, as second person recipients and as third person observers. It is the third person role which is the most unusual and special role, for it takes special training to become a fully objective observer; it is one's ability to adopt the third person role which is increased by videotape technology. In any social transaction, one's *usual* position is, seemingly, as a first person performer or as a second person recipient. In both such positions one has a status quite different from that of third persons: occupation of the first-person role *requires* one to direct one's expressions outwards; if one does not perform as and when expected to do so, then the flow of the exchange breaks down and embarrassment ensues. Occupation of the second person role gives one a right to intervene in and to modify the action—to assume at appropriate moments, in fact, the first person role. In both such roles one is involved in and requires to maintain the flow of the joint action. Not to do so renders one liable to blame and to recrimination. To maintain the flow one *must* attend only to what performers intend one to attend to, and one is supposed to ignore whatever else happens (what is not intended by the performer); one's *duty* is to attend only to expressions 'given' and to ignore those 'given off' (as Goffman, 1971, p. 16, puts it).

Because they do not face the same demands as second persons, third person observers may attend to the unintended aspects of people's performances (but they forego the right to intervene in the action in so doing). Hence our unease when, as first persons attempting either a tricky interpersonal encounter or as a Sartrean voyeur, we notice ourselves observed. Suddenly, the otherwise unintended and spontaneous aspects of our behaviour—revealing aspects of ourselves we would rather hide—require our control. We must pay attention to them and attempt direction of them, and often it is a task beyond our capacity to achieve. Hence our desire, in such circumstances, often to be enshrouded in darkness, so that what we cannot control is still hidden from another's view. All three statuses exist only within an interlocking structure of social relations; they are mutually constitutive and reciprocally determine one another—hence my claim that the relations between them are essentially *ecological* ones.

Evidently, people can be seen as functioning to a degree in all three roles simultaneously, with a degree of awareness at each moment of the possibilities (the meanings) available to them in each one. However, which of all the possibilities available they attempt to actualize is another matter, a matter of how they *direct* themselves. Their direction of their actions and their direction of their attention is, to a degree, up to them—but only to a degree, for that in its turn is influenced by what their circumstances signify to them, the range of opportunities they afford. To stare at another without offering to enter into a first or second person relation with them, to resolutely claim the right to observe them and to attend to what they do not intend us to attend to, is inimical to the ecology of the social relationships necessary to the proper workings of a social order (Shotter, 1981). Only certain modes of mutual relation are constitutive of an enduring and continually self-reproducing social order. Videotape technology offers the possibility of adopting a third person role divorced from the ecological pressures upon people to reproduce their social order in all their actions; hence people's feeling that, in using videotape or in making films, something really rather awesome is taking place. Unsophisticated peoples talk of it, as we shall see, as having their 'souls stolen', while we may see the process both as a matter of their relations to their *selves* being changed as well as their general conception of human nature, and thus their whole way of life.

Viewing recorded behaviour

Being observed

What is the meaning of being confronted, not with other people in the flesh but with videotape records of their (or of perhaps one's own) behaviour? Let us consider first the situation in which we notice ourselves being observed. The classic account here is Sartre's (1958, p. 259 *et seq.*) account of noticing—after having been moved by jealously, curiosity or sheer vice to glue one's ear to a door or to look through a keyhole—that one is being observed oneself: 'What does this mean? It means that I am suddenly affected in my being and that essential modifications appear in my [intentional] structure—modifications which I can apprehend and fix conceptually . . .' (p. 260). It means, suggests Sartre, that before being observed I existed as an unreflective consciousness. Initially, all my conscious attention was directed outwards, solely upon the world (as seen through the keyhole); my self as such was absent from my field of consciousness. All of a sudden, however, I find myself conscious of my self in a particular way: as wholly *an object for another consciousness*, completely at the mercy of other people.

This is both an unfamiliar and unhappy situation in which to be, for it means that while I am caught empty of intentions regarding *them*, they are able to direct themselves in one way or another towards me. In fact, suggests Sartre (1958), I apprehend my whole situation with them '*as not being for me . . .* since on principle it exists for the *Other*' (p. 261). In such circumstances I find myself blocked; the phase or aspect of my *self* called out by them in their role only as a third person observer of me and not as second person recipients, is afforded no form of expression regarding them. It is a most unusual experience.

> Nevertheless I *am that Ego*; I do not reject it as a strange image, but it is present to me as a self which I *am* without *knowing it*; for I discover it in shame and, in other instances, in pride. It is shame or pride which reveals to me the Other's look and myself at the end of that look. It is the shame or pride which makes me *live*, [but] not *know* the situation of being looked at (p. 261).

We may know *of* such experiences, *that* they are possible, and we may in directing our attention in a detailed way to our memories of such experiences in the past be able to describe their features, but we do not know how to intend within ourselves alone the situation of being looked at. It is something only constituted within us in interaction with an Other.

The essential point of Sartre's analysis is, however, not that it is an experience only available in joint action, but that the social context instituted between oneself and the Other is such that it neither affords one the usual stance as a first person performer nor as a secondperson recipient. In such circumstances, one becomes an object, if not literally then at least functionally. One becomes the object of a thirdperson observer, one who can see in the unintended aspects of one's behaviour what second person recipients usually have a duty to ignore. One is thus momentarily rendered transparent and as a result, robbed of a social context 'open' to one's actions. Some aspects of this analysis clearly applies to the videotape experience.

Being depicted

Viewing a depiction of oneself is different from merely being observed; the Other's object is your picture, not your *self*. Yet there is a similar element of self-consciousness in the experience—a feeling of being made in some vague way into an object for others, of being robbed of some of one's powers in social life at large. Carpenter (1976) provides numerous anecdotes of what happens when a person—*for the first time*—sees him or herself in a mirror, in a photograph, or on film; or hears his voice; or sees his name; etc. In the Territory of Papua and New Guinea, when hired to go there in 1969–70 as a communications consultant, Carpenter took the opportunity to carry out such tests. Everywhere New Guineans, he claims, responded in the same way to these experiences: they ducked their heads and covered their mouths. A *self*-conscious reaction—but why does consciousness of self produce *this response*?

Proceeding hermeneutically, we may follow Carpenter (1976) and offer as an initial interpretation the possibility that the acute anxiety of sudden self-awareness leads people everywhere to hide or conceal those aspects of themselves through which others gain access to them, mentally: their eyes and their mouths. They are suddenly made aware of themselves as others can see them—not just the surface properties of their mediatory behaviour, but what mentally can be seen through it. Usually they are only known to themselves in terms of the parts they play, the positions they occupy in relation to one another in the ordinary activities of everyday life; their *selves* are context-bound selves it would seem. They do not see themselves as isolable, detachable individuals, able to live a life apart, and one possibly different from that lived by the others with whom they currently share their lives.

Such an interpretation is strengthened by another, somewhat tragic observation of Carpenter's (1976). Studying people in one of the Sepik villages of New Guinea—a village in which stone axes were still in use when he first arrived—Carpenter, after first giving them experience of themselves on photographs, showed them *films* of themselves. At first (and he recorded their reactions on film in infra-red light) they viewed the films in silence, but with a terror that revealed itself in an uncontrolled stomach trembling. However, in an astonishingly short time the villagers, including the children and even a few women, were making movies themselves, taking Polaroid shots of each other and playing endlessly with tape recorders. No longer fearful of their own portraits, as they had been initially—for they felt they were being robbed of their souls(!)—men wore them openly on their foreheads. The tragedy, as Carpenter saw it, occurred later.

Returning to the village some months afterwards, Carpenter found some of the houses rebuilt in a new style, men wearing European clothing, people carrying themselves differently, with some of the people having wandered off in search of a new life at the government settlement:

> In one brutal moment they had been torn out of a tribal existence and transformed into detached individuals, lonely, frustrated, no longer at home—anywhere. . . . Their wits and sensibilities, released from tribal restraints, created a new identity: the private individual. For the first time, each man saw himself and his environment clearly and saw them as separable (p. 120).

Carpenter feared that their visit had precipitated the crisis. No one, he suggests, who ever comes to know him- or herself with the detachment of a thirdperson observer is ever the same again—evidently they can become objects of evaluation, etc., for themselves in a way quite impossible for them before.

Another observation of Carpenter's is also worth mentioning here; it is to do with people's reactions to cameras *when they already know what cameras are* and what they can do. Filming the behaviour of villagers already knowledgeable about cameras produced far more pronounced changes than those produced by simply observing them. A camera holds a potential for *self*-viewing, for *self*-awareness, in a way that simply being viewed by another person does not. Carpenter made the following three-way comparisons:

1. Using telescopic lenses, they (his group) filmed people who were unaware of the group's presence.
2. Then someone stepped from concealment and stood silently watching but not interrupting the villager's activity.
3. Finally the cameraman set up his equipment in full view, urging everyone to go on with whatever they were doing. Almost invariably, body movements

became faster, jerky, without poise or confidence. Faces that had been relaxed froze or alternated between twitching and rigidity.

People's self-conscious performances bore little relation to their unselfconscious behaviour. Thus, for New Guinea at least, Carpenter concludes: comparing footage of a subject who is unaware of the camera and then aware of it—fully aware of it as an instrument for self-viewing, self-examination—is to compare different behaviour and different persons. Do we (as camera-conscious Westerners) fail to see these kinds of camera-produced changes in people's behaviour, Carpenter asks, because they are so common among us, so much a part of our lives that we fail to recognize them as alien in others? The fact is, once again, that the experience of being not just an object for another but also an object for oneself alters the whole ecology of people's social interrelationships, the interlocking pattern of rights and duties in terms of which people hold themselves and one another responsible for their actions and evaluate each other's and their own performances.

Deautomatization and our 'real selves'

Holzman (1969), in discussing the experience of being confronted with audio or videotape recordings of oneself, introduces the idea of *deautomatization* to account for the results apparently observed. Like Sartre and Carpenter, he notes that people are astonished, shocked or even frightened by the self-confrontation experience. He, however, gives it a rather different interpretation: he suggests that, in shifting the role of behaviour from that of being a *mediator* of expression and communication to that of being a *percept*, one is permitted to experience incompletely censored aspects of it. One comes to notice aspects of it one would rather keep concealed. Seeing or listening to recordings of one's own behaviour 'deautomatizes', Holzman claims, people's inattention to the actual objective nature of their own behaviour. Deautomatization involves the redirecting of attention onto those highly practised processes for which it has ceased, normally, to be necessary.

Holzman makes two points here, one intentional and the other functional. I think that the first is correct but the second wrong. Essentially, Holzman sees the major consequence of self-viewing intentionally, as a redirection of one's conscious awareness. However, unlike Sartre and Carpenter, he offers a functional rather than an intentional interpretation as to what such a redirection of attention means. Whereas they both see the change as taking place in one's very *being* in the world, a change motivated by the changed ecology of people's relations to both themselves and others, Holzman (1969) sees the matter as being one of us 'facing an image of ourselves which we had learned *not* to see' (p. 208). He sees the self-confrontation situation as momentarily deautomatizing, what he regards as people's *defensive stance* towards themselves—a stance which is supposed to issue from the fact that most people's ideal self clashes with their selves in reality (Wolff, 1943).

The clash which *is* evident here is that between Holzman's account and those more phenomenologically based. Phenomenologists would suggest that Holzman has fallen victim to a 'prejudice in favour of an already objective reality', that the self projected back to us by others, by mirrors, by audio and videotape is no more our 'real self' than the self we ordinarily experience in reflection upon our first and second person encounters. They would suggest that our 'self' consists of an indefinite number of phases or aspects, each one called out or motivated by an appropriate context and where each phase or aspect of ourselves is experienced by us as carrying with it its own environment of opportunities for and limitations upon action. It is this which we must understand if we are to understand the meaning of having our behaviour recorded in a way which allows us to be confronted by it; what we see of ourselves from a third-person standpoint is only a phase or an aspect to be seen in relation to all the other phases of our selves, none of which is any more basic than any other. In all of this, the overall meaning of the experience of having one's behaviour recorded is clear: people are, as Sartre says, affected in their *being*. The particular way in which they are affected will depend, however, on their social, historical and personal context, and upon how they are attempting to modify it. The experience will produce a redistribution of the relations constituting the social ecology in which the person is embedded.

Conclusions

Human actions can only be understood through interpretations of their meanings for the people performing them; at least, this is what is assumed in taking a hermeneutical approach (Dreyfus, 1980; Gauld and Shotter, 1977; Taylor, 1980). Human phenomena 'release' one another, not by one being the efficient cause of the other but by what it means in relation to the other—no matter how vague or open to further specification that meaning may be. Vague and incompletely specified meanings can still determined the *style* of one's action, even if in the context the action is experienced as appropriate or bizarre. The meaning of the videotape experience must be interpreted in this light. In other words, its meaning is dependent upon the context in which it is used. Its primary consequence, obviously, is an increased *self*-awareness, but the use to which that self-awareness is then put and the aspects of one's self to which one then pays attention is clearly open to further investigation. In our culture at the moment, one feels that almost an opposite change in our being would be desirable: a decreased self-awareness and an increased spontaneity. However, the special and distinct realm of experience which video recordings supply will surely continue to provide new uses and new meanings—some desirable, others not. However, in such research, it will be not so much a matter of further research leading to final definitive conclusions—as if one day our ignorance as to the precise meaning of the experience can be totally overcome—but is a matter of genuine experimentation, the participation in an experience that alters our being. As Sartre puts it, some experiences cannot be simply *known about*; they can only be *lived*.

References

Brentano, F. (1973). *Psychology from an Empirical Standpoint* (Trans. L. L. McAlister), Routledge and Kegan Paul, London (original publication 1874).

Carpenter, E. (1976). *Oh, What a Blow That Phantom Gave Me*, Paladin, St Alban's.

Dreyfus, H. (1980). Holism and hemeneutics, *Review of Metaphysics*, **34**, 3–23.

Eiser, R. (1980). *Cognitive Social Psychology*, McGraw-Hill, New York.

Fingarette, H. (1967). *On Responsibility*, Basic Books, New York.

Garfinkel, H. (1956). Conditions of successful degradation ceremonies, *American Journal of Sociology*, **61**, 420–424.

Gauld, A., and Shotter, J. (1977). *Human Action and its Psychological Investigation*, Routledge and Kegan Paul, London.

Giddens, A. (1979). *Central Problems in Social Theory: Action, Structure and Contradiction in Social Analysis*, Macmillan, London.

Goffman, I. (1968). *Asylums*, Penguin Books, Harmondsworth.

Goffman, I. (1971). *The Presentation of Self in Everyday Life*, Penguin Books, Harmondsworth.

Heider, F. (1958). *The Psychology of Interpersonal Relations*, Wiley, New York.

Heron, J. (1970). The phenomenology of social encounter: the gaze, *Philosophy and Phenomenological Research*, **31**, 243–264.

Holzman, P. S. (1969). On hearing and seeing oneself, *Journal of Nervous and Mental Disease*, **148**, 198–209.

Jones, E. E., and Nisbett, R. E. (1971). The actor and the observer: divergent perceptions of the causes of behaviour, in E. E. Jones et al. (Eds.) *Attribution: Perceiving the Causes of Behaviour* (Eds. E. E. Jones *et al.*), General Learning Press, Morristown, New Jersey.

Laing, R. D. (1960). *The Divided Self*, Tavistock, London.

Merleau-Ponty, M. (1962). *The Phenomenology of Perception*, Routledge and Kegan Paul, London.

Sartre, L.-P. (1958). *Being and Nothingness* (Trans. H. Barnes), Methuen, London.

Searle, J. R. (1979). The intentionality of intention and action, *Inquiry*, **22**, 253–280.

Shotter, J. (1980). Action, joint action, and intentionality, in *The Structure of Action* (Ed. M. Brenner), Blackwell, Oxford.

Shotter, J. (1981). Telling and reporting: prospective and retrospective uses of self-acriptions, in *The Psychology of Ordinary Explanations of Social Behaviour* (Ed. C. Antaki), Academic Press, London.

Taylor, C. (1980). Understanding in human science, *Review of Metaphysics*, **34**, 25–38.

Wolff, W. (1943). *The Expression of Personality*, Harper, New York.

Using Video
Edited by P. W. Dowrick and S. J. Biggs
© 1983 John Wiley & Sons Ltd

Chapter 15

Choosing to Change in Video Feedback: On Common-sense and the Empiricist Error

Simon J. Biggs

Department of Social Services, Newham, London

Introduction

Video has enjoyed an uneasy relationship with training and therapy, being able to both provide and inhibit change. I intend here to explore the issues of choice in video feedback (viewing the self on tape). The main thrust of the argument has been to look at elements of both viewing and being taped in terms of implicit power relationships and associations with the medium. In the present article, I suggest that the video user (the therapist, trainer or whatever) may be overly directive because of an unequal distribution to technical knowledge and status in the video session. Video users should respect viewer's superior personal knowledge and work with them to discover the meaning of any insights gained in the context of the viewer's own sense of history. Viewers should resist any attempt to convert them into external observers in line with the user's ideology or inferior informational position. However, as video is played back on a television monitor, comparisons with idealized social situations may bias the view of the self that arises. This may be related to what the viewer is used to viewing through the medium. Although users may need to work equally as hard as viewers to unravel this societal ideology, they often have an interpretive system which can help the latter to become conscious of this source of bias and change in spite of it. In order to do this, it is important to understand the dialectical relationship between taping and viewing rather than focusing upon the recorded product alone.

Firstly, then, the reader will be asked to consider a video session as a social situation. The social influences involved in both taping and viewing will be explored. These will then be related to the way in which all the participants construct a meaning for the session and the ways in which different meanings can inhibit or enhance self-understanding and change.

Video and common-sense

In any social situation there are rules of conduct commonly understood and adhered to by participants. This common ground is often taken for granted by the actors involved and has the status of what Schutz (1962) has called a 'common-sense' construct. That is to say, it is that which 'the wide-awake, grown-up man who acts in it and upon it amidst his fellow-men experiences with the natural attitude as a reality' (p. 533). When actually involved in a social interaction, the actor does not need to think about these assumptions and, as the world is largely pre-interpreted, very little mental work is involved in accepting the pre-conditions and associations that are involved in a certain social activity. It may only be when someone, such as Garfinkel (1967), comes along and breaks these rules that actors become aware of them. At other times people participating in an event mutually construct and maintain a meaning for the behaviours in which they are involved.

This is no less true of the video user and the actor/viewer than it is of any other social activity. Both parties will have expectations which are not necess-arily explicitly acknowledged or even recognized, and are just accepted as the correct way of going about taping and being taped. In this particular situation, it is also unlikely that the knowledge needed to fulfil the two roles is equally socially distributed. For example, the video user will be expected to have specialist knowledge about the equipment being used and the image being recorded. On the other hand, the subject is left to hope and trust that the final result is suitably flattering (and/or truthful!). Even when the tape is being played back, it is not at all clear that viewers understand the rules of television production that may be used to create the picture that they see of themselves. Even if the tape is played back immediately, in a relatively 'raw' state, it is quite possible that viewers hold expectations to do with other images seen through the same medium. How far do they feel that the self seen should conform to the talking-heads and soap-opera characters who normally appear on the monitor screen?

Although subjects have participated in the original event caught on tape and have perhaps the most complete record of their own personal history, they may have minimal access and control over the medium through which they now experience themselves. If being taped and seeing events on television have a 'common-sense' of their own, then it is quite possible that the viewer accepts it without recognizing that it contaminates the video image that they see of themselves. This may be particularly important if, as Schutz has claimed, one also takes it for granted that one's perspective on an object of common know-ledge is essentially the same as anybody else's. In such a situation the trap is twofold. Firstly, the viewer may undervalue his or her unique knowledge of the self because of the norms associated with the medium. Secondly, one might feel that one is seeing what everyone else sees and understands, while really applying one's own perceptual style to oneself. (This second point has been elaborated elsewhere (see Biggs, 1980), where it is argued that because viewers can remember how they felt at the time of taping (any secret motivations and so on) their 'hit-rate' for potential recognition of emotions and idiosyncratic meanings increases because they know what to look for, whereas others do not).

Being recorded

To understand the whole experience of the video situation, one needs to look at the relationship between the camera user and his or her subject. Experimental evidence is quite sparse in this area. Some investigators have examined the effects of video recording (Gelso, 1974; Tanney and Gelso, 1972) on client and therapist's feelings of confidence in therapy and found that video recording appears to inhibit client self-expression and to increase defensiveness. For the present discussion, perhaps the most startling finding was that the assumptions of the video user may be seriously awry when compared to the subject's experience: whereas the former expected video to stimulate 'unblocking', the latter experienced inhibition. A possible reason for this might be that video makes subjects objectively self-aware (see Trower and Kiely in Chapter 13 of this volume). Video has indeed been used for precisely this purpose (Arkin and Duval, 1975; Duval and Hensley, 1976). However, as a rule, these studies have looked at the intrapsychic effects of being recorded rather than the influence that the whole situation has upon participants and the meaning that they create together.

Expectations on the camera user

Significantly more has been written about the relationship between the 'stills' photographer and the person whose photograph is being taken. Bender (1981) has identified four key relationships or interactions, these being between the photographer and the camera, the subject being taken, the people he or she is with at the time and, finally, the potential audience. He points out that the act of taking a photograph is almost never an end in itself. What, then, do the parties involved expect? Milgram (1975) and Hughes (1980) suggest an implicit contract between the camera user and the subject, namely that the former 'beautifies' what is seen. One is expected to search for the most flattering angle and so on. So, 'We count upon the photographer to function as a kind of ego-supporter and photograph us as we would like to be presented to that generic constituency which is the audience of all photographs' (Milgram, 1975, p. 341).

Indeed, when Hughes attempted to place control over self-presentation in the hands of his subjects, several objected, wishing to gain his professional opinion as an artist.

From these examples, it would seem that the subject is intent upon visualizing the finished product as part of the actual process of being photographed. To a large extent one 'knows' what one wants to see. An important element in this process is the final context in which the visual record is used. Is the image to be shown in a family album, on the home video, in a public gallery or to a scientific audience? A distinction has been made here between personal and public use (Berger, 1978). The private use of photographs has a certain continuity as the people photographed are likely to still be known personally to the owner. In contrast public use often isolates an image, it becomes decontextualized and becomes an example of type. Nielsen (1962) reports that this happens to videotapes of other people and even to ones of the self over time.

It is hardly surprising that viewers often become concerned over how a tape is used once it has been made (Willener, Milliard and Ganty, 1976). As such, personal use is far closer to participation while public use is like observation, where the former allows more control over the construction of meaning, even when the events themselves are over and done with.

Power and the camera user

Another important element in the context of taping is the degree to which the equipment intrudes and influences the events being recorded. As far as possible investigators have tried to give themselves the status of 'non-persons' in order that the natural rhythm of an interaction is left undisturbed. As Shanklin (1979) has shown, the trick is to become accepted as part of the ongoing scene. This may not be as simple as it seems, for as Milgram (1975) notes, there are norms associated with the obtrusiveness of passers-by. People rarely step into the visual field between the photographer and subject until the recording ritual has been completed.

Much of this writing focuses upon the relative passivity of the camera user. However, Sontag (1979) has argued convincingly that creating such a 'non-person' role, one that can go anywhere expecting to be ignored even though being an observer, is a singularly aggressive stance. By hiding behind a camera the appearance of participation can be given, while the camera effectively 'masters' the situation. This process means that the camera user is less able to react to events as they happen and frees an observer from responsibility for them. Again, when these expectations are challenged and the subject wants or is invited to interact directly with the camera user, Willener, Milliard and Ganty (1976), report that their interviews changed in quality. Interviews became more 'authentic' as a more intimate relationship began to evolve when video was used in this way.

Before going on to examine the context in which this feedback is given, it is important to note that video is not entirely the same as photography here. Firstly, video records over time. This can have implications for the forms of self-presentation that arise and the way that the roles already discussed are maintained. With video the possibility of sustaining a particular version of the self becomes more difficult. It is no longer merely shrunk to the moment of trust when the camera clicks. Under such circumstances it seems that the norm involves ignoring the video user rather than 'facing' him. It is unclear how this norm is learned. The video user may tell the subject. On the other hand, the subject might notice during feedback that when the video is looked at, the continuity of an event is broken. Unfortunately, there seems to be no experimental evidence on this point. Secondly, the video camera is often left recording on its own. This could be seen as a non-person *par excellence*. In such a situation the subject is completely unable to interact with the video user while at the same time being aware that observation is taking place. In these circumstances, any meaning is mutually constructed in the sense that a presence, or possible audience, is felt; however, it can hardly be called social in the sense of being open to equal influence by both parties involved.

Summary

So, there seems to be good reason to see the act of being taped as one with a projected end outside of the social interaction itself. At the same time it is one with norms and expectations which influence the quality of social behaviours which, when challenged, can change the meaning of the events taking place. The degree to which the image caught on video ties in with these expectations may be important when this image is accepted or rejected during feedback.

Television and feedback

Discussion about making a video recording is important because the record itself can later be used as feedback, specifically in training and therapy. In this situation, viewers already have access to their own history and mood at the time of taping with which to compare the self as seen from the outside. Reports in the literature suggest that certain events stand out on video (Biggs, 1979; Holzman, 1969; Rackham and Morgan, 1977) almost as if an implicit norm were being broken. As this image is mediated by the television monitor, it is important to ask whether common-sense interpretive assumptions also play a part at this stage. This is not a concern about a physical distortion of the image so much as the presence of a well-learned code which is taken for granted by viewers as they watch.

Idealised images from television

Both Sontag (1979) and Williamson (1978) have noted the way in which people freely accept media images as they are presented. Sontag has called the attraction of such images 'knowledge at bargain prices' because these 'carefully manicured' fragments of social reality come to represent the whole social world. She sees them as helping the viewer define what is really worth perceiving in an overwhelming world full of potential bits of information. Our interest here lies in the fact that they are primarily presented on the television screen in almost the same way as video feedback. However, the production of television images is quite different to that used by the 'objective' researcher or therapist who would be interested in a raw record of social events which can be repeatedly observed and re-coded. One of the products of the media-edited version of reality, as Williamson (1978) has shown in her study of adverts, is that the image is unattainable in everyday terms. It leaves the viewer dissatisfied and needing to consume more. She argues that one is being sold 'Something else besides consumer goods; in providing us with a structure in which we, and those goods, are inter-changeable, they are selling us ourselves' (p. 13).

In other words, viewers may internalize an idealized version of the situations and people seen and a set of standards by which to judge themselves. Williamson claims that although people's conscious attitude to such images will usually be one of scepticism, there is an unconscious tendency to absorb an underlying message which offers a mirror to the viewer's own social relationships. For example, the housewife may not believe that Brand X washes whiter but will internalize and feel a certain security in the relationships expressed within the television family.

The role of editing

Any standard work on television production (see, for example, McRae, Monty and Worling, 1979) will show that idealization is by no means the sole preserve of the ad-man. Camera angles, make-up, lighting and editing are manipulated as a matter of course to produce a stylized series of images which can be decoded and implicitly understood by the viewing public. This process is perhaps made most clear when marginal groups are represented on the television screen. Nunnalley and Ross (1957, 1961) have studied the presentation of the mentally ill. They isolated two major sources of distortion: the need for excitement to boost viewing ratings and simplification, dictated by time constraints on programme producers. This was largely achieved by selective editing.

Video users are by no means immune to the tendency to use editing to produce easy viewing. Willener, Milliard and Ganty (1976) have distinguished between the 'duration' of a tape and 'real' time or the time that naturally observed events take to unfold. Any shortening of real-time by editing out the time that an actor takes to move from one interaction to another, for example, did not seem to lead to a shortening of the duration of events as experienced by the viewer. This suggests that viewers have already learned a code which allows them to accept events as if they were experiencing them at first hand. Indeed, Lovell (1980) has argued that a distinction should be made between 'showing things as they really are' and producing exact replicas of events. She points out that even though marriages on television soap-operas often result in a shower of presents for the happy couples involved, most viewers are well aware of the differences between a television pub and their own local. What seems to be important is that the finished product is 'realistic'. She concludes that 'The critic's or the viewer's naive complaint that such and such is not realistic frequently masks a complaint that the rules have been broken' (p. 80).

The acceptance of such rules, that is to say rules of 'realistic' television production as distinguished from rules of social behaviour, takes place at an early age. Noble (1975) has shown that children from the age of five years upwards preferred a variety of camera angles and were able to indicate a sense of continuity across close-up, medium range and long shots. He links this ability to Piagetian age stages, but also reports that children recognized television characters who were similar to people that they knew in everyday life. Some children actually conversed with these characters and accepted what Noble calls an illusion of intimacy. He argues that viewers can increase their social skills by learning from the wide selection of role-models that television provides. Such an argument implies that there is both a common-sense for social behaviour and for interpreting images mediated by television and that in some cases these codes might actually be learned simultaneously and even become confused.

So far, then, there is some evidence to suggest a code which is largely taken for granted but is used to interpret images seen primarily through a television monitor. The way that these images are edited can be read by observers as if events were taking place in real-time and constituted real social interaction, although the level at which it is accepted and the generality of the effect is unclear. The image created by such manipulation is often skewed towards an idealized and simplified social world. (Indeed, similar techniques have been used by Miklich and Creer, 1974, and Dowrick in Chapter 9 of this volume to produce therapeutic change.) The process by which this common-sense understanding can influence a viewer's self-perceptions is not yet clear. It may be related to the segmenting of social behaviour into meaningful chunks which Newtson (1973, 1976) has shown to influence causal attribution and might take place at both a global and detailed level (Ebbesen, 1980).

Summary

For the present discussion it is sufficient to point out that both video recording and feedback include social expectations and assumptions which are often taken as given. These may influence choices made to accept or reject events seen on tape as the viewer compares the 'raw' record used in therapy with the highly processed products that are usually seen on television screens.

Lack of change and the 'empiricist error': The common-sense of therapy

Reviews of video feedback (Bailey and Sowder, 1970; Fuller and Manning, 1973; Nadelson and coauthors, 1977) indicate that there are two contradictory processes associated with the use of the medium in therapy and training. Firstly, video can be instrumental in reinforcing an existing picture of the self, 'crystalizing' suspicions that one might have had about the self which were not previously open to direct verification. Secondly, video can make people aware of the possibility of change, partly because of a dissatisfaction with what is seen on tape. Both of these effects may be useful at different times. However, it is unclear why the viewer should choose, or be persuaded, to adopt one strategy or another.

The primacy of the video image

It has been argued above that the actor/viewer often has little control over the way in which a tape is made and played back. This process may influence the value that is attached to the superior access that viewers have to their own mood and personal history when confronted with an external record which is visually concrete and immediate. As with photography, video allows one to 'possess' an image of oneself and give permanency to events which would otherwise not exist outside of memory. Following feedback the viewer has been left with a visual memory with few competing memories to compare and contrast with it. It is also very rich in information which doubly demands attention, firstly because it is about the self and secondly because it is not usually available. These factors may help to reinforce the existing self because the tape shows one's own existing repertoire of skills, largely without the opportunity to model new responses. A parallel danger here is that, rather than merely being faced with a lack of new personal strategies, the viewer will accept what is seen as what is known, or at least give it a high priority over other sources of information about the self. This second factor will be referred to as 'the empiricist error' because it is based upon *accepting the validity of a particularly impactful piece of sense-datum, which seems to have an objective and external status and discounts the social and personal historical contexts which surround it.* Other elements, such as the 'common-sense' of video recording, have been ignored.

A collusive role for therapists

This 'error' has, I feel, a particular importance for people using video, because it is in many ways precisely what the therapist has been looking for. By using this external 'unbiased' source, the denial shown by many clients can be challenged (Nadelson and coauthors, 1977). Fuller and Manning's (1973) review quotes viewers who 'changed toward objective reality' and 'increased realism about the self' while Reivich and Geertsma (1969) point to the value of giving both trainer and trainee access to the latter's actual performance during supervision. While I agree that the possibilities for distortion are radically reduced here, these reports merely re-describe rather than attempt to analyse the social context within which such events take place. Video users may unwittingly collude with a viewer's need to see the video image and one's consciousness of it as a copy of objective reality and thus establish an underlying message which reinforces what already exists. This process can become more complicated still if both parties overlook associations or the common-sense implicit in the mediating video and as such undermine an ability to transcend, to step outside one's conditioning by it. The response of depressed patients gives an example of this process. Biggs, Rosen and Summerfield (1980) found that video feedback increased the negative self-image that these people had of themselves and suggested that it should not be used with them in future. Now, given that these depressed women already had a tendency to see feedback about themselves in a negative light and generally exert little power over their immediate social context (the hospital ward), taping and viewing may covertly reinforce these trends. The relationship between the patient and the camera user was biased as mentioned previously in terms of power over equipment and in terms of the expectation that the two roles involved. The viewer then saw herself on a television monitor where she was used to seeing idealized and often stereotyped examples of impression management. These common-sense associations may have contributed to these viewers assessing the video images of themselves unfavourably by comparison. The message that video feedback was objective would then emphasize this conclusion; after all, the camera does not lie, does it?

Externality and objectivity

Two more general trends are also involved in the 'empiricist error'. Firstly, it is wrongly believed that this source of information about the self is independent of theories held by that self because it is external from personal memory.

Admittedly, new information becomes available as viewers see themselves 'from the outside' or 'as others see them'; however, choices about how that information is used may fail to acknowledge the new motives and associations which come into play when one is not involved in the heat of the moments held on tape. These new motives may not be part of the meaning which was mutually constructed by participants in the original context and should not be assumed by viewers to be immediately obvious to other people, nor to be an enduring part of the self.

Secondly, the viewer has been encouraged to develop a viewpoint more akin to that of an uninvolved spectator concentrating upon his or her own behaviour as an object for observation. This move from the private to the public arena facilitates the perception of behaviour as an example of 'type' cut off from the dialectical flow between the historical self and other social actors. While so doing, the opinions of others paradoxically become more important as other, internal frames of reference such as consistency and distinctiveness become devalued.

In such a situation, where one's own idiosyncratic memories become less important because an 'external' observer would not ordinarily have access and thus could not use them, it also becomes easier for a particular instance of behaviour to come to stand for the whole. The particular instance of interest here is the one seen on video. It becomes important because it is external and is open to the self and other alike, once the viewer's introspective information has been made irrelevant.

Summary

To summarize the argument so far, it is suggested that in some cases the external status of the video image and the value given to it by therapists as an objective source of information can lead viewers to underuse (in a theraputic sense) the information that they gain about themselves. Firstly, the therapist may collude with viewers with low self-esteem because influences implicit in the taping and feedback sessions are ignored. Secondly, viewers may be encouraged to value this new source of information as being objective, as least in the sense of how others see them, while undervaluing personal memories which are not open to empirical investigation in the same way. Both of these points follow from an empiricist ideology which assigns value to external observation in itself.

The 'empiricist error' and social skills training

Both of these problems are particularly important when video is used in social skills training. Trainers using this technique have largely concentrated on using video to facilitate the breaking down of complex social situations into small component parts which can be reconstructed with clients in a more appropriate manner (Hargie, Saunders and Dickson, 1980; Trower, Bryant and Argyle, 1978). In such a situation, it is important for the skills learned to be compatible with the client's existing social 'style' if they are to generalize to wider social contexts. Trower (1980) has recently pointed out that it is important to take the client's existing beliefs into account so that one can understand how skills are perceived in relation to his or her own plans. Others (Cooper, Biggs and Bender, in press) have emphasized that it is important to encourage client participation and improvisation during training so that new behaviour can be integrated into a client's natural social repertoire. Both of these studies have reflected a shift towards acknowledging that personal information held by the client has to be respected in training if it is to be successful. Now, if viewers take the role of a disinterested observer and choose to discount much of their own internal processes (by adopting the trainer's preoccupation with behaviour) it becomes unclear how far new performances are seen as part of the wider social milieu of the viewer as actor. They may concentrate upon the behavioural meaning of an interaction while excluding other meanings as the fragment caught on tape comes to represent the whole. It may then become increasingly difficult to associate this with a variety of social contexts where it is necessary to construct different social meanings to that of the video session.

All of these points hinge upon an implicit decision that the viewer has made, namely that the taped behaviour can be seen as an object with an immutable external status. This is partly because of its perceptual impact and partly because it has been extracted, decontextualized and can be looked upon as a discrete event rather than as an integral part of social episodes which are continually changing. Somehow choices can be made to accept the empiricist error which inhibit change. These may either be because the viewer feels that video is external and is therefore independent of his or her own thoughts and associations (and may paradoxically be used to support them) or because it is thought to be of greater value in and of itself than internal sources of information.

Video and change

Video can also be a catalyst which promotes change and one needs to ask what the preconditions of such change are. A distinction needs to be made between alienating forms of distance, ones which have immersed the viewer in the events on tape for their own sake and ones that have been integrated with personal motives and history.

Stepping outside the common-sense of social interaction

To understand this process one needs to look more closely at the differences between self-observation during normal social interaction and what happens when the self is seen on video. When involved in a social event actors have primarily been concerned with effects being made on the outside world (Jones and Nisbett, 1972; Kuiken, 1976). Monitoring of other aspects of their personal behaviour would have been minimal. Video allows actors to 'step outside' in a way that was previously unavailable. The events can still be seen although they have ceased to happen, so although one can no longer influence the events themselves they can be reflected upon in a very concrete way. This means that viewers are potentially no longer immersed in an activity. Freire (1972) has pointed out that only beings who can reflect upon the fact that they are 'determined' become capable of freeing themselves. Friere was concerned with the awareness of action upon the material and social world which can be grasped once various cognitive skills for reflection, such as reading, have been acquired. The objects of this sort of reflection are already 'out there' in a way that one's own behaviour is not. Video would be one way of making the raw material of self-reflection available.

Memory alone

This process would need to be distinguished from recognizing 'things only just suspected' about the self, which would involve relying increasingly upon memory at the expense of novel insights. Although one's preconceptions would undeniably be involved here, there would be a danger that judgements have become increasingly awry because they have only been based on an internal source without enquiry into alternative orientations. The viewer has shut intersubjective meanings out. Just as viewers who have looked for minute behaviours in a single performance have become immersed purely in the empirical meaning of an event, those who have relied entirely upon personal memory in order to confirm their suspicions have become immersed in their own past. Both positions are ultimately self-contained and static.

Stepping outside and change

So, how can the ability to distance oneself from one's behaviour lead to increased choice and change? An expansion of this process has been given in Sartre's *The Psychology of the Imagination* (1972). It is suggested here that the very fact of making something an object that one can consciously 'step outside' means that one's consciousness is now separate from that object (in this case one's own behaviour). Almost simultaneously one becomes able to distinguish oneself from it. A space emerges between the viewer and the object of attention, the self as actor. This distance leaves room for an area of what has been called 'free play' around the object of attention, which means that it can be more easily described in different ways and from different points of reference. Immediately that one is sufficiently distanced from events, questions arise. Sartre would say that the possibility of agreement or disagreement with what has been seen also arises. One becomes aware of alternatives to the existing state of affairs, or at least the possibility of what the self is not. Similar reports can be found about video. Willener, Milliard and Ganty (1976) have noted that viewers 'migrate' from the social role that they played while being taped and have attempted to assert their individuality in relation to the role expectations themselves. Holzman (1969) has spoken of 'de-automatization', a process whereby viewers experience 'a shake-up' of habitual attitudes or typical defensive stance towards the self. This provides an opportunity for 'advancing, retreating from, or maintaining the status-quo of a function' (p. 207).

Naming the social world and change

The problem of choice, whether the viewer accepts or rejects this opportunity, may largely depend on the position that the video user takes. Although viewers may have superior access to information about the self, they may not feel safe or confident enough, or be provided with a framework flexible enough to use video as a springboard towards alternative 'selves'.

In fact, this possibility of being different from the image seen is already implicit in the video session once other 'common-sense' associations have been cleared away. The video image is, or more correctly was, the self in a different role. However, the viewer is also watching that image and exists separately from it. In this sense the first event represents the self, as an analogue, apart from the whole. Indeed, the very act of replaying a tape of events that have just happened emphasizes the fact that it is not what it represents. These events do not now exist in themselves. This may seem a ludicrously obvious point were it not that television images constantly invite us to suspend this 'temporal' reality and merely accept a perceptual one. Sartre indicates that this confusion, a fusion of being something and at the same time not being something, leads to a new sense of freedom and flexibility.

It seems, then, that seeing oneself on video can lead to an awareness of the different roles that the self assumes and to a realization that alternatives to the former are possible. The point of learning has changed from an analysis of events caught on tape to a comparison between past events and one's present state. However, this reflection would seem to be short-lived once the demands of 'common-sense' reality flood back into consciousness. The problem is still faced that these rules that influence behaviour and lead to expectations during taping and viewing are largely unspoken. Therapists and trainers have often emphasized the need for directive strategies when using video feedback (Alger and Hogan, 1967; Nadelson and coauthors, 1977). It has been said that seeing video is not therapeutic in itself because viewers rarely have the cognitive tools to interpret behaviour which is ordinarily ignored. People have not developed an adequate language to use on their own behaviour. Freire (1972) has discussed a similar situation among illiterate peasants: 'To exist humanly is to name the world, to change it. Once named, the world in its turn reappears to the namers as a problem and requires of them a new naming' (p. 61).

In many ways our own behaviour is unspoken. It is unnamed and exists in a silence of action in the immediate present. A few people, those involved in scientific study or in radical critiques of existing role-relationships, have attempted to articulate this behaviour, especially that of other people. Naming one's own behaviour is usually more difficult because one rarely sees more than the results left in its wake. It is in this sense that video presents an opportunity for an existential self-appraisal in which a viewer becomes aware of dissatisfactions and the possibility of alternatives. However, this very personal revelation may need the help of therapists and trainers if it is to be articulated and extended once it has occurred.

Conclusions

There seem to be certain contradictions in the way that video has traditionally been used in training and to a lesser extent in therapy. The video user has emphasized the viewing part of the session, while the viewers themselves may be well aware of what they expect to see, even while they are being taped. Viewers may thus become more aware of the relationship between the acting and viewing situations and give more meaning to the whole event. Viewers may not be as 'literate' as the video user when it comes to understanding how images are produced. Neither are they so skilled at decoding the situation so that dissatisfactions can be articulated and thus reflected upon critically, rather than being seen to be of superior value because of the way in which they have been fed back.

A change of emphasis

These points mark a move away from a preoccupation with the record, the product to be analysed, towards a reevaluation of a critical point in the subject's experience. Elements in the early stages of video feedback have often been dismissed as 'cosmetic shock' or 'image impact', as something to be endured until the 'real' process of training can be started (Alger and Hogan, 1967; Hargie, Tittmar and Dickson, 1977). They may also be the point at which the viewer gains insight into the way in which he or she is dissatisfied. This dismissal has usually happened in the past because viewers have commented on hand movements, fidgetting or 'leaked' messages (Biggs, 1979) and personal appearance (Rackman and Morgan, 1977), which are rarely the behaviours which the trainer feels to be important. (In any event they soon spontaneously disappear because they are not what the viewer associates with a polished television appearance!). These cues have been recognized primarily because they reveal idiosyncratic meanings which the trainer, as an observer, may not be able to decode (Biggs, 1980). However, they are useful cues to the viewer's dissatisfaction with the self and role-relationships. For example, viewers may feel the need to hide their 'real' feelings, present a socially acceptable front or be an 'attractive person'. In other words, they are at once a reflection of societal norms and an expression of dissatisfaction.

Suggestions

Having discussed some of the problems inherent in the use of video, many of which have been overlooked by researchers and therapists, it is essential to examine the ways in which the use of video can be improved. Suggestions are made in four areas.

Firstly, video users must recognize that although they have specialist knowledge, this is only part of the picture. The viewer has superior personal knowledge about the events on tape and neither exist separately. In terms of subject matter, *both the client and user should be seen on tape*. As Alger (1969) says, this makes the latter's behaviour an object in the same sense as that of the client. This may go some way to sensitize the latter to the expectations and associations surrounding the medium and emphasizes the relationship between both participants. This is particularly important if the empiricist error is to be confronted and a single meaning with immutable status be challenged.

Secondly, *the whole session, both taping and viewing, should become a focus of attention.* If the implicit meaning of the social situation is to be uncovered, it is important that both user and viewer concentrate on the same aspects of the session. The viewer would seem to link the two parts, with expectations from one merging into the other. By concentrating largely upon feedback, the user may be encoding it differently to the viewer. This is important if the implicit meaning of the social situation is to be uncovered and both parties are to unravel it together.

Thirdly, *if the tape is to be edited, the viewer's opinion is needed.* The way that video is artificially segmented is probably the most powerful way of manipulating its meaning. Unless the viewer has been consulted, they may not fully accept the authenticity of the product and become mistrustful. It may also become less 'realistic' in Lovell's (1980) sense and thus less likely to aid generalization to other social situations. A problem arises here because time would have elapsed between acting and viewing and the impact effect reduced. Perhaps editing should be used as a separate technique to uncover the viewer's 'life-world' once impact has helped to articulate points of dissatisfaction. In both cases, the content of the image can then be subject to critical analysis. There would also be ways of using editing to emphasize role-relationships and thus capitalize on the impact mentioned earlier. As has been shown, the technology of editing can be used to 'telescope' time so that events which may take place some way apart in real-time can be seen next to each other. So, the subject could be taped in several different roles and at different times in order to associate different themes, blank areas and unfulfilled needs and make them more obvious. Alternatively, a continuous recording over a longer period of time would emphasize the contradiction between the spectacularized social relationships associated with the medium (television) and the speed and structure of everyday events.

Finally, it is suggested that *a distinction needs to be made between the impact of seeing the self on tape and its use to articulate dissatisfaction and insight aroused by the experience.* Information held by the video user and viewer varies in importance at different times during video use. The viewer has greater access to personal history and is more able to become aware of dissatisfactions expressed but not necessarily acknowledged until roles or behaviour are seen from the outside. The impact of the feedback reflects this and should be used as a starting point. The video user, by virtue of being an outside observer as well as a specialist, would be more able to see the empirical value of the tape, but not its idiosyncratic meaning. However, the specialist may use a language which can help the viewer articulate and critically analyse contradictions about role-relationships expressed during taping. These should be made available following an expression of dissatisfaction with these contradictions. Both taping and viewing have been complicated, however, because of unequal power relations implicit in both taping and viewing. As they are likely to be taken for granted by both participants, particular care should be made to use the medium in such a way that such common-sense expectations are unveiled.

References

Alger, I. (1969). Theraputic use of videotape playback, *Journal of Nervous and Mental Diseases*, **148**, 430–436.

Alger, I., and Hogan, P. (1967). The use of videotape recording in conjoint marital therapy, *American Journal of Psychiatry*, **123**, 1425–1430.

Arkin, R., and Duval, S. (1975). The focus of attention and causal attribution of actors and observers, *Journal of Experimental Social Psychology*, **11**, 427–438.

Bailey, K. G., and Sowder, W. T. (1970). Audiotape and videotape self-confrontation in psychotherapy, *Psychological Bulletin*, **74**, 153–181.

Bender, M. P. (1981). The camera as relationship, *British Journal of Photography*, **128**, 778–781.

Berger, J. (1978). Ways of remembering, *Camerawork*, **10**, 1–2.

Biggs, S. J. (1979). *Videotape Feedback and Self-awareness*, Unpublished doctoral thesis, Senate Library, University of London.

Biggs, S. J. (1980). The me I see: acting, participating, observing and viewing and their implications for video feedback, *Human Relations*, **33**, 575–588.

Biggs, S. J., Rosen, B., and Summerfield, A. B. (1980). Video feedback and personal attribution in anorexic, depressed and normal viewers, *British Journal of Medical Psychology*, **53**, 249–254.

Cooper, A. C., Biggs, S. J., and Bender, M. P. (in press). Social skills training with long-term clients in the community, in *Social Skills Training in Practice* (Eds. S. Spence and G. Shepherd), Academic Press, London.

Duval, S., and Hensley, V. (1976). Extensions of objective self-awareness theory: the focus of attention, causal attribution hypothesis, in *New Directions in Attribution Research* (Eds. J. H. Harvey, W. J. Ickes and R. F. Kidd), Vol. 1, Earlbaum, Hillsdale, New Jersey.

Ebbesen, E. B. (1980). Cognitive processes in understanding ongoing behaviour, in *Person Memory: The Cognitive Bases of Social Perception* (Eds. R. Hastie, T. M. Ostouch, E. B. Ebbesen, R. S. Wyer, D. L. Hamilton and D. E. Carlston), Earlbaum, Hillsdale, New Jersey.

Freire, P. (1972). *Pedagogy of the Oppressed*, Penguin, London.

Fuller, F., and Manning, B. (1973). Self-confrontation reviewed: a conceptualisation for video playback in teacher education, *Review of Educational Research*, **43**, 468–528.

Garfinkel, H. (1967). *Studies in Ethnomethodology*, Prentice-Hall, New York.

Gelso, C. (1974). Effects of recording on counsellors and clients, *Counsellor Education and Supervision*, **14**, 5–12.

Hargie, O., Saunders, C., and Dickson, D. (1980). *Social Skills in Interpersonal Communication*, Croom-Helm, London.

Hargie, O., Tittmar, H., and Dickson, D. (1977). Social skills training: applying the concept to a careers' guidance course, *Bulletin of the British Psychological Society*, **30**, 214–216.

Holzman, P. (1969). On hearing and seeing oneself, *Journal of Nervous and Mental Disease*, *148*, 198–209.

Hughes, M. (1980). Portraits: ways of taking, *Camerawork*, **20**, 14.

Jones, E. E., and Nisbett, R. (1972). The actor and the observer: divergent perceptions of the causes of behaviour, in *Attribution, Perceiving the Causes of Behaviour* (Eds. E. E. Jones *et al.*), General Learning Press, Morristown, New Jersey.

Kuiken, D. (1976). Immediacy in self-representation, *Journal of Humanistic Psychology*, **16**, 29–50.

Lovell, T. (1980). *Pictures of Reality: Aesthetics, Politics and Pleasure*, British Film Institute, London.

McRae, C., Monty, A., and Worling, D. (1979). *T.V. Production: An Introduction*, Methuen, London.

Miklich, D. R., and Creer, T. L. (1974). Self-modeling, in *Behaviour Modification in Rehabilitation Settings: Applied Principles* (Eds. J. C. Cull and R. E. Hardy), Charles C. Thomas, Springfield, Illinois.

Milgram, S. (1975). The image freezing machine, *Journal of Photography in Communications Bulletins*, **75**, 339–350.

Nadelson, C., Bassuk, E., Hopps, C., and Boutelle, W. (1977). Use of videotape in couples therapy, *International Journal of Group Psychotherapy*, **27**, 241–253.

Newtson, D. (1973). Attribution and the unit of perception of ongoing behaviour, *Journal of Personality and Socail Psychology*, **28**, 28–38.

Newtson, D. (1976). Foundations of attribution: perception of ongoing behaviour, in *New Directions in Attribution Research* (Eds. J. Harvey, W. Iches and R. Kidd), Vol. 1, Earlbaum, New Jersey.

Nielsen, G. (1962). *Studies in Self-confrontation*, Munksgaard, Copenhagen.

Noble, G. (1975). *Children in Front of the Small Screen*, Constable, London.

Nunnalley, J. U. M. (1961). *Popular Conceptions of Mental Health*, Holt, Rienhart and Winston, New York.

Nunnalley, J. U. M., and Ross, L. (1957). The communication of mental health information, *Behavioural Science*, **2**, 222–230.

Rackham, N., and Morgan, T. (1977). *Behaviour Analysis in Training*, McGraw-Hill, London.

Reivich, R., and Geertsma, A. (1969). Observational media in psychotherapy training, *Journal of Nervous and Mental Disease*, **148**, 310–327.

Sartre, J.-P. (1972). *The Psychology of the Imagination* (Trans. M. Warnock), Methuen, London.

Schutz, A. (1962). *Collected Papers*, Vol. 1, Martinis Nijhoff, The Hague.

Shanklin, E. (1979). When a social role is worth a thousand photographs, in *Images of Information* (Ed. J. Wagner), Sage, London.

Sontag, S. (1979). *On Photography*, Penguin, London.

Tanney, M., and Gelso, C. (1972). The effects of recording on clients, *Journal of Counselling Psychology*, **19**, 348–349.

Trower, P. (1980). Situational analysis of the components and processes of behaviour of socially skilled and unskilled patients, *Journal of Consulting and Clinical Psychology*, **3**, 327–339.

Trower, P., Bryant, B., and Argyle, M. (1978). *Social Skills and Mental Health*, Methuen, London.

Willener, A., Milliard, G., and Ganty, R. (1976). *Videology and Utopia*, Routledge, London.

Williamson, J. (1978). *Decoding Advertisements*, Marion Boyars, London.

Author Index

Subject Index